JOHN HENRY

Popular Culture Bio-Bibliographies: A Reference Series
Series Editor: M. Thomas Inge

Crockett: A Bio-Bibliography
Richard Boyd Hauck

Knute Rockne: A Bio-Bibliography
Michael R. Steele

JOHN HENRY
A Bio-Bibliography

Brett Williams

Popular Culture Bio-Bibliographies

Greenwood Press
Westport, Connecticut • London, England

Library of Congress Cataloging in Publication Data

Williams, Brett.
  John Henry, a bio-bibliography.

  (Popular culture bio-bibliographies ISSN 0193-6891)
  Discography: p.
  Includes index.
  1. John Henry (Legendary character) 2. John Henry
(Legendary character)—Bibliography. 3. Afro-American
songs—History and criticism. I. Title. II. Series.
PS461.J6W54 1983   016.3982'2'0973   82-12056
ISBN 0-313-22250-9 (lib. bdg.)

Library of Congress Catalog Card Number: 82-12056
ISBN: 0-313-22250-9
ISSN: 0193-6891

First published in 1983

Greenwood Press
A division of Congressional Information Service, Inc.
88 Post Road West
Westport, Connecticut 06881

Printed in the United States of America

10 9 8 7 6 5 4 3 2 1

Copyright Acknowledgment

The author would like to thank the following authors and publishers for permission
to use their works:

Excerpts from Guy B. Johnson, *John Henry: Tracking Down a Negro Legend.*
1929. Reprint. New York: AMS Press, 1969.

Excerpts from Sterling Brown's "Strange Legacies" in *The Collected Poems of
Sterling Brown,* selected by Michael S. Harper. New York: Harper & Row, 1980.

Every reasonable effort has been made to trace the owners of copyright material
in this book, but in some instances this has proven impossible. The publishers will be
glad to receive information leading to more complete acknowledgment in subsequent
printings of the book and in the meantime extend their apologies for any omissions.

John Henry was a little baby boy,
Sittin' on his daddy's knee,
Said "That old steam drill on the C & O Line
Gonna be the death of me, Lord, Lord,
Gonna be the death of me."

John Henry said to his Captain,
"A man ain't nothin' but a man,
And before I'll let your steam drill beat me down
Gonna die with my hammer in my hand, Lord, Lord,
Gonna die with my hammer in my hand."

John Henry walked in the tunnel,
Had his captain by his side,
But the rock so tall, John Henry so small,
Lord, he laid down his hammer and he cried,
Lord, he laid down his hammer and he cried.

John Henry told his shaker,
"Shaker, you better pray.
If I miss this piece of steel,
Tomorrow be your buryin' day,
Tomorrow be your buryin' day."

John Henry's captian sat on a rock,
Says, "I believe my mountain's fallin' in."
John Henry turned around and said,
"It's just my hammer singin' in the wind,
It's just my hammer singin' in the wind."

John Henry had a little woman,
Her name was Polly Ann,
When John Henry lay sick down on his bed,
Polly drove steel like a man,
Polly drove steel like a man.

John Henry had just one only son,
He could hold him in the palm of his hand.
Very last words that John Henry said,
"Son, you're gonna be a steel-drivin' man,
You're gonna be a steel-drivin' man."

CONTENTS

ILLUSTRATIONS

PREFACE

For the last one hundred years, ballads celebrating John Henry have captured the imagination of Americans. We know from these songs that as an infant the hero foresees his own fate; that as a man proclaiming "A man ain't nothin but a man," he acts it out; that he dies in a race against a steam drill with which his destiny seems somehow entangled. The story told in song is remarkably sparse, posing more questions than it answers. Who was John Henry and why did he choose to die in such a contest? And why, when we know so little about him, have Americans admired him and been fascinated by the sketchy story of his life?

It was a love of trains that first caught my own interest in John Henry, for I was intrigued by the fact that he is the only black man and the only menial laborer celebrated as a railroad hero. But writing this book has taken me far beyond the world of American railroading. Again and again I have been surprised to discover disparate portraits of John Henry which have emerged in a wide variety of traditions that honor him. Yet he has never entered our cultural mainstream, and we have commemorated him almost solely through song. Most of us do not know the details of his life or his heroic act; indeed, it is quite possible that he never lived at all. John Henry's legend is a powerful but ambiguous one, and I have come to believe that its ambiguity gives it its power.

In this book I have drawn together what I believe we need to know in order to understand John Henry and his heroic career in American culture. Chapter 1 suggests a life for him. Because we have no conclusive biographical information, the life I propose is one that joins ballad lore to nineteenth-century history: the lifeways of emancipated slaves, the course of railroad and tunnel construction in the south, the marketing of new steam-drill technology. I am concerned here with heroic possibilities: could a man in

John Henry's circumstances have seized the moment celebrated so vividly in song? In chapter 2 I explore the problem of John Henry's authenticity through oral history, through retracing the steps of two earlier researchers who gathered rich testimony from laborers, railroaders, and many black Americans who claimed to know or know of the heroic steel driver. I have organized these interviews so that they speak systematically to questions of when and where John Henry lived. But I am also interested in recapturing an exciting quest that led both scholars to West Virginia's Big Bend Tunnel and in conveying a sense of the special, intimate admiration surrounding John Henry during the 1920s.

Chapters 3, 4, and 5 treat John Henry's life in American culture. Chapter 3 explores his career in song, from the ballad fragments collected during the early years of this century through the numerous folksong treasuries which rarely fail to include "John Henry." Chapter 4 considers the rather scarce portraits of John Henry that we find in other art forms: literature, drama, poetry, dance, sculpture, and engraving, and an Appalachian festival that honors him each year. While these media have not commemorated John Henry as often as other heroes, his characterizations there are intriguing as they speak to the versatility of his legend. Artists have shaped him into many different kinds of men.

Chapter 5 examines John Henry scholarship, including efforts to assess his authenticity, to disentangle his life from the life of executed desperado John Hardy, to understand his heroic appeal or place him in a particular tradition, and to explore his place in music or art. Here again we see that John Henry has emerged as many different kinds of men and that he has provoked heated personal controversies.

I consider chapter 6 the heart of the volume, for here I offer my own analysis of his heroic appeal. Although ethnographic research has persuaded me that John Henry is no longer an appropriate hero to black Americans, I can place him in traditional black culture, where he speaks powerfully to the pain and the promise of the post-Emancipation era. At the same time, John Henry is lodged firmly in southern culture, particularly and ironically in a bitter and fearful Reconstruction South, but also in white southerners' dreams for a New South. John Henry surely figures prominently in the lore of laborers, especially those in the hammering tradition, and he has also bolstered the passions of those polarized around railroads. He seems to have been a hero to those enraged by the impersonality and corruption of the institution as well as to those who like trains and admire railroad workers. Chapter 6 explore each of these heroic contexts and John Henry's appropriateness to all of them at different times and for very different reasons. I believe that it is the ambiguity of the legend that allows for his cultural versatility. Because it is song that best preserves this ambiguity, it is song that best communicates to us his story. What is not ambiguous, however, is John Henry's place in a family trapped by a tragic destiny. I argue in concluding chapter 6 that we have mourned John Henry because he joins extraordinary courage and prowess to the most ordinary and universal human sentiments about kin.

Chapters 7 and 8 are resource chapters: one a bibliography of printed and visual John Henry materials, the other a discography of John Henry recordings. Chapter 7 also is the source for full bibliographic information on works cited in short form in other chapters. The organization of the volume and the context of each chapter reflect my hope that the book will be both valuable and flexible as a reference text. Each part can stand on its own, so that readers with particular research interests can consult individual portions of the book. Much like an encyclopedia, the book lists and briefly describes all that has been written and sung about John Henry. Scholars and teachers seeking films, stories, articles, or songs can locate and learn about them here. More than an encyclopedia, the volume offers biographical, ethnographic, historical, and critical analyses. Taken as a whole, it is the only comprehensive work available on John Henry, his legend, and his cultural career.

I am most indebted to my husband John Henry Pitt III and our son John Henry Pitt IV, who inspired this book. Julie Burns and Dante Dant spent long hours listening to John Henry songs and helping me transcribe and evaluate them. Chapin Vasilake assisted me in every step of preparing the manuscript: she pored over volumes of ancient small-town newspapers; she perused John Henry fiction; she read and critiqued drafts of every chapter. I consider myself fortunate to have had such a cheerful and able research assistant who is also a writer and critic in her own right. The librarians at the Library of Congress, especially in its Music Division and the Archive of Folksong, were patient and resourceful in locating sometimes arcane texts and in guiding the research. My fellow anthropologists at American University, folklorist Jo Radner, historian Kathleen Dalton, and American Studies scholar Kay Mussell, all helped immeasurably with the problems I faced in trying to draw together the interdisciplinary tools essential for studying an American hero. Patricia Rabain and Blanche Smith graciously and ably typed the manuscript. Finally, I am grateful to the residents of Hinton, West Virginia, and of the Mt. Pleasant neighborhood of Washington, D.C., who not only filled in many details on John Henry's life and lore, but also helped me understand why we have loved him. All errors of course are my own.

JOHN HENRY

1

JOHN HENRY: A LIFE

Even among heroes John Henry is extraordinary, for his fame rests on a single epic moment when he raced and defeated a steam drill destined to take away his job. That moment has captured the imagination of balladeers and storytellers for the last century, and in their songs and tales they have woven for John Henry a whole life: an infant's prophecy, a woman he loves, a heroic test, a martyr's victory. Although this heroic tradition tells us much about John Henry's appeal, it tells us little about his real and probably rather ordinary life. Reconstructing his biography is complicated further by the problem that his is the sort of life often lost to history: as a southern black laborer born a slave and most likely dead before the nineteenth century closed, his experience would not have been chronicled in official accounts. Oral tradition offers the biographer clues to John Henry's life; from there one must look to history for evidence that such a man might have lived such a life and that he might have had the opportunity to seize a heroic moment. Ultimately, to believe that John Henry actually lived is an act of faith, bolstered somewhat by the testimony cited in the following chapter. In this chapter I join the clues of oral tradition to a nineteenth-century southern setting in suggesting a life for John Henry.

Regrettably, we do not even know what to make of his name. John Henry would have lived at the most complicated time possible for discovering who he was. Because he was born a slave, some plantations might have recorded his birth. Those records that survive indicate that John and Henry were the two most common names for nineteenth-century male slaves. These records generally list only one name for each person, supporting assumptions that Henry was a surname, perhaps a slave family surname, linked ultimately to a white man such as the owner of the large and populous Henry plantation of Winchester, Virginia. In the 1920s Guy Johnson found further evidence that Henry might have been a surname: in researching Carter Woodson's *Free Negro Heads of Families, 1830*, Johnson found eleven John Henrys and believed that the actual number of men with that name would have been many more.[1]

But it seems just as plausible to assume that John Henry was a first and middle name, especially when we consider the complexity of slave-naming customs, the likelihood that plantation birth records would have ignored that complexity, and finally, the fact that many ex-slaves transformed their old names once free. Slave parents, or often grandparents, generally named children for kin as a way of rooting them in extended, though often dispersed, families. Naming was crucial in linking generations of blood kin, so that they might stand as a family although they could not share a household. Because naming was symbolically so significant, John Henry, like many others, quite possibly bore the names of two male relatives. Further, some slaves took unofficial nicknames as well as surnames other than their owners', probably to assert their separate social identities. After Emancipation, those former slaves who so desired often transformed their names, relinquishing a master's name or adding double names, perhaps to dramatize their new status. That double names were common among southern blacks once they were free is indicated by the testimony of those volunteering information on John Henry in the 1920s: all assumed that he had yet another surname. Finally, among black Americans today, John Henry is most often a double name.[2]

However, the very ordinariness of John Henry's name makes him not only impossible to trace but perhaps suspect as well. It symbolizes his heroic role as a sort of Everyman and also links him to traditional slave heroes such as John the Conqueror or the slave John of the John and Master story cycle.[3]

In any event, John Henry would have been born a slave in the 1830s or 1840s. Although every southern state has at some time claimed him as a native son, we cannot be sure where he was born. Most evidence seems to point to either North Carolina or Virginia. As a slave in either of these upper South states, he would have grown up in a community woven together by the kin ties of extended families who struggled to bind kin in spite of the terrible obstacles slavery imposed on family life. He would have participated in a society unique to that time and place, rooted in the Afro-American experience, joining African, American, and slave traditions to carve out in juxtaposition to the institution of slavery a culture rich in ritual, music, stories, and heroic lore. This heritage is crucial in understanding the heroic tradition, especially the poignant ballad that it produced to commemorate John Henry and the type of hero it celebrated.

In either North Carolina or Virgina, John Henry may have participated in, and surely witnessed, the great migration of slaves out of the upper South between 1815-1860, as the export shipping trade shifted to the less depleted and more prosperous plantations of the deep South. Only one of many practices that ripped apart slave families and disrupted slave communities, it was an especially dramatic one. One of every ten people experienced forced separation from kin: most typically this person was a single male between the ages of fifteen and twenty-nine. Everyone who witnessed it must have been struck by the arbitrary power of their owners to toy with human life.[4]

Finally, in either North Carolina or Virginia, John Henry may have participated in, and again surely witnessed, the industrial slavery common to both states. Throughout the South owners leased out their slaves to work on railroad, canal, and levee construction or in textile factories, and in the upper South to work in ironworks and coal mines (for labor not unlike that John Henry would do as a free man). Coal mining was a particularly hazardous endeavor: plagued with accidents from rock falls, fires, and explosions, the mines had such a bad reputation that many owners sent their slaves there as punishment. Others sought insurance on their slaves, but found that by the 1850s most insurance companies were too wary of the hazards of mining to grant it. Industrial slavery was another business venture that ruptured family life; often slaves refused to go to the mines or, once there, ran away.[5] Like the great migration, industrial slavery testified to the abandonment of human priorities to economic goals. John Henry must have come to freedom with these lessons well in mind. His heroic act, appropriately, was addressed to just this conflict.

Once free, a few former slaves found skilled jobs as blacksmiths, carpenters, or shoemakers; many more remained in farm labor, often as sharecroppers; and still others, like John Henry, joined a virtual army of inexpensive workers to build and rebuild the industrializing South. Because there were so many workers with so little bargaining power, they faced conditions in factories, on steamboats, railroads, and cattle ranges, in lumbering and turpentine camps, and in coal mines that were often terribly exploitative. Some employers still thought black laborers were little better than brute animals and worked them from sunup to sundown for wages as low as one dollar a day and punished them harshly if they performed poorly.

In many cases those supposed to be free actually worked under debt peonage, either as sharecroppers so indebted to landowners that their share of the crop could never repay the debt, as convicts on hire, or as laborers under contract to men functioning much like today's agricultural crew leaders. A great deal of migration characterized this labor force, as much of the construction work available was large scale and short term. Workers sometimes moved to the North or the Midwest seeking better positions or from one site to another at the behest of labor contractors to whom they were sometimes also in debt.[6]

Someone who might have provided us with information about John Henry was Captain W. R. Johnson. He died in 1911, leaving no accessible records; and because he became a father only late in life (at the age of fifty), he did not have the opportunity to tell his children and grandchildren stories they might have been able to pass on.

Captain Johnson was a contractor who moved his force to various sites around West Virginia. He would have been John Henry's employer at the Big Bend Tunnel, one of many projects contracted out by the C & O Railroad on its way from Washington, D.C., to Cincinnati, in the hope of linking the shipping lanes of the Chesapeake Bay to the fertile Ohio Valley.[7] Halfway there, engineers following the Greenbrier River through Summers County, West Virginia, met Big Bend Mountain. To tunnel through meant driving a mile and a quarter in treacherous red shale, but the expensive alternative was laying track along the river's great southerly loop, which after meandering for about ten miles returned to within about a mile from where it had begun. Choosing to save miles of track, the C & O hired Captain Johnson, who brought some one thousand men and boys, mostly blacks, to build Big Bend Tunnel between 1870 and 1872. It may be no reflection on Captain Johnson that *The Richmond Dispatch* reported of such laborers during those years: ". . . the majority are negroes. (They are preferred) because you can cuss a nigger but whenever an attempt is made to abuse a white, there is a row."[8]

The closest towns were Hinton, nine miles to the east, and Talcott, one mile to the west. Both were railroad towns, incorporated at the insistence of C & O officials, sustained by freight that travelled through, and by the employment opportunities offered in the rail yards, the mailroom, and on the trains. At the time of Big Bend tunnel construction, the area was a wild and desolate frontier wilderness, and the tunnel itself was not only remote from but possibly closed to the public press.[9]

We can realistically assume, however, that the C & O's decision to tunnel through the mountain probably cost hundreds of lives. Tunneling is arduous, hazardous, and extremely intensive labor. America's longest tunnel at the time, Big Bend was much too deadly for the technology available to cope with it; and safety measures do not seem to have been a priority for railroading and contracting officials concerned with wresting the greatest possible profits from their endeavors. Many tunnel workers died from tunnel sickness (also called miner's consumption or silicosis) inflicted by the horrible foul air and smothering heat encountered in the poorly ventilated underground. The thick stone dust, the noxious blasting fumes from the 833 pounds of nitroglycerin used daily, and the smoke from the lard and blackstrap oil which fueled each day's 115 pounds of candles, were nearly intolerable.[10]

Workers also suffered frequent accidents from bungled blasting or crashing rocks. As evidence of Big Bend's treacherous formation, Assistant Engineer James Nelson reported in 1870: "The rock formation is very hard, but disintegrates under the weather, so much so that at the time of construction of the brick arch, large cavities, sometimes fifty feet deep were found above the timber arch."[11] The *Railroad Gazette* noted one slide of eight thousand cubic yards at the west portal: "In fact the side of the mountain 'let go' and came down into the cut."[12]

Most often the dead were simply buried in the big rock fill near the east portal, their deaths unreported. Chappell claims that the press reported that Negroes who died at Big Bend "hailed from nowhere and had not been christened," a telling remark which helps to explain a seemingly unfathomable lack of concern for working conditions at the tunnel. Most likely the work force was kept quite separate from the townspeople, whose race relations were problematic at best. (The county historian reported a bloody race riot in tiny Hinton several years later.)[13]

The most dangerous tunnel work is at the heading, which is a tube-like horizontal cross section initially cut through the mountain so that the tunnel can be completed by drilling shafts downward from the tube and then blasting out the mountain's lower parts. Heading work is especially hazardous because workers must drill at a horizontal angle under a fragile, unsupported roof. Most witnesses agreed that John Henry worked at the heading near Big Bend's east portal, with other workers boring simultaneously from the west end and then through three vertical shafts as the headings progressed.

John Henry was a driver or hammer man, which meant that he spent his days driving steel drills into Big Bend's red shale in order to bore holes in which to place explosives. The drills were one-and-a-half inches in diameter and varied in length from two to fourteen feet. When a steel driver first opened a hole, he used a shorter drill, substituting longer and longer ones as he bored deeper. He worked with a partner, a shaker or turner, whose unenviable job it was to shake the drill after each blow to rotate the cutting edge and prevent rock dust from impacting around the point. Depending on whether the driver was hammering up, down, or sideways, the shaker might lie flat on his back, holding the drill between his legs, or plaster himself against the rock face with the drill crooked in his arm or close to his chest. Shakers needed very steady nerves and profound faith to steady the drills as hammers flashed by them in the tunnel's dim light: if they slipped or the drivers missed they might easily find their flesh mangled or their bones crushed.

Every few minutes the drill dulled—drivers used thousands each day—and the shaker had to exchange it for a fresh one without breaking the driver's pace. He reached out blindly to hand the old drill to blacksmiths stationed at the portals for resharpening. Once the holes had reached a depth of about fourteen feet and were ready for blasting, the powder men inserted shots of black powder or nitroglycerin. Great buckets powered by steam engines hopefully hoisted the workers high enough up the shaft to be safe from the blast. Because the equipment was primitive and the timing close, they didn't always get clear. Many accidents occurred at this point. After the rock was blown free, workers mucked it out by hand to be hauled away from the tunnel in mule-driven carts. This work was not only labor intensive but also very slow: six steel drivers working twelve-hour shifts needed a full day to bore the holes for just one blast, which advanced the heading only ten feet.[14]

To proceed relatively quickly with the deadly and monotonous work, drivers needed to find and keep a steady pace. (In this way, steel-driving is similar to the work of a lumberjack or the effort of a long-distance runner.)

Workers found that, as had been true on the plantation as well, music helped them find the necessary rhythm. Writing on railroad songs in 1899, William Barton eloquently described the tunnel work song:

> To hear these songs, not all of which are religious, at their best, one needs to hear them in a rock tunnel. The men are hurried in after an explosion to drill with speed for another double row of blasts. They work two and two, one holding and turning the drill, the other striking it with a sledge. The sledges descend in unison as the long low chant gives the time. I wonder if the reader can imagine the effect of it all, the powder smoke filling the place, the darkness made barely visible by the little lights on the hats of the men, the echoing sounds of men and mules toward the outlet loading and carting away the rock thrown out by the last blast, and the men at the heading droning their low chant to the chink! chink! of the steel. A single musical phrase or a succession of a half dozen notes caught on a visit to such a place sticks in one's mind forever. Even as I write I seem to be in a tunnel of this description and to hear the sharp metallic stroke and syncopated chant.[15]

Thus singing was important for setting a rhythm and a pace as well as for amusement in the foul and dreary tunnel. Some witnesses and most song writers and storytellers remember John Henry as a wonderful, enthusiastic singer of these songs. Certainly his destiny has been interwoven with song; it seems likely that the first commemoration of his contest with the steam drill was through workers' hammer songs, perhaps composed and improvised by drivers and shakers moved to incorporate his heroic act into the music of the work place.

Thus far, although we cannot prove that John Henry worked in Big Bend Tunnel, we can easily demonstrate that many men like him did. His heroic contest with the steam drill is more problematic and perhaps less likely. No records exist. All we can show is that there might have been a steam drill at Big Bend, there might have been a contest, and that John Henry might have won it. In the following pages I discuss each issue in turn.

Although hand laborers drove Big Bend Tunnel through, Captain Johnson might well have experimented with a steam drill there. He used other kinds of steam machinery to hoist men up through the shafts and to drill wells.[16] Moreover, the latter nineteenth century witnessed many technological innovations in railroading, such as the introduction of the air brake and the automatic coupler to replace hand operations. Tunneling too was revolutionized during that time by the introduction of modern explosives (already in use at Big Bend) and by mechanical rock drills.

As early as 1813, well before the great rock tunnels in Europe and the United States were built, inventors were experimenting with increasingly successful drills. Tunneling projects seem to have inspired even further innovation, perhaps because hand drilling was so tedious, expensive, and slow; or perhaps because contractors, hoping to finish their projects as quickly as possible to make their bids and increase their profits, were especially energetic hustlers. Rock drill technology progressed rapidly during the fifty years of great railroad tunneling and expansion, with numerous classic Yankee innovators tinkering with the first 1849 patents of Couch and Fowle until by the 1870s and 1880s they had refined drills which could be used successfully in certain kinds of rock.

Fowle's drill, hurled like a lance into the rock face against the motion of a hollow piston, was especially influential. It inspired the clumsy 240-pound Brooks, Gates, and Burleigh drill and later the much improved Burleigh drill of 1865. Also clumsy at 372 pounds but robust enough to withstand much of the punishment in tunnel work (in which the drill's tendency is to pound itself to pieces), the Burleigh drill was a spectacular success at Massachusetts' Hoosac Tunnel.[17] Pioneering contractors imported it there to replace the Brooks, Gates, and Burleigh which, priced at four hundred dollars, was too expensive for them to tolerate its constant breakdown.[18]

Hoosac engineers used Burleigh drills from 1866 until they had completed the tunnel, and although they had to ship out approximately 250 machines a month for repairs, they were nonetheless pleased with the Burleigh's effectiveness. Before 1865 engineers had found hand labor at Hoosac terribly slow: they estimated that they had required fifty days' man labor to advance the tunnel a single foot. Each man had been able to bore only about nineteen inches of holes for explosives a day. Contractor Shanley compiled an extensive report comparing the cost of power drilling to the expense of hand labor during the years 1869-1874. At the tunnel's east heading, Shanley estimated that power drilling had cost four cents per inch, and hand labor nine and one-third cents per inch; in the harder rock at the west heading, machine work had cost seven and one-tenth cents per inch as opposed to thirteen cents for hand labor. On the average Shanley found he needed five and one-eighth feet of holes to remove one cubic yard of rock. Converting his estimates on the comparative cost of labor to cubic yards, he estimated that the Burleigh drill cost him 75.2 cents per cubic yard, while hand drilling required $2.9640. (Shanley's calculations include the expense of mining labor, mechanical labor, blacksmith work, iron, steel, oil, coal, interest, and depreciation. He does not indicate if he took repair costs into account, but I believe that he must have.)

Shanley's glowing report concluded that hand labor would have involved an additional twelve years and three times the expense to complete the Hoosac Tunnel. (This latter estimate was based on tests which showed that in the Hoosac micha-schist machines progressed 167 feet for every 40 feet by hand.) Similar claims from Pennsylvania's Nesquehoning Tunnel that explicitly include running and repair costs confirm his estimates. Nesquehoning engineers concluded that hand drilling cost 26.2 cents per foot, while machines required only 14.1 cents per foot. The Burleigh drill also was used successfully at Nevada's Sutro Tunnel and throughout the western mining region in 1875.[19]

Although the Burleigh was an influential and popular innovation, it was not without its problems in certain kinds of rock and certainly not without serious rivals. American inventors patented 110 rock drills between 1850-1875; Europeans patented 86. Some of the best drills emerged during the years of Big Bend construction, and although most scholars have assumed that John Henry must have raced the Burleigh, his opponent might well have been one of these newer inventions. For example, the Ingersoll drill was patented in 1871 by Ingersoll Rand, which eventually merged with the Burleigh Company to produce a very highly regarded rock drill used successfully at Musconetcong Tunnel in New Jersey from 1872-1875.[20] Perhaps Johnson experimented with an early Ingersoll model at Big Bend.

Another possibility would have been the American Diamond Drill Company's black diamond drill. Praised by *Scientific American* in 1871, the black diamond model sounds well equipped to meet the challenge of Big Bend. It was much simpler and more portable than earlier models and designed to drill in any position or direction (a considerable asset in tunnel work). The drill's most exciting feature was its ability to adjust to the varying hardness of different kinds of rock, although in doing so it ran erratically at vastly varying speeds. The diamond drill could bore through eleven inches of brittle sandstone in just fifty-five seconds, while four inches of much harder blue limestone required three minutes. Although its hard black diamond drill bits were too brittle to stand percussion for long, the drill's flexibility was appealing to contractors.[21]

Throughout the 1870s rock drill technology continued to improve, with an impressive innovation in the middle of the decade: new hammer drills which ironically imitated more closely the movements of a man and thus avoided the Fowle drill's costly, stressful reciprocating motion between drill and piston, a feature that also was characteristic of its imitators.[22]

At the C & O's Lewis Tunnel, the contractor tried the Burleigh drill for perhaps as long as nine months. Several separate reports established its presence there during part of 1870 and most of 1871, although these reports might have referred to distinct instances and several different drills.[23] Big Bend was only forty-three miles away, but 2,046 feet longer and composed of brittle shale much more likely to clog and choke the steam drill than the sandstone at Lewis. C & O engineers interviewed during the 1920s did not recall the steam drill in use at Big Bend.[24] But the C & O was in difficult straits during the early 1870s, overextended and overcapitalized, facing court orders to repay back taxes it had dodged, and anxious to complete the route and recover its investment.[25] For his part, Captain Johnson wanted to finish the tunnel quickly, and he lived at an historic moment when many possibilities presented themselves for expediting the work. Manufacturers were aggressively marketing the new drills; engineering and scientific journals exulted in the time and money they could save.[26] It seems impossible that Johnson would not have tested the Burleigh, Ingersoll, or Black Diamond drill. The affair might have been brief and unofficial; perhaps it occured at the prompting of a salesman who had brought the drill to the tunnel for a promotional trial. Most likely there was no sale, but just a test—or a contest— between Johnson's star driver, John Henry, and the steam drill.

Contests between two steel drivers were quite common on tunneling and mining projects—perhaps to provide amusement or build morale, perhaps to encourage free overtime. Festivity sometimes surrounded the race in the form of drinking, wagers, and prize money. Since contests were commonplace, that some of the witnesses at Big Bend do not particularly recall John Henry's particular test is not especially surprising. It is also possible that this was one race his supervisors did not want publicized: the steam drill might have distracted and angered the workers, and John Henry's victory certainly would have impressed them with their employer's dependence on manual labor. Moreover, Big Bend was a mile and a quarter long, worked at five different points by one thousand laborers. Some might easily have missed an isolated race in such a mammoth project.

Those who did recall the contest placed it at a logical time and place, just a few months after Johnson had assumed the tunnel contract (during the summer or fall of 1870) and at the east heading, completed in November of 1870 and closest to the Greenbrier River—the only convenient source of water to power the steam drill. Because this also was the first point to be drilled, the place witnesses named was consistent with the time; and it also seems probable that Johnson would have tested the steam drill soon after starting tunnel construction.

We must turn to the ballad for speculation on why John Henry might have agreed to a contest; Big Bend witnesses volunteered no motive. Some versions of the ballad label the hero a hammerin' fool, while others suggest that just five years out of slavery and with no place much to go, he purposefully took a stand to save his job. Perhaps his captain offered him a share of a wager, or perhaps he acted out of personal loyalty to his captain or his fellow employees. We cannot demonstrate that he raced the steam drill, but only that he might have, that history supports the claims of the ballad and the testimony of those who remember him. Re-arching of Big Bend's east portal in the 1880s concealed the holes allegedly left by the contest.

Could John Henry have won? This is perhaps the murkiest matter. We do not know how long the contest lasted or how far the contestants drove. Claims concerning the contest's duration range from thirty-five minutes to two days.

Once again we can look to recorded history for clues. A series of Massachusetts tests in 1865 using six different drills concluded that on the average they could drive 2.01 inches a minute.[27] This particular rate would not be impossible for a man to outspeed; if we look at contest records, they vary from William Shea's 25.31 inches through Rocky Mountain granite in fifteen minutes in 1892 to the Tarr Brothers' all-time double-jack record—again through granite—of 59.5 inches in fifteen minutes (set in 1912 in Butte).[28] Since Shea drove one and two-thirds inches a minute and the Tarr Brothers almost four inches, we can assume that John Henry could have driven over two inches, especially if he were using two hammers. Of course, an 1871 drill would have been faster than those of 1865, but if the Burleigh Drill were used, it would have had difficulty getting through the brittle shale at Big Bend. As many versions of the ballad taunt: "Your hole's done choke and your drill's done broke." The Burleigh would likely have hung up in cracks and clogged with dust. This musical detail is so consistent with what engineers claimed was the Burleigh's chief flaw that it seems more plausible as an eyewitness report than merely as the product of a balladeer's imagination.

The outcome may have depended on how long the contest lasted, although it is difficult to say which contestant would have profited from a longer race. John Henry would have tired, and the drill might have required numerous repairs or even broken down completely. Often ballads claim that John Henry drove fourteen feet, and the steam drill drove only nine feet. If, as many contests did, this one lasted thirty-five minutes, we can check John Henry's distance against the Tarr Brothers' record of 59.5 inches in fifteen minutes. Given twenty more minutes at the same pace, they would have bored eleven and one-half feet. If John Henry, wielding two hammers through less resistant rock, drove fourteen feet in the same amount of time, his feat would have been heroic indeed, but just within the realm of human possibility.

Often the ballad claims that John Henry died as a result of the race, from a rollin' or a roarin' in his head (which might refer to a stroke), or because he busted his "intrels" out or simply hammered himself to death. Several witnesses believed, however, that he died later in the tunnel, possibly during a rock fall, or from a fever. Especially because he worked in the tunnel's most dangerous place, and especially because the longer the shale was exposed the more likely it was to crumble, John Henry might well have died later on. Residents of Hinton and Talcott and laborers in the tunnel ever since have firmly believed his ghost haunts Big Bend.

Tales of death have surrounded Big Bend Tunnel for many years. Although local lore for the most part ignored its black builders, many of whom must have died there, white passengers and workers who were killed later provoked the resentment and ire of area townspeople. Nineteenth century railroading was a hazardous business generally, and the C & O was no exception. The Summers County historian notes many deaths in the rail yards at Hinton, and several local disasters, including one especially tragic event when the Big Creek trestle, flimsily built from wood, collapsed and burned along with the freight train crossing it at the time. Big Bend, also carelessly constructed, was particularly deadly. The fumes that once had suffocated its workers continued to plague those riding through. One engineer died of suffocation by smoke when his train was forced to stop in the tunnel for several minutes, and eventually public outcry over such tragedies as his death and also Big Bend's generally hazardous and unpleasant conditions forced the C & O to install fans. Throughout the 1870s the tunnel's roof was crumbling as well; one particularly scandalous accident occurred when a freight train met a mass of debris crashing down from the roof, killing the fireman and burying the engineer who survived, however, to be killed twenty years later in the Hinton yards. Finally in 1883, Big Bend virtually caved in, killing several people and forcing the surviving passengers to take a long hike around the mountain. At this point, Hinton's District Attorney courageously took the C & O to court, where the tunnel was condemned, forcing the railroad to spend a great deal of money and ten years' time re-arching it in brick.[29] Residents, however, continued to associate it with death: a favorite tale recounted in the 1920s portrayed two brothers—Irishmen—who, finished with their work there and preparing to leave, decided to walk through one last time for sentiment's sake. As the story goes, Big Bend crashed in on them and they met an ironic death.

But most of those who died at Big Bend remain relatively anonymous. It is John Henry's death that popular culture commemorates, his ghost that workers and residents believe haunts the tunnel most vividly. We shall never know what actually became of him, but chances were probably less than even that he would have left Big Bend alive. His might have been just another unsung death; instead the heroic tradition surrounding the moment that he may have chosen to die encourages us to build a life for him. I like to envision some anonymous worker, inspired by John Henry's heroic act to weave his death into a hammer song, pacing his own toil to the life affirming refrain: "This ol' hammer, That killed John Henry, won't kill me." Through song drivers and shakers could comment discreetly and indirectly on working conditions and consequences which they were not allowed to discuss. They could also defy death. And that death which they both commemorated and defied has inspired those of us who will never face such grinding, hazardous toil to explore and appreciate the lives of those who did, as personalized in their hero, John Henry.

NOTES

1. Newbell Niles Puckett, "Names of American Negro Slaves," p. 163; Guy B. Johnson, *John Henry: Tracking Down a Negro Legend,* p. 12.

2. On the significance of naming to slave family life, see Herbert G. Gutman, *The Black Family in Slavery and Freedom, 1750-1925,* pp. 230-56; for one person's slightly ethnocentric account of the tendency of former slaves to take new names, see Elizabeth Kilham, "Sketches in Color," pp. 31-38; on the 1920s speculation about John Henry's last name, see Johnson, *John Henry,* p. 12.

3. For a lively discussion of John the Conqueror, see Zora Neale Hurston, "High John de Conquer," in *Mother Wit from the Laughing Barrel*, edited by Alan Dundes, pp. 541-48. The best recent exploration of the John and Master story cycle is in Lawrence Levine's *Black Culture and Black Consciousness*, pp. 127-33.

4. See Gutman, *Black Family*, pp. 144-45.

5. See Ronald L. Lewis, *Coal, Iron and Slaves*, pp. 90-96.

6. Pete Daniel, in *The Shadow of Slavery*, writes eloquently on debt peonage in the Reconstruction South; Paul Oliver in *The Meaning of the Blues* (pp. 48-49) and Eileen Southern in *The Music of Black Americans* (p. 245) describe laboring conditions. Orra Langhorne, in *Southern Sketches from Virginia*, (pp. 10-11), writes of meeting a black woman on a train in 1881. The woman was "just returning from six months sojourn in a mining district in Iowa." Langhorne adds:

> I had seen in the Valley papers that Major Schumate, an ex-Virginian now in the employ of a mining company in the West, had carried seven-hundred Negroes from the Valley of Virginia to Iowa in the last year or two.

This system, which may have been quite common, sounds very similar to the mining companies' use of commissioned agents to rent slaves, described by Lewis, *Coal, Iron and Slaves*, pp. 84, 134.

7. On 2 April 1870, the *Railroad Gazette* reported that the C & O had contracted out all work to some twenty different contractors. On 2 November 1872, in noting the completion of Big Bend Tunnel, the *Railroad Gazette* reported, revealingly, of Johnson and his workers: ". . . the greater portion of Captain Johnson's force has been dispatched to Miller's Ferry in charge of Capt. Steele." This report indicates that Johnson may have been the type of labor contractor who moved his men from one site to another; it also reveals why it was difficult later on to trace John Henry's co-workers.

8. *Richmond Dispatch*, 30 April 1872.

9. Charles Nordhoff described the Big Bend region in the *New York Weekly Tribune*, 1 November 1871:

> When we mounted our horses . . .we bade good-bye to roads and entered the New River country—a howling wilderness, through which the engineer parties of the Chesapeake and Ohio Railroad have constructed what pleases them to call a path, by which path, if you have a sure-footed horse and steady nerves, you may ride at a slow and difficult walk. . . . If you have ridden into the Yo-Semite Valley, you will find here a trail steeper and more difficult than that curious descent, and not two miles but eighty long.

Louis Chappell complained in *John Henry: A Folk-Lore Study*, p. 69: "The press of Virginia and West Virginia, which apparently remained silent on casualties in the tunnels of the New River region, was able to give startling numbers of deaths from the construction of tunnels farther away."

10. Chappell, *John Henry*, pp. 65-66, estimates the quantities of nitroglycerin and candles from comparable amounts used in the Hoosac Tunnel.

11. James Nelson, *The C and O Railway*, p. 27.

12. *Railroad Gazette*, 15 June 1872, p. 257. On 12 October 1872, the *Railroad*

Gazette reported that work was retarded by rock slides caused by heavy rains.

13. James H. Miller, *History of Summers County, West Virginia,* p. 179.

14. For excellent, vivid discussions of Big Bend Tunnel work, see Chappell, *John Henry,* pp. 61-70; Johnson, *John Henry,* pp. 27-44; Hank Burchard, "In Quest of the Historical John Henry," Richard Dorson, "The Ballad of John Henry," and Jeffrey Miller, "John Henry."

15. William E. Barton, "Recent Negro Melodies," pp. 304-5.

16. *Richmond Dispatch,* 21 January 1871, describes a problematic steam drill used to bore for water.

17. Gosta Sandstrom, *Tunnels,* pp. 288, 290, 291; Henry Drinker, *Tunneling, Explosive Compounds, and Rock Drills,* pp. 54, 160.

18. Drinker, *Tunneling,* p. 460, estimates that ten drills were shipped out for repairs each day.

19. Ibid., p. 165, 217, 244, 249-51.

20. Sandstrom, *Tunnels,* pp. 291-93.

21. *Scientific American,* 18 November 1871.

22. Drinker, *Tunneling,* pp. 964-65.

23. Chappell, *John Henry,* p. 45.

24. Johnson, *John Henry,* pp. 48-51.

25. Miller, *History of Summers County,* p. 185.

26. *Richmond Dispatch,* 18 November 1871, and *Scientific American,* 18 November 1871.

27. Drinker, *Tunneling,* p. 159.

28. *Engineering Magazine,* September 1892, p. 886.

29. Miller, *History of Summers County,* pp. 164, 181, 190.

30. Johnson, *John Henry,* pp. 28-29.

2

THE TRAIL OF JOHN HENRY

During the 1920s two southern professors, Guy Johnson and Louis Chappell, vigorously pursued the trail of John Henry and gathered the only existing testimony from witnesses who claimed to know something of the steel-driving hero. When Johnson and Chappell began their research, John Henry lived only in song; folklorists had no notion of the background to the ballad. Both began by soliciting correspondence from all around the United States, and both were drawn eventually to the Big Bend Tunnel region. Both concluded their investigations through interviews with elderly residents of Hinton and Talcott. With the exception of one letter written to folklorist John Harrington Cox, I have relied solely on Johnson's and Chappell's materials for my information.

I have reorganized the interviews so that they speak coherently to the crucial issues surrounding the John Henry tradition. Thus, those cited first illustrate the age, vitality, and variety of John Henry lore; and they culminate, as does the weight of the evidence, with witnesses who knew John Henry at the Big Bend Tunnel.

Louis Chappell was interested in dating the event he knew only from ballads as a step toward locating its place of origin. Much of the testimony Chappell gathered was too vague to help with even an approximate date. He read, for example, a report from clergyman J. T. Baker:

> I was reared in South Carolina, and there I often heard the colored men, while driving with heavy hammers, sing this much of the song in question, which seemed to be the chorus:
>
> > 'This is the hammer that killed John
> > Henry, but can't kill me;

This is the hammer that killed John
Henry, but can't kill me.'

I heard one man relate to another that John Henry was a negro con-
vict (possibly of the state of South Carolina) who at that time was hired
out to a quarry company, that John was such a powerful man a bet
was made on him and a race was staged with the steam drill. The drill
beat him ten inches in a day and that night John Henry died.[1]

Other written reports Chappell was able to pin down through further re-
search. In the following case he visited Mrs. Susan Bennett at her home in
Landisburg, West Virginia, where she told him that she had known about
John Henry since around 1870 or 1872.

Wish to say that there was a man of that day in making the big ben
tunnell that whipped the steam drill down. I live in about 25 miles of
the tunnell and it was as true as the song Pearl Bryant or Jessie James
or George Alley and you may write to the Bureau of Information and
get the History of John Henry and his captains name. We have 3 records
of Johnie so I will close and listen at him drive that steel on down.[2]

Several others remembered hearing of John Henry from the late nineteenth
century. Chappell felt that their testimony demonstrated that the tradition
was widely diffused by the 1880s:

Joe Wilson, Norfolk, Va. In 1890 people around town here were
singing the song about John Henry, a hammering man, hammering in
the mountains four long years. I was working in an oyster house here
for Fenerstein and Company, and I am 66 years old and still working
for them people.
Tishie Fitzwater, Hosterman, W. Va. I have heard of him for 40
years. A old colored man told me that John Henry was a colored man,
and he was a cousin of him. I have never heard any one say that John
Henry was any relation to John Hardy, and I am sixty years old.
R. H. Pope, Clinton, N.C. Well I know of the song 41 years. I went
to Georgia 1888, and that song was being sung by all the young men.
I am now 60 years of age. In those days I knew all the words of that
song but can't remember all of them now, but it was that he would die
with the hammer in his hand before he would be beat driving steel. . . .
He was a negro and a real man so I was told.
O. W. Evans, Editor of *The New Castle Record,* New Castle, Va.
The writer is a man in the 50's, but as a boy and young man I can dis-
tinctly remember the song, the tune, and some of the verses, which
I remember were quite a number . . . The negroes of forty years ago
regarded him [John Henry] as a hero of their race.

W. C. Handy, New York City. As a composer of Negro music I seized on a melody that I used to hear when I was a little boy, at Muscle Shoals Canal in Alabama. I printed this under the title JOHN HENRY as I had heard it.

Andy Anderson, Huntington, W. Va. About 45 years ago I was in Morgan County, Kentucky. There was a bunch of darkeys came from Miss. to assist in driving a tunnel at the head of Big Caney Creek for the O & K. R R Company. There is where I first heard this song, as they would sing it to keep time with their hammers.

Jesse Sparks, Ethel, W. Va. My father is 87, and he says it has been a song ever since he can remember. He says he has heard his grandpa sing it. . . . I am 37 years old myself, and I have been knowing it ever since I have been big enough to sing.[3]

Two witnesses testified to the popularity and extraordinary vitality of John Henry lore. Mr. N. A. Brown, stationed on the U.S.S. *Pittsburgh* at Shanghai, wrote Chappell:

I've heard the song in a thousand different places, nigger extra gangs, hoboes of all kinds, coal miners and furnace men, river and wharf rats, beach combers and sailors, harvest hands and timber men. Some of them drunk and some sober. It is scattered over all the states and some places on the outside. I have heard any number of verses cribbed bodily from some other song or improvised to suit the occasion. . . .

The opinion among hoboes, section men and others who sing the song is that John Henry was a negro, 'a coal black man' a partly for-gotten verse says, 'a big fellow' an old hobo once said. He claimed to have known him but was crying drunk on 'Dago Red,' so I'm discounting everything he said. I have met very few who claim to have known him.

There was a giant yellow negro with only one arm who helped to put the Tennessee Central through the mountains between Nashville and Rockwood, Tennessee. His name was John Henry and his thumb was said to be as large as an ordinary man's wrist. He could pick up a length of the steel they were laying, straighten up, turn himself completely around, still holding the rail, and lower it back into place. I am not cliaming this fellow as the original John Henry. He wasn't anything above the ordinary with a hammer.[4]

And Mr. Leon Harris, secretary of the Rock Island Railway Colored Employees' Club and contributor of a folktale cited later in this text, wrote Guy Johnson:

The ballad, by special right, belongs to the railroad builders. John Henry was a railroad builder. It belongs to the pick-and-shovel men,— to the skinners,—to the steel drivers, to the men of the railroad con-

struction camps, which they call the "gradin' camp." It is a song by
Negro laborers everywhere, but none can sing it as they can sing it,
because none honor and revere the memory of John Henry as do they.
I have been a "Rambler" all my life,—ever since I ran away from the
"white folks" when twelve years old,—and I have worked with my
people in railroad grading camps from the Great Lakes to Florida and
from the Atlantic to the Missouri River, and, wherever I have worked,
I have always found someone who could and would sing of John Henry.

And I have tried faithfully to get the story of John Henry. No folksong fiend has searched more diligently than have I. But I have failed.
Anyone who tries will fail. I believe, however, that the following are facts:

1. John Henry really lived.
2. He beat a steam drill down and died doing it.
3. Li'l Bill was his "buddie" or helper.
4. He worked for a railroad construction contractor.
5. His wife, or his woman's name, was "Lucy." (I have never heard
   any other woman's name in a "John Henry" song.)

These are probabilities:

1. He died in the early 1870s.
2. He was a Virginian.
3. He worked on the C. & O. road or on a branch of that system.
4. His "captain's" name was Tommy Walters—probably an assistant
   foreman however.

In a later communication Mr. Harris makes these additional statements:

I have always been deeply interested in John Henry. I knew that his was
a story worth preserving and about fifteen years ago I wrote a short story
built around the incident, but could never find a publisher. This winter I
revised it some and sent it to the Opportunity contest. I got most of my
information from an old Negro grader who was called John Camp. This
was not his name for I know he was a fugitive from justice. He claimed
to have known John Henry personally—said he was present when he died,
but he prevaricated so much that I could not believe much that he said
was true. He was a good banjoist, and it is his version of the song and tune
that I sent. He said that John Henry died during the Civil War, also that
he was a "free" Negro—but that is hardly possible for no steam drills
were used in this country prior to that time. None that I know of.[5]

Johnson cites another interesting letter he received from the Ohio State Penitentiary:

Having seen your advertisement in the *Chicago Defender,* I am answer-
ing your request for information, concerning the Old time Hero of the Big
Bend Tunnel Days—or Mr. John Henry.

I have succeeded in recalling and piecing together 13 verses, dedicated to such a deserving and spending character, of by gone days. It was necessary to interview a number of Old Timers, of this Penitentiary to get some of the missing words and to verify my recollections; so I only hope it will please you, and be what you wish.

In regards to the reality of John Henry, I would say he was a real live and powerful man, some 50 years ago, and actually died after beating a steam drill. His wife was a very small woman who loved John Henry with all her heart.

My Grand Father, on my mother's side, was a steel driver, and worked on all the big jobs through out the country, in them days, when steam drills were not so popular. He was always boasting about his prowess with a hammer, claiming none could beat him but John Henry. He used to sing about John Henry, and tell of the old days when hammers and hammer men, could do the work independent of steam drills.

Being pretty young at the time, I can not now recall the stories I heard, but I know John Henry, died some time in the eighties about 1881 or 1882, I'm sure which was a few years before I was born.

I am setting price on this information, I am a prisoner here in the Ohio Penitentiary and without funds, so I will be pleased to except what ever you care to offer.[6]

Some informants confused John Henry with the legendary desperado John Hardy, who was executed for murder in West Virginia in 1894. John Harrington Cox quotes the Honorable W. A. McCorkle, Governor of West Virginia from 1893-1897, in a 1916 letter to Dr. II. S. Green of Charleston:

"He [John Hardy] was a steel-driver and was famous in the beginning of the building of the C[hesapeake] & O[hio] Railroad. He was also a steel-driver in the beginning of the extension of the N[orfolk] & W[estern] Railroad. It was about 1872 that he was in this section. This was before the day of the steam drills and the drill work was done by two powerful men who were special steel drillers. They struck the steel from each side and as they struck the steel they sang a song which they improvised as they worked. John Hardy was the most famous steel-driver ever known in southern West Virginia. He was a magnificent specimen of the genus homo, was reported to be six feet two, and weighed two hundred and twenty-five or thirty pounds, was straight as an arrow and was one of the handsomest men in the country, and, as one informant told me, was as black as a kittle in hell.

"Whenever there was any spectacular performances along the line of drilling, John Hardy was put on the job, and it is said that he could drill more steel than any two men of his day. He was a great gambler and was notorious all through the country for his luck at gambling. To the dusky sex all through the country he was 'the greatest ever,' and

he was admired and beloved by all the negro women from the southern
West Virginia line to the C. & O. In addition to this he could drink
more whiskey, sit up all night and drive steel all day to a greater extent
than any man ever known in the country. . . .His story is a story of one
of the composite characters that so often arise in the land. A man of
kind heart, very strong, pleasant address, yet a gambler, a roue, a
drunkard, and a fierce fighter.'''[7]

Others simply assumed John Henry and John Hardy were the same man.
Journalist Erskine Phillips of Fayetteville, West Virginia, reported a characteristic example of this confusion to Chappell:

> I had a very interesting conversation with an old negro here sometime
> ago. He, Ben Turner, and his brother, Sam, are natives of Old Virginia,
> and migrated to West Virginia, along with hundreds of other 'niggers,'
> to work on the C and O Railway. They both worked in the Big Bend
> Tunnel. John Henry was a powerful man, large all over, but possessed
> of the 'most powerful arms and shoulders I ever saw. Why,' he said,
> 'his arms was as big as a stovepipe. Never seen such arms on a man in
> my life.'
>   'Could he drive steel the way the song says he could?' I asked. 'Law—
> I reckon he could. Make that steel ring just like a bell. But look here.
> John Hardy (he spoke of him both as Henry and Hardy) had a steel
> turner almost as big and strong as he was. Just the same as two men
> driving. That man could turn the steel and hit almost as hard as John
> Henry could. John Henry wouldn't let no one else turn steel for him.'
>   The John Henry song was not the one that was generally sung by the
> steel-drivers. If some one were hurt or killed in the tunnel, the foreman
> would yell, 'All right, boys, let's hear "John Henry." ' The song had
> the effect of sobering the workmen, taking their minds off the accident
> and restoring order.[8]

And C. J. Wallace of Charleston, West Virginia, testified:

> I am a steam shovel operator or 'runner,' and have heard steel drivers
> sing John Henry all my life and there are probably lots of verses I never
> heard as it used to be that every new steel driving 'nigger' had a new verse
> to John Henry.
>   I never personally knew John Henry, but I have talked to lots of old
> timers who did. I have been told by some old Rail Road construction
> men that John Henry and John Hardy were the same man and by some
> others that they were not, but I believe that John Hardy was his real
> name. He actually worked on the C & O Ry. for Langhorn & Langhorn
> and was able to drive 9 feet of steel faster than the steam drill could in

Big Bend Tunnel. Then later he was hanged in Welch, W. Va., for murdering a man. After shifting out the 'chaff' think I can assure you the above is correct.

I have heard the two songs sung mostly in the same section of the country that is, West Virginia, Virginia, Kentucky, Tennessee, and North Carolina, seldom elsewhere except by men from one of the above states. I have worked all over the South, South West, and have heard the John Henry song almost ever since I could remember, and it was an old song the first I ever remember of.[9]

Others such as B. E. Thompson of Sutton, West Virginia, objected vehemently to this confusion:

Having been born and raised in the state of Tennessee and, therefore, in sufficiently close contact with the negro element there, it happens that I have heard these songs practically all of my life, until I left that section six years ago . . .

I have been informed that John Henry was a true character all right, a nigger whose vocation was driving steel during the construction of a tunnel on one of the southern railways. I heard the John Henry song long before I did John Hardy. It has always been my understanding that John Hardy was a western character, probably a train robber.[10]

Lee Holley of Tazewell, Virginia, was also adamant:

I've lived 'round here all my life. I've been acquainted with the camps in this section forty or fifty years. I remember seeing John Hardy pretty often, and know all about him.

He was black and tall, and would weigh about 200 pounds, and was 27 or 8 when he was hung at Welch over in McDowell County. He was with a gang of gamblers 'round the camps. Harry Christian, Lewis Rhodes, Cooper Boots, and Ben Red, and Jim Mason, and others besides were all about as bad as he was. They were all loafers and gamblers, and robbed the camps at night often after pay-day. Harry Christian was hung for killing Bill Crowe, and most of the gang got killed sooner or later.

My Cousin Bob Holley drove steel with John Henry in Big Bend Tunnel. John Henry was the famous steeldriver there in building that tunnel. I heard Bob talk about him several times, but Bob's dead now. He's been dead ten years. I know John Hardy didn't drive steel in Big Bend Tunnel; he couldn't because he wasn't old enough when it was built, and he didn't work anyway. He got his living gambling and robbing 'round the camps.[11]

Several informants insisted that John Henry was white. Chappell quotes Hazel Underwood of Huntersville, West Virginia:

> My father has often told me about John Henry. He says he was a man of about 35 years old, strong built, had muscles was supposed to be like iron. He drilled holes in the big rock cliffs with his strong arms and his two hammers one in each hand day by day.
>
> There is no mistake about his being a white man. Papa says his last drive was made in the big ben tunnel on New River. Father says he has heard when he was a boy all about him and learned the song when he worked in the log camps, but had forgotten it till he heard part of it on a Record we have, it is just a part of it. Mamma and Pa says they can't believe this is all.[12]

George Roberts of Sweetland, West Virginia, believed that John Henry was an Englishman:

> John Henry was a white man, an American born English by birth. His weight—240 lbs at the age of 22. The muscle of his arm was 22 inches around. Many times have I seen his woman but never John Henry personal, but have worked in the mines for years with the old Welshman that sharpened tools for him by the name of Billy McKenzie.
>
> John Henry was a native of Virginia and did actually kill himself driving steel at the Big Bend tunnel on the C. & O. R.R. in the year of 1873. He was in the penitentiary for killing a man and the contractors got him out to drive steel. He was no relative of John Hardy at all.
>
> I am nearly 70 years old, and I was a miner for a great many years in the Kanawha Valley at Paint Creek after the C. & O. was built, and that is the place I used to see John Henry's wife a little ugly freckle face woman. She would come around the mines where the work was going on.[13]

And Harvey Hicks wrote from Evington, Virginia:

> John Henry was a white man they say. He was a prisoner when he was driving steel in the Big Ben tunnel at that time, and he said he could beat the steam drill down. They told him if he did why they would set him free. It is said that he beat the steam drill about two minutes and a half and fell dead. He drove with a hammer in each hand, nine pound sledge.[14]

Johnson found persistent efforts to place John Henry in Alabama. Glendora Cummings wrote:

My Uncle Gus (the man who raised my father) was working by John Henry and saw him when he beat the steam drill and fell dead. This was in the year 1887. It was at Oak Mountain, Alabama. They were working for Shay and Dabney, the meanest white contractors at the time.

The steel drivers were the highest salaried men. But John Henry's salary was higher than theirs. Nobody ever drove steel as well as him. I mean when I say the steel drivers were the highest paid; that for a negro in those days in South.

John Henry wielded a nine pound Hammer. So the words of one of the songs: Is: "A nine pound hammer killed John Henry but this old hammer wont kill me." Both my Uncle and my father were steel drivers. So I have heard several different kinds of the John Henry songs. In one John Henry song a man named Lazarus is mentioned, and also George Collins. These people are not myths. They all lived in the camp with my Uncle Gus and my father. My father arrived after John Henry dropped dead, but my Uncle Gus and John Henry were friends.[15]

Also writing Johnson was F. P. Barker of Birmingham:

I take great Pleasur to write and informing you that there was a real Man John Henry. Brown skin Colored 147 lb a steel driver He driv against a steam drill and beate it down a shaft advancin. He song before He wowed let it beat him down that He wowed die with his Hammer in his Hand and He did it. F. P. Barker I was driving steel on Red Mountain at that time 45 years ago sown where about that time. Just as true as you see the sun. there was a real man John Henry. He was the champon of wowld with a Hammer.

. . . I was Driving steel on Red Mountain at the time of the contest. John Henry was on Cursey Mountain tunnel in His song he told his shaker to shak that drill and turn it around John Henry is Bownd to Beat the steem Drill down the steem Drill Beat men of every other Race down to the sand. Now Ill gaive my life before I let it beat the Negro man. I tell you more a bout it when I see more of my old mates I am 73 years old and it been nerley a half a century.[16]

The most emphatic and thorough of the Alabama advocates was C. C. Spencer of Salt Lake City:

. . . John Henry was a native of Holly Springs, Mississippi, and was shipped to the Cruzee mountan tunnel, Alabama, to work on the A.G.S. Railway in the year of 1880. In 1881 he had acquired such a skill as a hand driller that every one along the road was singing his praise. It happened that at about this time an agent for a steam drill company (drills used now are compressed air) came around trying to sell the contractor a steam drill. The contractor informed the agent that he had a Negro who could beat his damned old drill any day; as a result of this argument the company owning the drill offered to put it in for nothing if this man could drill more rock with the hammer than he could with the drill. And, so the contractor (Shea & Dabner) accepted the proposition.

This man John Henry, whose real name was John H. Dabner, was called to the office and they asked him if he could beat this steam drill. He said that he could, the fact of the matter was he had never seen a steam drill and did not know what one could do. The contractor told him that if he could beat this steam drill he would give him a new suit of clothes and fifty dollars, which was a large amount for that day and time. John Henry accepted the proposition providing they would buy him a fourteen-pound hammer. This the contractor did.

Now the drills that we had in those days were nothing like the drills we have today. The drills they used then in hard rock could only drill a hole twenty-five feet deep in a day and the average man could only drill a hole about fifteen feet deep in a day working by hand.

Well—preparations were being made for the race for about three weeks, and on the 20th of September, 1882, the race took place, the agent from New York using steam, and the man from Mississippi, using the fourteen-pound hammer, in the hardest rock ever known in Alabama.

The agent had lots of trouble with his drill, but John Henry and his helper (Rubin Johnson) one turning the drill and the other striking, kept pecking away with that old fourteen-pound hammer. Of course the writer was only about fourteen years old at the time, but I remember there were about three or four hundred people present.

When the poor man with the hammer fell in the arms of his helper in a dead faint, they threw water on him and revived him, and his first words were: "send for my wife, I am blind and dying."

They made for his wife, who took his head in her lap and the last words he said were: "Have I beat that old steam drill?" The record was twenty-seven and one half feet (27½′). The steam drill twenty-one (21′), and the agent lost his steam drill.

In a second letter to Johnson, Spencer added:

I have just received your letter and am indeed pleased to know that it was of some assistance to you in writing the history of John Henry.

Now, my Dear Sir, I feel sure that you do not expect one's mind to be clear concerning the minor things which were connected with this story forty-four years after the Actor has passed from the stage. As I kept no diary in those days, I must quote from memory the facts as near as I can recall them.

No. 1. The name of the Railroad was the Alabama Great Southern.

No. 2 His name was John Henry Dabner, but we called him John Henry.

No. 3 I think he was born a slave in Dabner family.

No. 4 I should judge that he was at least 25 or 26 years old at the time of his death. His weight was near 180 lbs; his color very dark he was about 5′ 10 or 11 inches in height.

No. 5 I do not recall the name of the County if I ever knew it, but the tunnel is near the line which divides Georgia and Alabama. I was told by the older men that there was a town on the Georgia side by the name of Riseingforn. At that time I was under the care of a white man, the young Master of my people and I was never left to wander around very much, so I never went to this town in Georgia. There was, also a town fifteen miles to the north in Alabama (in which was an Iron-Ore mine) by the name of "Red Mountain."

Now, Sir, as this Railroad was in the process of construction, there was no train's running upon it, so the names of these towns may have changed ere this time.

No, John Henry never was in West Virginia, but his wife stayed with the older men and cooked for many of them after we came to West Virginia, in 1886, for the purpose of working on the Norfolk & Western Railroad in the Elkhorn tunnel.

The above is about all that I know of my importance about John Henry.

. . . John Brown was the man of the "Big Bend tunnel fame." This man lived and probably died before this writer ever came upon the stage. In my younger days I saw old men who claimed to have worked with this man—but no two told me the same story.

This tunnel was put through with slaves, and if John Brown was one of the men who worked there as a slave, or in the Big Bend tunnel at any time, he never raced against a steam drill. There never was a steam drill in there. If you will write to any Railroad Journal you will find that the "C. & O." road was put through in 59-69, long before the steam drills came into use.

This is a trend of the song about John Brown, sang when I was a boy some forty six years ago: "John Brown was a little boy, sitting upon his Mother's knee. He said the Big Ben tunnel on the C. & O. Road will sure be the death of me."[17]

Johnson found these Alabama claims inconclusive, but he was troubled by his inability to locate the Cruzee/Cursey tunnel to which they repeatedly referred. In evaluating Johnson's evidence, Chappell felt that the reference could be to the Santa Cruz Mountains in Jamaica, where the ballad might have originated and spread later to Big Bend. He cites two reports, the first from H. R. Fox, Chief Engineer of the Jamaican Government Railway, and the second from C. S. Farquharson of the Public Works Department:

Excerpts from Mr. Fox's report:

The No. 9 Tunnel (now known as No. 12 Tunnel) at the 32 Mis. 2 Chns. from Kingston was built during the construction of the Extension (54 miles of track) from Bog Walk to Port Antonio which started in June 1894 and finished on July 1896. This tunnel is 464 feet long.

This construction was carried out by an American Syndicate headed by a Mr. J. P. McDonald and was more locally known as the McDonald Company.

A Jamaican labourer named John Henry is said to have died from the effects of constantly striking drills with a 10 lb. hammer on the work at No. 9 Tunnel, which was then notoriously regarded as a difficult task in the construction. In Jamaica, particularly at those times, any incident of the kind was bound to attract great notice, and somebody thought of the idea of commemorating it with a song, the words and rhythm appealing to the imaginative spirit of the labourer. The song, 'Ten pound hammer kill me pardner' soon took the hit, and was not alone popular among the labourers on the Railway construction but was everywhere sung by labourers in Jamaica.

The West Indian Improvement Company from the U.S.A. built the Railway from Porus to Montego Bay 1891-94 and sublet to the McDonald Company who built Bog Walk to Port Antonio Line 1894-96.

Mr. Farquharson's report begins enigmatically:

The bridge foreman on the road Frankfield John's Hall Corner Shop Road, Road Policy Works, worked on the extension of the Railway to Port Antonio and I saw him on the 7th Inst., and asked him if he knew anything about the incident at the No. 9 tunnel. He gave me the following information:

This song originated when the No. 9 tunnel was in course of construction.

In fixing the centering for the lining of the tunnel, wedges were being driven up by a man using a 10 lb hammer. The structure collapsed and killed some 11 people. The name of the man alluded to in the song as 'me pardner' was John Henry. The song therefore runs—'A ten pound hammer him kill me pardner.'

No accident of the kind ever happened as far as I know on the New Castle Road and none of the cuts were numbered, they never are, at least I have never known this to be the case. At times appropriate names are given to cuts, such as 'Smellhell,' 'See me no more' etc.

Steam drills were used on the construction of the line, but nothing is known of any competition having taken place between steam drills and hand drills.

The following names are known:

Dabner, in charge of blasting operations.

John Henry, checking up cuts and embankments.

Shea, Engineer in charge.
Tommy Walters, Assistant Pay Master.[18]

Chappell collected several reports holding that John Henry worked in Kentucky. The most vivid of these claims was Newton Redwine's in the *Beattyville Enterpriser:*

Newton Redwine reports another John Henry of that region, a smaller man in some respects:
John Henry the steel driving champion was a native of Alabama and from near Bessemer or Blackton. This is no doubt the man in question as he died when I was just a boy and I have heard my uncle tell of his exploits a number of times. The steel driver was between the ages of 45 and 50 years and weighed about 155 pounds. He was not a real black man, but more of a chocolate color. He was straight and well muscled.
For several years John Henry worked around the iron mining region of Alabama. Later he became a steel driver and worked on the Western & Atlantic, now the N.C. & St. L., also on the Memphis & Charleston, now the Southern from Memphis to Salisbury, N.C. His fame as a steel driver grew each year and he was in great demand on every construction job and drove steel on practically every road under construction during his day. The Queen & Crescent was his last job.
He was well known to all the old contractors and when he had finished a job he would walk thru the mountains to another, if he had the time. He finally landed at the Kings Mountain tunnel on the route between Danville, Ky., and Oakdale, Tenn., where he worked until his death. He drove steel for four years for the Cincinnati Southern.
John Henry drove steel with a ten pound sheepnose hammer with a regular size switch handle four feet long. This handle was made slim from where the hammer fitted on to a few inches back where it reduced to one half inch in thickness, the width being five eights in this slim part. It was kept greased with tallow to keep it limber and flexible, so as not to jar the hands and arms.
He would stand from five and one half feet to six feet from his steel and strike with full length of his hammer. The handle was so limber that when it was held out straight the hammer would hang nearly half way down. He drove steel from his left shoulder and would make a stroke of more than nineteen and one half feet spending his power with all his might making the hammer travel with the speed of lightning. He would throw his hammer over his shoulder and nearly the full length of the handle would be down his back with the hammer against his legs just below his knees. He would drive ten long hours with a never turning stroke.
John Henry could stand on two powder cans and drive a drill straight

up equally as fast as he could drive it straight down—with the same long sweep and rapidity of the hammer. He could stand on a powder can with feet together, toes even and drive all day never missing a stroke. He was the steel driving champion of the country and his record has never been equalled.

There was a white man brought from some point near South Pittsburgh, Tennessee, to work in the Kings Mountain tunnel who was a good steel driver. I think his name was Duffin. They drove steel in the tunnelheading together. They were so far under the mountain that the air was bad and stale. John Henry thought the Tennessee man would drive his hole down first and became fatigued and fell. His last words were 'Give me a cool drink of water before I die.' This was before the completion of the tunnel. He was buried not far from the South end of the tunnel. My Uncle Solomon Archilus Knox worked with him for two and one half years. This is what I have personally heard from my uncle and other old men who worked there. The best I remember it was about 1880 when John Henry died.[19]

Chappell largely discounts Redwine's information because of the fundamental inaccuracies about the drilling contest, and because efforts to follow up the testimony proved fruitless.

In the course of their investigations, Johnson and Chappell received many letters pointing to the Big Bend Tunnel. Rev. J. F. Glaze from Packard, Kentucky, wrote:

While reading *The Defender* I fine where yo ar Trieing to get the True statement a boute John henry. yes the statement is True I am a man that work with John henry I new him and I new his wife I new the little Song he use ter sange. he use ter drive with a man purnd the name of Abe. Burndis. But ther ar borth dead now at that time ther wars men and I wars a boy I pack watter at the Big Bend Turnel where the 2 men druve steale.

. . . as far as the real date of Con Test I cant tell But I will rite to mi Bruther and see if he cant tell But it has Bend a long time and I was just a boy at the time wars packing water fer the men But I will Tri and see if he new the date or a bout the time. But I new his song he Sang all the time so yo rite and tell me price yo pay.[20]

Several had heard of John Henry from kin who had worked at Big Bend. Pete Sanders of Franklin County, Virginia, reported:

I didn't drive no steel in Big Bend Tunnel. Uncle Jeff and Eleck did though, and say John Henry drive against the steam drill, and died in five minutes after he beat it down. They said John Henry told the shaker how to shake the steel to keep it from getting fastened in the rock so he couldn't turn it. He told him to drive it two quick shakes and a twist to make the rock dust fly out of the hole.

I heard the song of John Henry driving steel against the steam drill when they were still working on the C and O. It was all amongst us when I was a boy. When we boys there in Franklin County worked on the extension of the railroad up in Pocahontas County, we carried the song with us there and carried it back home when we went. It was the leading railroad song, but they've tore it all to pieces and sp'iled it. I heard it the other day on the machine, but it ain't noways like it used to be.

They said Big Bend Tunnel was a terrible-like place, and many men got killed there. Mules too. And they throwed the dead men and mules and all together there in the fill between the mountains. Uncle Jeff and me come in West Virginia together when I first come, and he showed me the big fill and said they tried to put Henry there first, but didn't do it and put him somewhere else. The dumper at the fill was the man that knowed all about it. Uncle Jeff said one day a long slab of rock that hung down from the roof fell and killed seven men. He said he seen 'em killed, and they put 'em in the fills. The people in the tunnel didn't know where they went.[21]

George Johnston of Lindside, West Virginia, had heard of John Henry through his grandfather:

John Henry was the best driver on the C & O. He was the only man that could drive steel with two hammers, one in each hand. People came from miles to see him use the 20 lb. hammers he had to drive with.

It seems that two different contracting companies were meeting in what is called Big Bend Tunnel. One had a steam drill while the other used man power to drill with. When they met everyone claimed that the steam drill was the greatest of all inventions, but John Henry made the remark he could sink more steel than the steam drill could. The contest was arranged and the money put up. John Henry was to get $100.00 to beat the steam drill.

John Henry had his foreman to buy him 2 new 20 lb. hammers for the race. They were to drill 35 minutes. When the contest was over John Henry had drilled two holes 7 feet deep, which made him a total of 14 feet. The steam drill drilled one hole 9 feet which of course gave the prize to John.

When the race was over John Henry retired to his home and told his wife that he had a queer feeling in his head. She prepared his supper and immediately after eating he went to bed. The next morning when his wife awoke and told him it was time to get up she received no answer, and she immediately discovered that he had passed to the other world some time in the night. His body was examined by two Drs. from Baltimore and it was found his death was caused from a bursted blood vessel in his head.

The information I have given you came to me through my grandfather. He was present at Big Bend Tunnel when the contest was staged, at that time he was time keeper for the crew that John Henry was working with. I have often heard him say that his watch started and stopped the race. There was present all of the R.R. officials of the C. & O. The crowd that remained through the race at the mouth of the tunnel was estimated at 2500 a large crowd for pioneer days.

John Henry was born in Tenn. and at the time of his death he was 34 years old. He was a man weighing from 200 to 225 lbs. He was a full blooded negro, his father having come from Africa. He often said his strength was brought from Africa. He was not any relation of John Hardy as far as I know.[22]

C. E. Waugh, an Orange, Virginia, railroad worker, knew the story from work:

Yours to hand in regard to the old Darkey John Henry the old song is a true story while i was not present when the contest was made i was then imployed by the same firm wich was C,R, Mason, and Co of Staunton Va it was in the early seventys when the Big Bend was built Machinery was not known in them days all work done by hand the men that drove the headings in the tunnels was looked on as a little above the common labor and got some twenty five cts more pr day than the common labor there was always a rivality between the Irish and the Darkeys and often contest held to decide wich was the best hammersmon Mike Olery held the championship for some years but was defeated by the big darky John Henry about that time the steam drills was introduced and one sent to the big bend tunnel to try out of course all the hammersmon did not take kindly to the steam drill and the made everry effort to down the steam drill so the selected two of their best men to drive against the drill with a two days test the worked twelve hours in thm days John Henry drove against the drill 24 hours and won by severel enches but when the contest was over he colapsed and wear taken to his shanty and Died that night this story was told to me many times by the contractor, C, R, Mason i was quite a young man at that time imployed by the same Co for a number of years and was a member of the firm of Gooch and Waugh for many years and have every reason to believe the story true.[23]

Several of Chappell's informants also had learned the story from railroad workers. Sam Williams of Bluefield, West Virginia, had worked on another C & O tunnel:

I was working at Hawk's Nest, that tunnel there on the C and O, when John Henry drove steel with the steam drill at Big Bend further down below there. People coming down the line told us about it. They said John Henry and Bill Dooland drove steel together. That's what they said. I never did see old John, but they said he was a big powerful man.

I am 84. I turned steel for the steel-drivers. When I worked at Hawk's Nest, I worked for Major Randolph.

Mike Smith, seventy-three years of age when he made his report in 1925, had a somewhat wider range of experiences on the road, and thinks there was such a man:

I worked in putting the C and O from White Sulphur Springs to the big cut below Kanawha Falls. I worked a while with the surveyors, but later drove steel in tunnels. I didn't see John Henry. I think there was such a man, and he drove steel. I heard about him when they were working on the Big Bend Tunnel. They talked about him driving steel there, and getting killed.

J. M. Logan of Pownell, West Virginia, had labored at Big Bend during the preliminary stages:

I drove steel for Blevins four months at the east end of Big Bend Tunnel before they got the shafts in. Blevins was a foreman there, and he went from Smyth County right by Wythe.

I remember seeing Mike Breen and Jeff Davis. I didn't see John Henry. I didn't hear anything said about a great steel-driver.

When I went back to Ivanhoe, people would come in there from the tunnel and talk about John Henry driving steel with a steam drill. They had a song on it, and it was a whole lot longer than the John Henry song they sing now.

I heard the song often before Big Bend Tunnel was finished.

And W. M. Coleman of Mt. Carbon, West Virginia, who had worked all along the C & O in the state:

Dick Deans, and Aaron Bailey, and Anthony Jones worked on my first crew, and off and on for a long time afterwards. They were big strapping Negros from Campbell County, Va. They were always singing when they worked, and 'John Henry' was their best song, they liked it the best.

They worked in Big Bend Tunnel, and all of them said they'd seen John Henry drive. Dick Deans said he saw John Henry drive against the steam drill, but I don't recall anything he said about his death. They said John Henry was the most powerful man they'd ever seen, rawbony, and as black as he could be.

These Negroes are all three dead. Dick Deans was working for me at the time he got killed on the railroad track.[24]

Others had grown up in the area and knew of John Henry from local lore. I. F. Huston, a C & O telegraph operator at Big Bend since 1893, reported:

When I was a boy, we boys here in the neighborhood used to play steel-driving. We used sticks for hammers and sang as we played, 'This old hammer killed John Henry,' and so on.

The John Henry story has been in our family ever since we moved to Big Bend Tunnel in 1881. My father worked for the C and O Railroad, and they moved him to Talcott in 1881. After we moved here I heard him talk with the people around the tunnel time and again about the contest John Henry had with the steam drill.

My mother had two old Negro house servants, a man and his wife, who quite often spoke of the steel-driver. They were certain that he was buried in the big fill at the east end of the tunnel.[25]

Johnson and Chappell, each intrigued by such persistent reports, did extensive interviewing in the Hinton-Talcott area. Some of what they learned was of little value. For example, Sam Wallace, who lived about two miles east of Talcott and helped his father build a railroad bridge there, had watched the tunnel construction as a boy. Johnson reports the following conversation with Mr. Wallace:

"I never heard of John Henry until two years ago," said Mr. Wallace. "I was down at Talcott one day, and some of the men were talking about John Henry. They said that some fellow had been there asking for information about him. That was the first time I ever heard anything about John Henry."

"Do you think the steel-driving contest happened?" I asked.

"I certainly don't," he replied. "In the first place, if it had happened I would have heard about it at the time because I was at the tunnel a great deal and I knew most of the steel drivers. In the second place, I'm sure there never was any steam drill at the tunnel. No, I think this John Henry stuff is just a tale somebody started."[26]

Retired engineer W. H. Cottle, a boy of thirteen when tunnel construction began and a walker at the east end, was also doubtful:

"I carried water and tools at the east end of the tunnel," he said. "My father was on the tunnel work, so I worked too."

"Have you ever heard this John Henry tale before?" I asked.

"Oh, yes," he replied, "I have known of it for a long, long time, but I didn't hear it when I was working at the tunnel. I must have heard it after the tunnel was built."

"How long were you employed at the tunnel?"

"I was there all the time during construction, from the fall of 1869 to the fall of 1872. I can't recall ever having known of any driver named John Henry and I can't recall any drilling contest."

"Do you know whether there was ever a steam drill on the job or not?"

"No," he replied, "I can't remember exactly on that point. My impression is that we didn't have a steam drill. Still I seem to recall some sort of steam boiler apparatus at the east end of the tunnel, but I don't remember just what it was for. It might have been used to run a steam drill, but I don't think so."[27]

On the other hand, Mr. Banks Terry, who had come to Talcott in 1880 to help re-arch the tunnel in brick, had no doubts at all:

"Do you believe that he beat it?" I asked.

"I think it is a settled fact," he said. "I worked in the Croton aqueduct tunnel in New York, and I know something about air drills. Steam drills hadn't been used long when they build Big Bend Tunnel, and they were not as good as the air drills we have these days. I don't believe there is any doubt but that John Henry beat the steam drill."

While Mr. Terry was certain that John Henry beat the steam drill, his knowledge was secondhand. He could not give a description of John Henry, nor could he say whether John Henry died as a result of the contest.[28]

Johnson regretted very much that he had not begun his investigations earlier. Many of his informants found their memories fading:

There is the case of Uncle Beverly Standard, for example. This old colored gentleman was every bit of ninety. Thus he could have been thirty or thirty-five when he worked at Big Bend Tunnel. I visited him at his humble little cottage high up on a mountain side overlooking the enchanting Greenbrier River about four miles east of Talcott. His grandson, Herbert Standard, a youth who piloted me on several of my trips into the country around Talcott, accompanied me and acquainted the old man with my mission.

"John Henry, John Henry," Uncle Beverly said, as if he were speaking to himself. After a moment: "Which John Henry do you want to know about? I've known so many John Henry's."

"I want to know about the one who was a steel driver at Big Bend Tunnel," I explained.

"Big Bend Tunnel—John Henry—Yes, seems like I remember." He paused, and a faint smile came over his face, as if he were at the point of recalling something. But the something wouldn't cross the threshold of his memory. He frowned and added, "No, I guess I didn't know anything about that John Henry."

I stayed half an hour, talking about his age, his corn patch, his horse, his view of the river, hoping that he would suddenly recall something about Big Bend Tunnel days. But he did not. As we were driving back to Talcott, Herbert said, "I'm sorry granddaddy couldn't remember better. I know that he knew a lot about John Henry, because he used to tell us about John Henry and he sang a song about him. I learned the song from him, but now he can't remember the song or John Henry either."

Similarly, the widow of a man, who, according to the local tradition, drove steel as John Henry's partner, could or would not recall one thing her husband had ever said about John Henry. Yet her granddaughter said that only a few months previous to this she heard her grandmother speak to someone about the steel-driving episode.[29]

William Wimmer, however, fourteen when work began on the tunnel and also a walker, had an interesting explanation for not particularly recalling John Henry:

"I carried water and steel to shaft number one," said Mr. Wimmer. "That was down toward the west end of the tunnel. I have heard about that steel-driving contest, but I think I must have heard about it some time after the tunnel was finished. I don't believe there ever was a steam drill at the tunnel. However, I wasn't around the east end much, where all this is supposed to have happened."

"Do you think it could have happened without your hearing about it at the time?"

"Well, yes," he said after some hesitation. "You see, these steel-driving contests were pretty common. I don't mean between men and steam drills, but between two pairs of drivers. I have seen many a contest in my day. Back in North Carolina I've seen two or three hundred people gather on a Sunday afternoon to see a contest. There'd usually be a wager up. They'd agree to drive a certain depth or a certain length of time, and the winning pair, that is the driver and the turner, would get the money. I've seen them put up two or three hundred dollars on a contest—besides lots of bets by the spectators on the side. Most people who have worked around tunnels or quarries get used to these contests and sort of take them for granted; so I can see how this fellow, John Henry, could have had his contest without raising much stir around camp. Still, since it was a man against a steam drill, it does look as if the news would have spread around pretty well."[30]

It also seems likely that the supervisors discouraged the distractions from work that contests might have caused, or that at Big Bend they did not want to publicize the test for fear of demonstrating even greater dependence on their steel drivers when the steam drill failed.

These last witnesses offered the most vivid and convincing testimony of all. Both Johnson and Chappell interviewed the Hedrick brothers, who were seventeen and twenty-three during the construction of Big Bend and lived on their family farm just a few hundred feet from its west end. George Hedrick, in his seventies during the interviews, still lived there. He told Chappell:

> My brother John helped to survey the tunnel and had charge of the woodwork in building it. I often saw John Henry drive steel out there. I saw the steam drill too, when they brought it to east end of the tunnel, but I didn't see John Henry when he drove in the contest with it. I heard about it right after. My brother saw it.
>
> My memory is Phil Henderson and John Henry drove together against the steam drill. That was the usual way of driving steel in the tunnel.
>
> I saw John Henry drive steel. He was black and 6 feet high, 35 years old, and weighed 200 or a little more. He could sing as well as he could drive steel, and was always singing when he was in the tunnel—"Can't you drive her,—huh?''[31]

Chappell was especially impressed by George Hedrick's memory of John Henry's song, as the *Hinton Mountain Herald* in 1874 had attributed that line to the miners building the tunnel.[32]

George Hedrick elaborated a bit more to Johnson:

> "My father's farm was near the west end of the tunnel; so when they began to build Big Bend Tunnel, father did some work clearing trees and hauling things. I helped him, and so I was around the tunnel a great deal, though I never worked down at the east end where John Henry worked. But I would sometimes go down there, and I have seen John Henry driving steel. He was a powerful man—tall and heavy, but not fat. He was pretty dark, but not coal black, and I'd say he was rather young—around thirty. Sometimes I could hear him singing clear up at our farm. He would sing certain lines over and over, such as
>
> > Can't she drive 'em!
> > Can't she drive 'em!
>
> "Now I can't give you the details of the contest between John Henry and the steam drill, because I was not there at the time, but I heard the

men talking about it soon afterward, and I am absolutely certain that it happened. It must have been in 1871 or 1872. Just how it all got started I don't know, but there were some bets made, and John Henry drove against the steam drill. I think that either Jeff Davis or Phil Henderson—they were both white men—turned the drill for John Henry."

"Did John Henry beat the drill and die?" I asked.

"Oh, yes, he beat it, but he didn't die then. I can't say when he died."[33]

John Hedrick's testimony was even more important, and here the discrepancies between Johnson and Chappell's reports are a little troubling. Johnson wrote that John Hedrick did not work on the tunnel but knew many of the workers there:

"I did not see the contest myself," said Mr. Hedrick, "but I heard the men talking about it right after it took place. It was about 1870 or '71. I think there is no doubt about John Henry beating the steam drill. I have seen him drive, and he was a mighty strong man."

I asked Mr. Hedrick for a personal description of John Henry.

"John Henry was a low, heavy-set man," he said. "He was yellow, weighed about 160, and must have been about thirty years old at the time he was working there."

Mr. Hedrick could not say whether John Henry died after the contest, although his impression was that he did not. He gave the name of John Henry's partner as Wesley Eddleston.[34]

Chappell was outraged by this report, as he considered John Hedrick one of his star witnesses, well suited for the position of tunnel boss which he claimed to have held:

I was manager of the wood-working in putting through Big Bend Tunnel, and built the shanties for the Negroes there in the camp. The first work at Big Bend Tunnel was making the survey, and I helped with that. Then men came to put down the shafts, and took rock from them 50 feet down to send away for contractors to examine when they were making contracts for the work on the tunnel. Menifee put down the first shaft. When he came I went with him to help him find the place. I worked there till the tunnel was completed.

I knew John Henry. He was a yaller-complected, stout, healthy fellow from down in Virginia. He was about 30 years old, and weighed 160 or 170 pounds. He was 5 feet 8 inches tall, not over that.

He drove steel with a steam drill at the east end, on the inside of the tunnel not far from the end. He was working under Foreman Steele, and he beat the steam drill too. The steam drill got hung up, but John Henry was beating him all the time. I didn't see the contest, because it was on the inside of the tunnel, and not very many could get in there. I was taking up timber, and heard him singing and driving, and he was beating him too.

John Henry stayed 'round the tunnel a year or two, then went away somewhere. I don't remember when he left. He had a big black fellow with him that drove steel, but he couldn't drive like John Henry.

John Henry was there 12 months after the contest. I know. He was there when the hole was opened between shaft 1 and 2. Henry Fox put the first hole through, and then climbed through it. He was a foreman, and got a watch that Johnson offered for the first man to get through. He was from shaft 2, and people on the other side pulled him through and tore off all his clothes.

I don't believe a single man got killed at Big Bend Tunnel at work. A boy fell in the shaft, and one died from foul air. A man was killed in Little Bend Tunnel, but none in Big Bend.[35]

Hedrick's assertion that no one died at Big Bend is absurd but consistent with C & O efforts to downplay dangers there, with a near blackout by the press on the subject, and with another witness' report that to talk of accidents was to jeopardize one's job. Many of Hedrick's particulars are otherwise surprisingly accurate. He gives a sound account of the early phases of tunnel construction; he is correct in stating that a man named Menifee lowered the first shaft into Big Bend and in claiming that Fox and Steele were foremen there.[36]

Mr. C. S. (Neal) Miller was by far the most exciting witness. A conservative member of his community, who was regarded as honest and accurate, he came from a large railroad family and had carried water and steel at Big Bend.

Mr. Miller, who is seventy-four lives on his farm about a mile north along a creek which joins the river near the east end of Big Bend Tunnel.

"I came here when I was seventeen," said Mr. Miller, "It was the spring of 1869. In the fall of that year I began work at Big Bend. I carried water and steel for the gang of drivers at the east end. I would take the drills to the shop and bring them back after they were sharpened. I often saw John Henry, as he was on the gang that I carried water and drills for.

"John Henry was a powerful man. He weighed about 200, was of medium height, and was about thirty years old.

"The contest took place in 1870, as well as I remember. Jeff Davis, a white man, turned the drill for John Henry. There was a hundred dollar wager up between John Henry's foreman and the man who brought the steam drill.

"The steam drill wasn't very practical. It was operated by an eight horse-power steam engine. The drill was mounted on steel supports something like table legs, and it could be used only where there was a fairly level surface to set it on. The steam came through a pipe from the boiler to the engine. A belt ran from the engine shaft to a pulley on the drill. There was an apparatus to regulate the position of the drill. They would begin with a short drill and go down to its limit; then they would stop and insert a longer drill. The drill turned round and round instead of churning up and down, and this caused a lot of loose gravel around the top of the hole to slide down and pack the drill. Several times during the contest they had to take the drill out of the hole and clean the gravel out. John Henry outdid the power drill pretty easily, because they had so much trouble with it. After the test the steam drill was dismounted and the boiler was used to run a hoisting engine at shaft number one. The test took place at the east portal, and the steam drill was never taken inside the tunnel.

"Now some people say John Henry died because of this test. But he didn't. At least, he didn't drop dead. As well as I remember, though, he took sick and died from fever soon after that."

I asked Mr. Miller if the contest caused much excitement.

"No," he replied. "It was just considered a sort of test on the steam drill. There wasn't any big crowd around to see it. I was going and coming with water and steel, so I saw how they were getting along from time to time, but I didn't get excited over it especially. The test lasted over a part of two days, and the depth was twenty feet, more or less."[37]

Miller's knowledge of tunnel community life also impressed Chappell. Their interview is especially interesting in that he hints at a cover up of John Henry's death:

I saw John Henry drive steel in Big Bend Tunnel. He was a great singer, and always singing some old song when he was driving steel. He was a black, raw boned man, 30 years old, 6 feet high, and weighed near 200 pounds. He and Phil Henderson, another big Negro, but not so high, were pals, and said that they were from North Carolina.

Phil Henderson turned the steel for John Henry when he drove in the contest with the steam drill at the east end of the tunnel. John Henry beat the steam drill because it got hung in the seam of the rock and lost time.

Dave Withrow, who lived with his wife at our home, was the foreman in charge of the work on the outside of the tunnel where John Henry beat the steam drill, and Mike Breen was the foreman on the inside of the tunnel there.

The steam drill was brought to Big Bend Tunnel as an experiment, and failed because it stayed broke all the time, or hung up in the rock, and it could be used only on bench drill anyway. It was brought to the east end of the tunnel when work first commenced there, and was never carried in the tunnel. It was thrown inside, and the engine was taken from it and carried to shaft number one, where it took the place of a team of horses that pulled the bucket up in the shaft with a windlass.

John Henry used to go up Hungart's Creek to see a white woman, . . . or almost white. Sometimes this woman would go down to the tunnel to get John Henry, and they went back together. She was called John Henry's woman 'round the camps.

John Henry didn't die from getting too hot in the contest with the steam drill, like you say. He drove in the heading a long time after that. But he was later killed in the tunnel, but I didn't see him killed. He couldn't go away from the tunnel without letting his friends know about it, and his woman stayed 'round long after he disappeared.

He was killed all right, and I know the time. The boys 'round the tunnel told me that he was killed from a blast of rock in the heading and he was put in a box with another Negro and buried at night under the big fill at the east end of the tunnel. A mule that had got killed in the tunnel was put under the big fill about the same time.

The bosses at the tunnel were afraid the death of John Henry would cause trouble among the Negroes, and they often got rid of dead Negroes in some way like that. All the Negroes left the tunnel once and wouldn't go in it for several days. Some of them won't go in it now because they've got the notion they can still hear John Henry driving steel in there. He's a regular ghost 'round this place.

His marks in the side of the rock where he drove with the steam drill stayed there awhile at the end of the tunnel, but when the railroad bed was widened for double-tracking they destroyed them.[38]

Chappell considered Miller's and the Hedricks' testimony conclusive and was very critical of Johnson for, Chappell felt, undermining his own witnesses. Chappell found three additional men who supported Miller's claims, but all had come to Big Bend later and seen less. George Jenkins arrived at Big Bend with his father, a blacksmith, soon after construction was begun. He worked as a tool boy there and though he did not remember a contest, he did know John Henry:

John Henry was there when I went to Big Bend, and I remember he was under Jack Pasco from Ireland. He was very black, and he'd weigh about 160. Always singing when he worked. He was a sort of song-leader. He was 30 or 35 years old.

I don't know what he did when he wasn't at work in the tunnel. I don't know when he left the tunnel or where he went. No; I don't know anything about him driving steel against a steam drill. The tunnel was all hand work.

Jim Brightwell ran the hoisting engine at shaft 2, and my brother fired for him. Captain Johnson gave a barrel of liquor when they knocked through the heading from shaft 2 to 3. Mose Selby stabbed John Hunt that day, but didn't kill him. I saw Hunt in Roanoke a few years ago.

I saw one man killed in the tunnel. He was taking up bottom when a rock fell from overhead and killed him dead. I don't remember what they did with him, sent him home to his people I suppose.

When the mules came out of the tunnel some of them were blind as a bat. One went blind and stayed blind. Most of them got all right after a day or so. They put a cover over their heads for a while.

They burnt lard oil and blackstrap in the tunnel for lights.

After Big Bend was in I flagged on the work train between White Sulphur and Hinton about a year. Then I went with my father to work on a tunnel at King's Mountain, Ky. No; I knew John Henry only at Big Bend. I don't know what became of him.[39]

John Gilpin also came to Big Bend with his father, a foreman recruited by the contractor. Gilpin carried water and steel for the workers. Although he did not remember a contest, he offered many interesting details about John Henry. He is also explicit about the pressure on workers not to discuss the realities of tunnel life:

I know that he was from North Carolina, for he used to get Pearce, my brother-in-law and a foreman in the tunnel, to write letters for him to his people there. Pearce liked John Henry because he was sensible and used good manners, and keen and full of good jokes, and he could sing and pick a banjo better than anybody else I ever saw.

My mother used to help out when anybody got hurt in the tunnel. She'd come with clean clothes and medicine. She ran a boarding house there at the tunnel, and baked for John Henry. He cooked the rest of his food at the camp, but he couldn't bake bread and Pearce asked my mother to do it for him. I'd often carry it to him at his camp, and he'd give me a little extra for carrying it.

I've seen John Henry playing cards, but I never saw him gambling, and he didn't swear like the other Negroes did when he was at work.

My half-brother, Jim Wimmer, drove steel in the tunnel, and he drove with John Henry when he could get the chance, because John Henry was a good worker at driving steel, and he was sensible and safe, a man of good judgement with a good eye. There was not so much danger in driving with him in the heading like there was with some of the other drivers. John Henry was a reliable man in danger or in a risky job.

When the first light hole was opened from shaft number one to the east end of the tunnel, I dipped the liquor for the steel-drivers. Every crew tried to put their boss through the hole first, and they fought and yelled like mad men. John Henry was a mighty powerful man that day, I tell you. When thcy pushed my father through the hole, they pushed me through after him, and almost tore off one of my legs in doing it. Then Superintendent Johnson gave me a suit of clothes because I got hurt.

I don't know a thing about John Henry driving steel in a contest with the steam drill, and don't think I ever saw one at the tunnel. Hand drills were used in the tunnel. They were using an engine at shaft number one to raise the bucket up when we moved to the tunnel, but they didn't have any steam engine or steam drill in the tunnel.

The last time I saw John Henry, who was called Big John Henry, was when some rocks from a blast fell on him and another Negro. They were covered with blankets and carried out of the tunnel. I don't think John Henry was killed in that accident because I didn't hear of him being buried, and the bosses were always careful in looking after the injured and dead. They were afraid the Negroes would leave the tunnel.

I don't know what happened to John Henry after that accident, though. He may have left for a while and then come back again, but I can't say. I always thought John Henry died in the tunnel, but I didn't know anything about his death. I don't remember seeing John Henry after the day the rocks fell on him. I might have found out what happened to him if I had tried then, but we were not allowed to go round the camps asking questions about such things. Any man who walked around and talked about the hard life in the tunnel was allowed to stay there about two days, and that's all.[40]

Because Gilpin and Jenkins came late to the tunnel, and because they worked at the west end (far from the east portal where Miller and Hedrick claimed the contest took place and which would have provided the least expensive source of steam power from the Greenbrier River), it is not surprising that they did not see the actual contest.

Finally, Chappell considered William Lawson's report one of the least credible. It is very interesting, nonetheless, and the only report from a black worker in either researcher's account:

I was living on A. S. Massey's place up Falling Spring Valley when I went to Big Bend Tunnel in the spring. My brother Armstead was already there. I went to him there and stayed 'til time to cut corn in the fall. It was the year they put the hole through.

Armstead was along with John Christian and John Turner in the heading, and I drove steel under Armstead. He showed me where to drive. We were driving from the east end.

When we met a dispute arose between the two sides about who was the first man to drive a light hole through. My brother said he did, and they fussed about it all that evening. Next morning when we started working again they started the dispute again. My brother and Will Christian (Will was from the other side) shot each other dead. Armstead said, 'Your gun ain't no bigger than mine,' and they both fired about the same time. Will Christian hit my brother right plumb in the heart, and my brother hit him a little on the side further toward the middle of his breast. Both of them were dead in five minutes after the guns cracked.

I was the first to get to Armstead, and turned him over. He fell on his face. Then C. R. Mason come. They buried him on the mountainside in a government graveyard.

When the hole was put through there was a great deal of whiskey in the tunnel, and that's what started all the fuss. They fussed over who put the crowbar through first, but it was the drill.

The hole had been put through three or four months when John Henry was killed. He was the best steel-driver I ever saw. He was short and brown-skinned, and had a wife that was a bright colored woman. He was 35 or 36, weighed 150 pounds.

When I went there they had a steam drill in the tunnel at the east end. They piped the steam in. They had a little coffee-pot engine on the outside. They didn't use it in the heading, but on the bench and on the sides.

John Henry drove steel with the steam drill one day, and beat it down, but got too hot and died. He fell out right at the mouth of the tunnel. They put a bucket of cold water on him.

His wife come to the tunnel that day, and they said she carried his body away. I don't know. I never saw anybody buried at the tunnel except my brother. They said they shipped some of them away, but I didn't see anybody shipped away. I don't know where they buried Will Christian. They didn't bury him with Armstead.

The time John Henry killed his self was his own fault, 'cause he bet the man with the steam drill he could beat him down. John Henry never let no man beat him down, but the steam drill won't no good nohow.

John Henry was always singing or mumbling something when he was whipping steel. He would sing over and over the same thing sometimes. He'd sing

> 'My old hammer ringing in the mountains,
> Nothing but my hammer falling down.'

A colored boy 'round there added on and made up the John Henry song after he got killed, and all the muckers sung it.

C. R. Mason was the boss man at the tunnel. He was a good-hearted old man, but he was a tough man. He'd spit on you all the time he was talking to you. His son was named Clay Mason.[41]

Lawson is incorrect in naming the contractor at Big Bend as C. R. Mason. He might very well have worked under Mason at another tunnel, however; and as one of many black laborers working for a remote employer, he could easily have confused the two contractors. That Lawson is the only black informant illustrates a terrible gap in our testimony. The residents of Hinton and Talcott in the 1920s were permanent white residents of the two towns. Most had held upper supervisory positions in the tunnel. Those who had worked as walkers probably participated more fully in the community of black workers; but their testimony still could not be as helpful as the information provided by one of John Henry's fellow drivers or shakers. These men would have labored alongside him, sung with him and about him. Part of a migratory labor force, they left the Big Bend area soon after John Henry's death, and we have no way of tracing them.

It is unfortunate that researchers did not begin their investigations earlier. By the time that Johnson and Chappell reached the Big Bend area, fifty years had elapsed since the death of John Henry. Their informants confused many details or could not remember relevant and important points. It is difficult to know how badly they confused their knowledge of ballad lore with their own recollections, although one suspects that these particular witnesses may not have participated in the folk culture which celebrated John Henry.

They do, however, seem to confirm less direct evidence. Those who claim to have known John Henry at Big Bend place the contest at a logical site and at an appropriate time. The later comers were unlikely to have known about him. Others who did not remember John Henry worked in parts of the tunnel as far away as a mile and a quarter from where the contest would have been. Moreover, if contests were either frequent or unpublicized, workers would have no reason to remember a fairly brief affair fifty years later. Most scholars have considered the work of Johnson and Chappell very convincing, as I do.

Those who have attempted interviews since have found that it is much too late. When I began this study, I knew that it would be fruitless to try to locate people who remembered John Henry, but I thought that it might be possible to interview those who knew and were moved by the story. Despite an extensive search, I have not been able to locate anyone for whom this is true. However, a delightful interview with one man able to comment on John Henry's heroic appeal—Charles Lewis Choice, a resident of Washington, D.C.—is found in an appendix.

NOTES

1. Louis Chappell, *John Henry: A Folk-Lore Study,* p. 30.
2. Ibid., p. 30.
3. Ibid., pp. 31 and 32.

4. Ibid., p. 21.

5. Guy B. Johnson, *John Henry: Tracking Down a Negro Legend,* pp. 17-19.

6. Ibid., pp. 16-17.

7. John Harrington Cox, "John Hardy," pp. 505-6.

8. Chappell, *John Henry,* p. 34.

9. Ibid., p. 24.

10. Ibid., p. 27.

11. Ibid., p. 25.

12. Ibid., p. 26.

13. Ibid., p. 27.

14. Ibid.

15. Johnson, *John Henry,* p. 23.

16. Ibid., p. 22.

17. Ibid., pp. 19-22.

18. Chappell, *John Henry,* pp. 41-42.

19. Ibid., pp. 22-23.

20. Johnson, *John Henry,* p. 16.

21. Chappell, *John Henry,* pp. 33-34.

22. Ibid., pp. 32-33.

23. Johnson, *John Henry,* pp. 31-32.

24. Chappell, *John Henry,* pp. 35-36.

25. Ibid., p. 37.

26. Johnson, *John Henry,* pp. 34-35.

27. Ibid., pp. 37-38.

28. Ibid., p. 36.

29. Ibid., p. 33.

30. Ibid., pp. 38-39.

31. Chappell, *John Henry,* pp. 47-48.

32. *Mountain Herald,* Hinton, West Virginia, 1 January 1874, cited in Chappell, *John Henry,* p. 50.

33. Johnson, *John Henry,* p. 39.

34. Ibid., p. 40.

35. Chappell, *John Henry,* p. 48.

36. *Greenbrier Independent,* 22 January 1870 and *Railroad Gazette,* 2 November 1872, both cited in Chappell, *John Henry,* p. 50. *Border Watchman,* 6 June 1872, cited in Johnson, *John Henry,* p. 30.

37. Johnson, *John Henry,* pp. 40-41.

38. Chappell, *John Henry,* pp. 46-47.

39. Ibid., pp. 50-51.

40. Ibid., pp. 51-52.

41. Ibid., pp. 37-38.

3

JOHN HENRY'S CAREER IN SONG

John Henry has not been researched as thoroughly as some other American heroes; his life in our culture has been primarily a life told in song. In this chapter I offer an overview of the early work of folklorists who were interested in gathering samples of his song. I then turn to the printed versions of the ballad: in texts with extended commentary, in the personal collections of individual musicians, in folksong treasuries, and in published sheet music.

FOLKSONG COLLECTORS

Folklorists' earliest interest in John Henry stemmed from their activities in gathering folksong. In the first years of this century, folksong collecting was a relatively new endeavor; but several collectors seeking to record thoroughly, for example, the music of a particular region or ethnic group, encountered at least fragments of the John Henry song. The first to publish a two-line fragment was Louise Bascom, whose 1909 collection of songs from western North Carolina included: "Johnie Henry was a hard-workin' man, He died with his hammer in his hand." Two other folklorists gathered more complete texts at about the same time but did not publish them until several years later. Both E. C. Perrow and Josiah Combs were Kentucky natives; Combs had left Kentucky to attend the University of Paris, then returned as a professional folklorist. Both men's collections were thorough and respectful, speaking to the intimacy they felt with the region's lore. Perrow's ballad and several hammer songs that dated from 1905 were submitted as part of a collection of southern songs to the *Journal of American Folklore* in 1913. Combs first mentioned a ballad collected in 1909 in his 1911 *Syllabus of Kentucky Folk-Song* (coedited with Hubert Shearin) and published the full text in 1925. (That the ballad had indeed been popular in Kentucky for some time is indicated by William Bradley's comments in the

Berea Quarterly in 1915: describing life in Berea and particularly its music, he noted that one could frequently hear the "John Henry" song.)

Other versions appearing in these early years include one Henry Davis just mentions in his 1914 article on South Carolina folksong, "That's the Hammer Killed John Henry," and a lengthy and very interesting ballad published by John Lomax in the *Journal of American Folklore* in 1915. Lomax identified his version as a C & O railroad song from Kentucky and West Virginia. That same year Newman I. White gathered several versions of hammer songs from Alabama, West Virginia, and North Carolina, allegedly black songs but most likely submitted to White by his white college students. White's hammer songs were published in his *American Negro Folk Songs* of 1928. In 1918, Natalie Curtis-Burlin released four folksong booklets, including materials gathered by black students at Virginia's Hampton Institute and transcribed for male quartets. Her "Hammerin' Song" which mentions John Henry twice by name was submitted by a George Alston, who Curtis-Burlin identifies as a boy who'd brought the song to Hampton from the mines.

Most interesting about these early samples is the evidence they offer that the John Henry song had already become an integral part of southern white folk culture. Samples that emerged from all over the south from white and black singers revealed an extraordinary variety. They included both hammer songs such as "If I could drive steel like John Henry, I'd go home, Baby, I'd go home," and "This old hammer killed John Henry, Can't kill me, can't kill me," as well as complex ballads.[1] All of the traits which make the ballad unique occur in this early period: we see the baby John Henry with his parents predicting his own fate, the man with his loving woman, working in the tunnel, and the driver racing the steam drill. He makes many of his characteristic comments and often adds a request more common to the songs of this early period than those of later years. He asks that after his death "You take my hammer and wrap it in gold, And give it to the girl I love."[2]

In the 1920s a growing enthusiasm for black culture inspired numerous collections of black folksong, several of which contained "John Henry." Dorothy Scarborough's *On the Trail of the Negro Folk Song* included a few hammer versions that she considered the most famous of all black work-songs, and a ballad from Mississippi to the tune of "Come thy Fount of every Blessing." Thomas Talley's 1922 collection of *Negro Folk Rhymes* contains a ballad in poetry, with four-line stanzas differing from ballad stanzas in their deletion of the (usually repeated) last line. His poem is similar, however, to those ballads emphasizing John Henry's family life: most of the verse is devoted to John Henry's wife and son.

Two collectors of black music in the 1920s surpassed all others in their energetic gathering of John Henry lore. Howard Odum and Guy Johnson published two remarkable collections of black songs, one in 1925 and the other in 1926, within which many varied versions of the ballad and hammer song are presented. Their versions come from all over the south and midwest; and although the authors at this point were persuaded that John Henry was a mythical character, they were, rightfully, impressed with the vivid tradition surrounding him. Thus Odum and Johnson's work stresses the variety of that tradition rather than making any claims about origin or authenticity. Johnson continued the work, reprinting one sample in *Ebony and Topaz* and the *Southern Workman* in 1927. His book-length study *John Henry: Tracking Down a Negro Legend,* written in 1929, includes the best collection I know of ballads and hammer songs, almost fifty in all. Like his earlier work, this group is fascinating in its extraordinary variety of, as examples, women named to be John Henry's wife, and railroads claiming him as an employee.

In addition to those whose primary concern was black lore, two other folklorists briefly pursued the John Henry tradition in the 1920s. R. W. Gordon's "Ask Adventure" column was a regular feature in *Adventure Magazine* throughout the decade; there he presented musical contributions from readers and provided a forum for readers to discuss the songs he printed.[3] In April of 1923 a Kentucky reader contributed a very interesting version with several verses from "The Lass of Roch Royal," an Anglo-Appalachian ballad, beginning with "Who's going to shoe your pretty little feet?" Because this entry was similar in narrative structure to the ballad "John Hardy," it provoked a lively readers' debate over whether or not John Henry was really the executed black desperado. Many of these readers also mailed Gordon additional verses of the songs. In July of 1924, Gordon concluded that the weight of readers' testimony indicated that the two men and their songs were really quite different.

Also in the 1920s regional folklorist Arthur Hudson offered a very unusual example of John Henry music in his collection of Mississippi lore. Hudson's hammer song, dated 1928, began: "Oh, John Henry, where you been so long, Your clothes ain't on right and yo' shoes all untied."

Finally, it became apparent during these years that the John Henry tradition would be transformed. Carl Sandburg published a ballad in his collection "Songs of Old Frontiers" in the magazine *Country Gentleman* in 1927. It reappeared in Sandburg's immensely popular *An American Songbag,* signaling the beginning of John Henry's journey out of traditional folk culture. It is not altogether clear whether Sandburg gathered this ballad himself; while he did do some collecting, he also relied on friends and on the samples of others. I include it in this section because he does not credit another collector, and because his is a lengthy and interesting ballad which has been extremely influential. Its emphasis is on John Henry as a "natural man," a mysterious motif which reappears many times in popular culture. He also implies that John Henry had not one, but many women, and that Polly Ann received gifts from several men. These verses are reminiscent of several of Guy Johnson's ballads, and indicate that Sandburg's version is perhaps a composite.

During the 1930s many Americans grew enthusiastic about folklore, inspiring a number of popular endeavors such as Sandburg's. These are treated later in this chapter. Although their hero was moving into mainstream popular culture, folklorists continued to find traditional texts. In 1931, the *Railway Maintenance of Way Employees' Journal* printed a contribution from Alabama folklorist Peter Brannon, a song entitled "Jawn Henry" which places him on the Central of Georgia Railroad, describes a dramatic and detailed contest, and, like Sandburg's version, insinuates that Polly Ann was not quite the loving woman portrayed in other ballads. Brannon's version was labeled a black song, as was John Work's sample in *American Negro Songs.* The Lomaxes also gathered ballads from black singers, including "Little John Henry," from James Baker in Sugarland, Texas, which was published in their *American Ballads and Folk Songs* of 1934; and "John Henry," recorded by Arthur Bell at Cummins State Farm in Pine Bluff Arkansas in 1935. Bell's version is unusual in its beginning: "Well, every Monday morning, When the bluebirds begin to sing, You can hear those hammers. . . ." His song has been published in a number of the Lomaxes' collections, and presented on Folkways records as well, inspiring many imitators. Zora Neale Hurston, an anthropologist studying under Franz Boas, pioneered in ethnographic fieldwork by gathering black folklore (including songs, tales, and a unique description of hoodoo) in southern Florida. In 1935, her *Mules and Men* contained a hammer song and ballad, again with the Roch Royal verses, and much detail on the contest, which appeared to be increasingly popular in the 1930s. Hurston's discussion is also important in her emphatic claim that "John Henry has no place in Negro folk-lore except in this one circumstance," that is, in song.[4] Also focusing on black song, Muriel Longini included John Henry in her collection of Chicago Negroes' music. She hesitantly labeled her version corrupt, and it does seem to be blended with material from another song, with its last stanza for example beginning, "You'se a no good weed; I'm gonna let the cows come and moo you down."

Regional collections continued in the 1930s as well. Frank C. Brown's massive collection of North Carolina folklore devoted two volumes to songs, some gathered as early as 1915. His John Henry pieces ranged from ballads through hammer songs to several Brown thought might be related to the Henry-Hardy complex, namely "Ashville Junction" and "Swananoa Tunnel." Louis Chappell's *Folksongs of Roanoke and the Albermarle* is a sensitive and thorough volume of songs gathered from his relatives and friends in his home region of eastern North Carolina. One version he printed here of "John Henry" is especially intriguing because it is very close to Walter Jekyll's Jamaican songs of 1907, and has appealed to scholars who feel that the tradition may have originated in Jamaica. Arthur Davis' volume of Virginia songs lists six different versions of the John Henry piece under railroad songs, including two which Davis recorded on wax cylinders. Three 1930s masters' theses from Tennessee contained "John Henry": Mildred Haun's, submitted to Vanderbilt University in 1937, cites the John Henry ballad from Cocke County; while Ruby Duncan records it from Northern Hamilton County and Robert Mason from Cannon County. Mason's is the most interesting and unusual with its eery focus on death. Finally, a more general volume is Mellenger Henry's *Folksongs from the Southern Highlands,* with several John Henry pieces gathered during Henry's sojourns in Appalachia.

Since the 1930s the collection of folksongs about John Henry has been more erratic, and in some cases more urban-centered. Rural and regional samples continued to come in, of course, with Leach and Beck's unusual chant-fable of 1947 published in a 1950 group of songs from Rappahannock County, Virginia. One of the most unique of all John Henry ballads, this song is interrupted for a story about a fight with Stackolee and ends with John Henry's burial in a safe at the White House. Other regional collections included Alton Morris' *Folksongs of Florida,* also issued in 1950. Morris' version is a fairly traditional and solidly composed piece, contributed by a white singer who had learned the song from his black family's cook—an interesting example of the ballad's transmission from black to white singers in the south. Courlander prints a lengthy and complex ballad from Alabama in two collections of black music, one published in 1950 and the second in 1960. This song emphasizes John Henry's love life and the conflict he feels between his work and his woman. Bruce Buckley's selection of Ohio folksongs, published in *Midwest Folklore,* includes Uncle Ira Cephas' song recorded in 1951. Buckley found it one of the most stirring and beautiful versions he had ever heard; it is a compelling and unusual piece placing John Henry at the Hard Rock Levee Camp. The last regional sample I know of is in Burton and Manning's group of songs from East Tennessee, printed in 1967.

Finally, two folklorists in recent years have gathered urban ballads. Roger Abrahams' comes from black street men in Philadelphia. In this very erotic piece, John Henry "dies from too much cock." Bruce Jackson's samples come from a Texas prison; gathered in the mid-sixties they appear in his 1972 book of prison lore, *Wake Up Dead Man.* He provides a selection of both ballads and hammer songs, which also include some erotic allusions but seem to be very traditionally composed and performed pieces.

FOLKSONG COLLECTIONS WITH COMMENTARY

I turn now to academic and popular collections which include the ballad. I have classified the collections in three types: those volumes which intersperse their songs with extended commentary; those which are individual musicians' presentations of their personal repertoires; and those which are general treasuries of music, offering songs primarily to be sung and with little explanation.

Of the volumes which feature the ballad with explanation, one of the very best is *Ebony and Topaz,* the National Urban League's compilation of black literature and lore, edited by Charles S. Johnson and published in 1927, that is an eloquent tribute to the Harlem Renaissance. Guy Johnson contributed an article on John Henry to this volume; in it he offers his readers one interrupted version of the ballad and another which is dissected in order to discuss the story underlying each part. He usefully summarizes the heroic tradition, concluding that the truth of the matter may be irrelevant when posed against the heroic lore which seemed so appealing to black Americans, then ends this piece in the same prophetic way that he concluded his later book: " I marvel that some poet among the 'New Negro' generation does not sing John Henry's praises, that some playwright does not dramatize him, that some painter does not picture him as he battles with the steam drill, or that some sculptor does not fulfill the wishful fantasy of the Negro pick and shovel man who said to me, 'Cap'n, they tells me that they got John Henry's statue carved out o' solid rock at the head of Big Ben' Tunnel. Yes sir, there he stan' with the hammer in his han'.'"[5] Ironically, Johnson's dream was to be fulfilled by some artists he may have regretted inspiring.

Carl Carmer's *Stars Fell on Alabama* issued in 1934 is a narrative text describing Carmer's alleged experiences gathering Alabama folklore. In Part IV, "Conjure County," Carmer tells of being in River Falls, Alabama, and hearing convicts on their way from the mills to the barracks. After the convicts have passed, Carmer's companion Philip sings for him Brannon's Central of Georgia version of the "Jawn Henry" ballad, and talks to him about the hero, characterizing him as most importantly a "natural man," and attributing his prowess to his being double-jointed.

Although Benjamin Botkin included the ballad in three of his collections—the treasuries of southern, American, and railroad folklore, he discussed it extensively in only one, *The Treasury of American Folklore* of 1944. To accompany two of the Lomaxes' ballads, Botkin offered Newton Redwine's discussion of hammering techniques (from Louis Chappell), Chappell's interview with railroader George Johnston, Guy Johnson and Howard Odum's folktale, Guy Johnson's summary of the hero's appeal, and Roark Bradford's fictional piece on John Henry's birth.

In his 1945 book *Railroad Avenue,* Freeman Hubbard printed "Jawn Henry" (Peter Brannon's ballad published in the *Railway Maintenance of Way Employees' Journal* and in *Stars Fell on Alabama* as well), and briefly described the heroic tradition, adding some interesting information on the Alabama claims to the hero. His portrait of the "actual" Jawn Henry seems influenced by Roark Bradford's fictional account: Hubbard characterizes the hero as a mixture of "boomer, laborer, and minstrel" and claims that "When he felt in the mood for work—which was not very often—no man alive could outdo him at his particular job.[6]

A. L. Lloyd's "The Anatomy of John Henry" put out in 1947 was written in a more serious vein. Essentially a summary of Guy Johnson's work which includes a composite ballad culled from Johnson's selections, Lloyd's article stresses that John Henry is a laboring hero, "the vividest, saddest, and most impressive of all the heroes of the lower tenth."[7]

Albert Friedman's book of ballads in 1956 included, under "Outlaws, Pirates, Badmen, and Heroes," a brief discussion of what he considered to be the masterpiece of Negro balladry and a very concise summary of the hero's life story. Friedman selected an excellent sampling of ballads for his volume, joining two from Chappell (one the unusual Jamaican version), two from Johnson, and worksongs from the collections of Scarborough and White. His text is a remarkably useful overview of the quite varied forms the John Henry song has assumed.

John and Alan Lomax almost always included John Henry in their folk-song treasuries; and in 1960 Alan Lomax offered a lengthy introduction to the songs in his *Folk Songs of North America*. Crediting Chappell with sorting out the facts of the hero's life, Lomax vividly and elegantly summarized Chappell's portrait of tunnel life. He also discussed the origin and development of the ballad, its mountain influence, and what some scholars consider to be sexual allusions disguised as hammer songs. Lomax suggested that John Henry is the descendant of John the trickster slave, but a more appropriate hero for the "hard-working, hard-hitting, hard-boiled guys who opened up the modern South."[8] His samples included two he collected himself or with his father and a reprint from Johnson.

Maria Boette's *Singa Hipsy Doodle* includes an original song collected in Summers County in 1969 and a provocative newspaper article from the *Parkersburg Sentinel* in 1957. Its author Kyle McCormick quoted the grandsons of James Twohig, allegedly a contractor's foreman at Big Bend, who claim that their records fail to support the exploits attributed in 1872 to John Henry. Twohig added that John Henry's son went on to become a prominent Negro educator. Efforts to substantiate McCormick's story have not been fruitful, but the article is an interesting example of West Virginia lore.

Finally, Paul Glass' *Songs and Stories of Afro-Americans* of 1971 presents a composite, uninterrupted ballad, a ballad broken up by stanzas so that Glass can provide background on each verse, an elaborate and well told version of the traditional story as well as an evocation of the grim life in Big Bend, and Glass' suggestive comment that: "The railroad workers who related the fantastic accounts of John Henry emphasized that 'he was not a giant like you read about in fairy tales,' but 'a regular, natural man' who could 'sing, dance, and take care of his family.' "[9]

PERSONAL COLLECTIONS

Several American singers have thought of the John Henry ballad as part of their personal repertoires of songs. Among them are Huddie Ledbetter, whose version can be found in *The Leadbelly Songbook,* edited by Mose Asch and Alan Lomax; Harry Belafonte, who includes "John Henry" in his *Songs Belafonte Sings;* and of course W. C. Handy who may have been the first to do so in his *Blues: An Anthology* and *Treasury of the Blues.* Another blues singer, Josh White, found his own fame linked to John Henry's popular career. White played the minstrel Blind Lemon in Roark Bradford's Broadway play *John Henry* in 1939. Although the play was a failure, White's musical talents were striking as he strolled through the show providing background musical commentary. He moved from near obscurity to national popularity as a result, and presents his blues version of "John Henry" in the *Josh White Song Book* of 1963. Finally, Jane Sapp's short piece on Alabama bluesman L. C. (Bunk) Pippens features Pippins' quote on the role of "John Henry" in his repertoire—it was the first piece he learned to play.

Among white singers, Woody Guthrie, Burl Ives, and Pete Seeger, all in the folk/protest tradition, sang "John Henry." Guthrie sang mainly his own songs, but mentions singing the John Henry ballad for migrants on the Arizona Highway in an article he contributed to *Common Ground* in 1942. Guthrie reprints two stanzas of the ballad, which recount how Polly Ann picked up the dead John Henry's hammer and drove steel like a man. Guthrie also explains his choice of these two particular stanzas: the women among the migrants he had encountered criticized him for running women down in his music, so he offered to sing for them a song about a real woman! This strikes me as an unusual interpretation of the meaning of the John Henry song. Ives and Seeger sang "John Henry" much more frequently; Ives includes it in three collections of his own songs in 1953, 1962, and 1966; Seeger's version is presented in his *American Favorite Ballads* of 1961. Labelling the song the noblest American ballad of them all, Seeger attributed it to the Swananoa Tunnel of West Virginia, constructed in the 1880s, and mentioned that he had learned it from artist Thomas Benton who had played it for him on the harmonica when Pete was a child.

Several white Appalachian singers also present the ballad as one of their own pieces. In *Singing Family of the Cumberlands,* Jean Ritchie suggests that it spoke to the role of railroads in the life of her family. Her "John Henry's" last two stanzas testify to a mountain influence: "And the green leaves a-hangin' on the vine, Lordie babe, Green leaves a-hangin' on the vine."[10] Michael E. "Jim" Bush presents a more traditional ballad in his personal volume, *Folk Songs of Central West Virginia.* Finally, Dash Moore included a unique version in a pamphlet of his own songs printed in 1965, when the civil rights movement must have been very much on his mind. His talking blues piece opens with John Henry's long and troubled reflections on the nature of racial discrimination and particularly over his mother's warning: "You got a long row to hoe, Just because your skin ain't white, Lord, Lord."[11]

FOLKSONG TREASURIES

Since first appearing in popular form in Carl Sandburg's *An American Songbag* in 1927, John Henry ballads have reemerged in numerous treasuries of folksong. Among these are volumes devoted to black American music, beginning in 1937 with John Rosamund Johnson's remarkable potpourri of folksong ranging from spirituals and ring shouts through prison songs and street cries to blues and work songs. Clark's *Copper Sun* in 1957, Krehbiel's *Afro-American Folk Songs* of 1962, Brewer's *American Negro Folklore* in 1968, Spalding's *Encyclopedia of Black Folklore and Humor* in 1972, and Courlander's *A Treasury of Afro-American Folklore* of 1976, all feature John Henry ballads. Courlander's selection is reprinted from *Negro Folk Music USA;* he also contributes a Jamaican version similar to those of Chappell, Scarborough, and Jekyll, which is taken from Martha Beckwith's *Black Roadways* and Roark Bradford's fictional portrait of John Henry's birth.

Anthologies in the protest/worksong tradition often present "John Henry" as illustrative of laborers' ballads. Four railroad anthologies, Sherwin and McClintock's *Railroad Songs* of 1933, Landeck's *Git on Board* of 1950, Botkin and Harlow's *A Treasury of Railroad Folklore,* 1953, and McPherson and Williams' *Railroad,* 1976, feature the steel driver's song. Collections that seem to be rooted in the folksong revival and often term "John Henry" a protest song are: Siegmeister's *Work and Sing* of 1944; Hille's *The People's Song Book,* 1948; Fowke and Glazer's *Songs of Work and Freedom,* 1960; Jahn's *Blues und Work Songs* of 1964; Whitman's *Songs that Changed the World* in 1970; Greenway's *American Folksongs of Protest,* 1970; and Silber's *This Singing Land* (1965), *Folksong Festival* (1967), and *Folksinger's Workbook* (1973). John Henry appears in regional anthologies as well: Botkin's *A Treasury of Southern Folklore* of 1949; Maurer's *Mountain Heritage,* 1974; Burton and Manning's volume of eastern Tennessee folklore, compiled in 1969; and Gainer's *Folksongs from the West Virginia Hills.* (Gainer gathered his songs himself, over a fifty-year period, publishing them as a treasury in 1975. His ballad was contributed by a Mrs. Warren Mullens of Nicholas County, West Virginia.)

Among general treasuries, the best known are probably the Lomaxes': they included the ballad in their *American Ballads and Folksongs* of 1934; *Our Singing Country,* in 1941 (especially worth pursuing for its intriguing introduction by Leadbelly, in which he describes what it means to be double-jointed); *Folksong USA,* 1947; *Best Loved American Folksongs,* 1955: and *The Folksongs of North America,* in 1960.

In addition to the Lomax volumes, general collections include Houghton Mifflin's 1936 text, *Their Weight in Wildcats,* with compelling illustrations by the noted commercial artist James Daugherty. In 1940 Downes and Siegmeister published the ballad in their *A Treasury of American Song,* as did Carmer in *America Sings,* 1942; Botkin in his *Treasury of American Folklore,* 1944; Ewen in *Songs of America,* Scott in *Sing of America,* and

Boni in her *The Fireside Book of Folksongs,* all from 1947. In 1948, Ruth Seeger featured it in *American Folksongs for Children* and the Kolbs included it in their *A Treasury of Folksongs;* and it appeared in 1949 in Greenell's *Young People's Records Folk Song Book* and *Anthology of Ballads* published by Black, Sivalls, and Bryson with no editor listed. Several years lapsed before "John Henry" emerged again, in Leach's *The Ballad Book* of 1955; Bill Clifton's *Old Time Folk and Gospel Songs* of 1956 and Haufrecht's *Folk Sing* of 1959. A rash of folksong collections in the 1960s indicated that John Henry had been rediscovered. Ames's *The Story of American Folksong* in 1960; the *Life Treasury of American Folklore,* 1961; Grafman and Manning's *Folk Music USA* and Cazden's *American Folksongs for Piano,* both in 1962; Morse's *The Dell Book of Great American Folksongs* and von Schmidt's *Come for to Sing,* both from 1963; Tom Glazer's *A New Treasury of Folksongs,* 1964; Luboff and Strache's international collection *Songs of Man* and Morehead's *Best Loved Songs,* both in 1965; Leisy's *The Folk Song Abecedary* of 1966; Okun's *Something to Sing About,* 1968; and Poulakis' *American Folklore* of 1969. Finally, several anthologies appeared in the 1970s and featured John Henry: Hodgart's *The Faber Book of Ballads* and Stuart's *A Medley of Folk-Songs,* both in 1971; and Warner Brothers' *American Story in Song,* Arnett's *I Hear America Singing,* and Silverman's *Folk Song Encyclopedia,* all in 1975. The first two of the 1975 volumes were inspired by the approaching Bicentennial. Silverman has demonstrated a long-term interest in the John Henry ballad, including it in two workbooks, *The Folksingers' Guitar Guide* (1964) and *Folk Harmonica* (1974) as well as in his *Back Packer's Song Book,* published in 1977. Finally, the most recent volume that I know to commemorate John Henry is David Ewen's *Songs of America,* appearing in 1978.

PUBLISHED SHEET MUSIC

The first piece of what we might call sheet music was a printed broadside obtained by Guy Johnson from Mrs. C. L. Lynn of Rome, Georgia. The broadside was signed W. T. Blankenship, but undated. Johnson estimated from the typeset that it may have been printed as early as 1900; other scholars such as Leach have suggested that it was the work of a 1920s hack rearranging folk material for popular consumption. Phillips Barry felt that the broadside spoke to the influence of mountain whites on the John Henry tradition, and was intrigued that Cecil Sharp had encountered the name Blankenship while collecting English folk ballads in Appalachia. The mysterious broadside might hold many clues to the John Henry legend, were we able to trace it more carefully. Guy Johnson reproduced it as the frontspiece of his book, and Norm Cohen included it in his *Long Steel Rail* as well.

Since Blankenship's broadside was released, "John Henry" has appeared in many forms in printed sheet music. Often arrangers have simply adapted the traditional songs. John Work's 1933 arrangement is for a piano with four male voices, who sing variants of "This Ol' Hammer/Take this Hammer" almost as rounds. Similarly, Charles Seeger's monumental work "Three American Folksongs: John Riley, Wayfaring Stranger, and John Henry for Solo Voice and Orchestra" is based on the traditional ballad. This piece was performed for the seventy-fifth anniversary of the Department of Agriculture in 1937. Elie Siegmeister's "John Henry" of 1938, adapted for mixed voices and tenor solo, is a fairly traditional piece as well, with a gripping climax centered on the sweaty details of the contest. Performed by the Robert Shaw Chorale in 1948 over NBC, Gail Kubick's "John Henry: American Folk Song Sketch" was adapted from the traditional ballad for tenors, basses and piano, with the piano rhythmically mimicking a hammer. Brookhart's 1950 version is for soprano, alto, tenor, and bass with piano and adds a soaring baritone solo. Anita Kerr's 1953 adaptation of the ballad, arranged for "Four Gals," is much sparser, with little more than a tune and much room for improvisation by what she terms "Living Voices." Lonnie Donnegan's 1956 piece sticks very close to the Lomaxes' 1935 version of the traditional ballad as sung by Arthur Bell; Oster and Leyden's 1958 arrangement for mixed voices (two tenors and two basses) is based on folksong but takes much creative license with it in what is aesthetically a very exciting piece. Sue and Lionel Wood's arrangement of "John Henry" for soprano, alto, tenor, bass, and piano treats the story as Central of Georgia Railroad lore, emphasizing the contest and the ghost of John Henry. (I have not been able to find Dave Dudley's 1963 arrangement; however, its catalog entry describes it as a rearrangement of the traditional ballad.) Leonard Stone's 1965 piece is also for soprano, alto, tenor, and bass, a very traditional ballad, as are Walter Ehret's of 1973, and Joe Cavella and Tom McIntosh's lengthy work of the same year. Also arranged in 1973, Carl Miller's "John Henry" for two voices and piano is introduced by a Kansas City boogie beat.

Some composers have commemorated John Henry in instrumental works: notably Aaron Copland in his symphony for partial orchestra of 1953; Phillip Gordon in a "Folksong Fantasy for Band," in 1957; Chet Atkins in a solo instrumental of 1962; and Edward McLin, for the Red Band Series in 1966.

Finally, a number of composers have taken great liberties with the legend. The first to do so were Musser and Cohen whose 1937 "Ballad of John Henry" treats him as a sort of desperado on whom the authorities are closing in and the church has slammed its doors. His last refuge is music: "I'll belly my way up hell's high hill, And sing! And sing!" the song concludes. In this category I include four of the Wolfe/Bradford songs published from their play in 1939: "I've Trompled All Over," (written for Julie Ann and describing her search for the right man), "Got a Head Like a Rock," (John Henry's unflattering self-portrait which also describes his heart of stone and his itching feet); "Sundown in My Soul," (a weary blues piece); and an adaptation of the traditional "Careless Love." Mattie O'Neil's 1950 song "John Henry Blues" describes a woman in mourning for a man she feels can never be matched; Mosley, Jaffee, and Dresner's patriotic composition of 1952 terms John Henry the same "spirit of the USA," that, for example, inspired George Washington at Valley Forge. In 1963 Singleton's strange and sketchy "John Henry's Surf" offers repetitive lyrics and just a tune; also in that year Jeanie Lee's "John Henry's Woman" features a woman singing a variant of "This Old Hammer" as though she had, indeed, taken up the dead man's burden. "John Henry's Girl," arranged by Winkler and Hathcock in 1964, describes Little Joe creeping on Belinda Lou, again to just a tune. Finally, Triplett's "John Henry, Junior," of 1965 is the most irreverent of the lot, characterizing John Henry's son as a no good gambler who is stabbed in Atlanta and laid to rest by his father beneath the epitaph: "Here lies the Good and the Bad."

NOTES

1. Both hammer fragments come from E. C. Perrow's "Songs and Rhymes from the South," p. 163.

2. See Josiah Combs' ballad in *Folk Songs du Midi des Etats-Unis,* p. 192, and John Lomax, "Some Types of American Folk Song," p. 14. Perrow's lines are slightly different: "Wrapped up his hammer in paper and silk, And sent it to the woman he loved" (p. 165).

3. Drawing on the network of over two thousand readers which he developed through this column, Gordon was the first collector to mount a massive expedition to track down folksong all over America. See D. K. Wilgus, *Anglo-American Folksong Scholarship Since 1898,* p. 180.

4. Zora Neale Hurston, *Mules and Men,* p. 306.

5. Guy Johnson, "John Henry: A Negro Legend," p. 51.

6. Freeman Hubbard, *Railroad Avenue,* p. 80.

7. A. L. Lloyd, "The Anatomy of John Henry," p. 12.

8. Alan Lomax, *The Folk Songs of North America,* p. 553.

9. Paul Glass, *Songs and Stories of Afro-Americans,* p. 61.

10. Jean Ritchie, *Singing Family of the Cumberlands.* Ritchie's book is essentially an autobiography built around 44 songs. Wilgus notes (p. 209) that Ritchie's songs are not necessarily typical of the Kentucky counties of Knott and Perry where Ritchie grew up.

11. Dash Moore, "John Henry and Some Other Stuff," p. 26.

4

ANALYZING THE
JOHN HENRY TRADITION

In addition to collecting John Henry songs, scholars since the 1920s have
been intrigued by the heroic tradition. Certainly the most important works
on John Henry are two short but rich studies, from whose interviews I have
drawn in constructing Chapter 2. Black sociologist Guy Johnson's *John
Henry: Tracking Down a Negro Legend* appeared in 1929. Although it does
not conform to strict notions of scholarly form, his is a lively, readable,
fascinating account. As noted in Chapter 3, Johnson had been drawn to
John Henry through an initial interest in black music, which he felt could
reveal the story of black Americans. He was intrigued by the discovery
that the fame of John Henry was sung everywhere, especially by black laborers
and wanderers, who might not know Booker T. Washington, but unfailingly
recognized the story of John Henry. Johnson tapped the knowledge of these
people through advertisements in the black press, through well publicized
contests, particularly at black high schools and colleges, and through extensive correspondence and many interviews, particularly in the area of Big
Bend Tunnel. He corresponded with and interviewed many whites as well,
mostly railroad men in the vicinity of Big Bend who, ironically, provided
him with his most conclusive testimony. Johnson's book explored questions
of John Henry's authenticity and tried to match the details of legend to
historical possibilities. He felt the evidence that John Henry actually lived
was sketchy, but personally preferred to believe that John Henry was a real
man. He was primarily interested, however, in the folklore process, in how
John Henry's story had spread and changed, in why it was so appealing,
and in what John Henry really meant to Negro people.

Johnson was excited by the inconsistencies in the story, and felt that the
hero's career in folklore expressed what is best about folk creativity, enrich-
ment, and diffusion. He urged the writers of the Harlem Renaissance to

tap into this tradition, to write an epic play, an opera, a symphony which would celebrate black culture as symbolized by John Henry. I believe that Johnson's influence has indeed been most profound in the popular arts, as many John Henry enthusiasts have looked to his book as a resource in constructing fictional accounts. *John Henry* is invaluable not only for its exuberance and originality, but for its collection of ballads and hammer songs and its transcripts of letters and interviews from those who claimed to know the steel driver.

Three critics reviewed Johnson's book in 1930. In the *Journal of American Folklore,* Louise Pound praised Johnson's contribution to what she considered a novel and useful approach to folklore theory: a movement away from armchair generalities and toward an exploration of particular songs in the lives of real people. She felt that research such as Johnson's would eventually allow scholars to return to generalities, but with rich, vivid, detailed material to draw on as a foundation. Certainly her assessment of Johnson's success in grounding the tradition in its community of believers is indisputable.

Lowry Charles Wimberly reviewed Johnson's study for Botkin's annual publication *Folk-Say,* but found it somewhat disappointing. He regretted that Johnson had not been more persuasive or conclusive in demonstrating John Henry's authenticity. However, he enjoyed Johnson's skill at enlisting the reader as cosleuth, admired Johnson's lively style, and clearly found the hero and his song endearing: "And crude and rough as it is, our little song, composed years ago, is prophetic of that which has, in great measure, come to pass. It is a tiny epic of man's last stand against the machine."[1]

Writing for the journal *American Speech,* Louis Chappell was the third reviewer of *John Henry.* Unlike Pound and Wimberly, Chappell was distressed by Johnson's work, particularly by Johnson's change of heart on the hero's authenticity. (As mentioned earlier, in 1925 Johnson had felt fairly sure that John Henry was a mythical character.) Chappell also accused Johnson of mishandling his own evidence, and claimed that Johnson's reports differed from what informants themselves said that they had told him.

Chappell's seemingly unwarranted distress becomes more comprehensible when we examine his book, the other major contribution to John Henry studies, published in 1933. *John Henry: A Folk-Lore Study* opens with Chappell's carping criticisms of several other scholars, with the most venomous attack reserved for Johnson. Johnson and Chappell appear to have been rivals of a sort, both pursuing the John Henry tradition throughout the 1920s. Chappell charged that Johnson had been inspired to reverse his position after reading an unpublished report of Chappell's investigation at Big Bend, although he never credited either the report or Chappell by name. (As D. K. Wilgus notes, this very ugly charge was never answered.)[2] Chappell was also critical of Johnson's interpretation of the ballads (especially his casual dismissal of the more vulgar versions). He was most offended because he felt that Johnson had undermined his own evidence and constructed a more negative case against John Henry's authenticity than was justified.

Chappell's book thus began on an extremely petulant note, which may discourage many readers, but which is understandable if his charges are correct. After the first chapter, however, it is rich, like Johnson's, in oral testimony and ballad samples. Although both authors were interested in the factual basis for the story, Chappell researched it much more thoroughly and his conclusions are, therefore, more persuasive. He consulted many years' worth of all available local newspapers, scientific and engineering journals, and reports from the construction of other tunnels to supplement the letters and interviews he gathered from informants. This painstaking work is admirable and leaves few avenues for later scholars to explore. Chappell was much more certain than Johnson that John Henry really lived; he felt in fact that it was indisputable. He was not quite so intrigued by the folk tradition as Johnson but argued, provocatively, that John Henry is a tunneling hero rather than a railroad man, and that he speaks most vividly to the dreams and fears of underground workers. This book is an invaluable resource, a model of meticulous investigation, and a superb illustration of how to use historical evidence to untangle and document oral tradition. The two books complement each other very nicely, with Johnson's perhaps more useful to the artist, and Chappell's most helpful to those seeking substantive information on the Big Bend Tunnel community.

SCHOLARLY ARTICLES

Ironically, the first scholar to explore the John Henry tradition provoked a strange and murky controversy which continues to this day. While writing his doctoral dissertation on West Virginia folksongs, John Harrington Cox grew interested in the ballad hero John Hardy, a black man celebrated for his gambling, drinking, and ways with women, who was hung for murder in 1894. Cox pursued the story of Hardy from at least 1914-1927 and for most of those years argued that he and John Henry were the same man. Intrigued by the execution order documenting Hardy's death, Cox was persuaded by a letter from West Virginia's ex-governor McCorkle that before dying in 1894 Hardy had been Big Bend's legendary steel driver.

In a 1919 article for the *Journal of American Folklore,* Cox cited several witnesses' descriptions of Hardy and offered five ballads as evidence that he was also John Henry. Only McCorkle's ballad really confuses the two, including in a Hardy tale several stanzas about the steel-driving incident at Big Bend. Cox concluded that this version must be halfway between the John Henry steel-driving ballad mentioned in 1911 by Shearin and Combs and later Hardy ballads which, Cox believed, had dropped descriptions of the contest in order to concentrate on the details of Hardy's execution.

Cox was not disturbed by the several other John Henry ballads known to him, but rather concluded that he had discovered a ballad evolving to commemorate its hero's continuing adventures. He did find his informants' testimony slightly problematic, in that the three who claimed to have seen Hardy guessed his age at between twenty-five and forty, which would have made Hardy awfully young for the prowess he demonstrated at Big Bend Tunnel twenty-four years earlier. Cox resolved this problem by pointing to the vagaries of memory and to the tendency of whites to underestimate the age of a strong and healthy Negro.

In 1925 Cox's theory received wide circulation when he repeated it in his *Folk-Songs of the South.* Here he included what he labeled two versions and nine variants of the ballad "John Hardy." One, from Combs' collection, is clearly a John Henry song; McCorkle's is again a blend of the two ballads; and several others about Hardy include the traditional first verse of "John Henry," where he prophesies his own death while sitting on his daddy's knee.

By 1927, in *American Speech,* Cox had reconsidered this position. Struck by Odum and Johnson's extensive collection of John Henry songs and a folktale they reproduced which likened John Henry more to Paul Bunyan than to Hardy, Cox suggested that a "final statement (on the matter) must await further investigation."[3] But other authors had adopted Cox's earlier and more publicized position by this time. Scarborough in 1925 and Maud Cuney Hare in 1936 assumed that Hardy and Henry were the same man; Brown referred to what he considered the Hardy-Henry complex; and in 1942 parttime folklorist Charles Carpenter, describing how in his boyhood he learned songs from steel drivers on the C & O, quotes *Folk-Songs of the South* in bolstering his own recollections. Carpenter's article is fascinating in its evocation of early twentieth century railroading and the transmission of black workers' songs to southern white youth. Like Cox, Carpenter thought of "John Hardy" as a black song, recalling that he had heard it first among steel drivers in around 1904. Following Cox, he assumed that only the earlier versions contained the steel-driving stanzas. Because he did not know of "The Death of John Henry" until the 1930s, Carpenter also proposed that it probably originated on the C & O and was composed by an anonymous ballad maker elaborating the steel-driving stanza eventually dropped from the Hardy ballad. Although Carpenter's chronology differs from Cox's, his argument demonstrates the extent of Cox's influence.

By 1927 critics had begun to challenge Cox's theory. The first was Guy Johnson, who devoted an entire chapter of his book to the John Hardy question. Interested in Cox's confusion of both the men and the songs, Johnson was troubled most by the age which Cox's informants attributed to Hardy. Johnson wryly suggested that if whites do tend to underestimate the age of blacks, his own informants, guessing John Henry to be thirty, had probably seen a man of forty who would then have been sixty at his execution, and thus a steel driver of extraordinary longevity. Johnson felt that Cox should have assumed Hardy's age to fall somewhere in the middle of the estimates, which would have made him a man in his early thirties, therefore the same age as John Henry at Big Bend, and thus certainly quite a different man. Clearly, Johnson felt, McCorkle was remote from the folk tradition commemorating both men and had offered Cox a second-hand, composite, and confused report. (One might extend Johnson's critique to argue that all but one of Cox's witnesses were whites acting in an official capacity at the execution, and unlikely to be the most astute reporters of Hardy's life experience.)

On the subject of the ballad, Johnson politely noted that Cox's position in 1919 had inevitably suffered from a paucity of data, that many other versions of the ballad had been published since, and that it seemed clear by 1927 that the "John Henry" songs were both older and much more popular than the Hardy ballad. Johnson's interesting argument on the diffusion of the two songs held that black itinerant railroad workers had carried "John Henry" all over the country, singing it in construction camps to other migrant laborers and leaving John Henry relatively unknown among West Virginia natives. (As the folksong samples described earlier demonstrate, Johnson underestimates the ballad's influence among white West Virginians.) Hardy emerged after the black itinerants had left West Virginia and his song hardly occurs outside Appalachia, although its author seems to have cast it in the "John Henry" format.

Unlike Cox and Carpenter, Johnson felt that the Hardy ballad had been embraced by white singers who occasionally added snatches of the "John Henry" song (most notably the first stanza) which were still recalled in the area and which suited the ballad's similar structure very well. Finally, Johnson pointed to the two songs' very different tunes and rhythms, with "John Henry's" faster, syncopated rhythm attesting to its prominence in black culture. Thus, Johnson saw "John Henry" as a black song, carried far beyond West Virginia by black workers, and "John Hardy" as a mountain whites' ballad occasionally enriched by a bit of John Henry lore.

Reviewing Johnson's book in 1930 and slightly disappointed that Johnson's general findings were inconclusive, Wimberly nonetheless praised him for settling the Hardy-Henry matter "beyond the shadow of a doubt." In his 1928 *American Negro Folk-Songs,* Newman White agreed with Johnson that the ballads mingled and coalesced, but essentially differed, and that "John Henry" was older and much more popular among blacks. White also felt that John Henry certainly lacked Hardy's vicious personal traits. Gerould noted in 1932 that Johnson's work had clarified a confusion inspired by the mere similarity of the men's names, but he admitted that the songs' variants were indeed bewildering, "with complexities of relationships as baffling as any found in our oldest ballads."[4]

In 1933 Chappell launched his book with a renewed and vigorous attack on Cox. Critical that Cox had relied too heavily on hearsay evidence, Chappell was most venomous in his description of Cox's talents as an editor. He checked Cox's printings of various ballads in different editions and contrasted Cox's pieces with those transcribed by original collectors. Chappell concluded that the errors must have resulted from confusion, overwork, or an excessive reliance on memory, and suggested that such an untrustworthy editor's mixed-up ballads may have been simply errors unworthy of scholarly debate!

In 1934 Phillips Barry used the occasion of reviewing Chappell's book for the *Bulletin of the Folk-Song Society of the Northeast* to address the Henry-Hardy question, under the larger issue of who had composed the John Henry ballad. Raising questions largely ignored before and since (until Norm Cohen returned to them in 1981), Barry's argument is provocative. Barry felt, as had Johnson, that the John Henry and John Hardy songs belonged to black and white traditions, respectively. But he saw them as more fluid than had Johnson, and was most intrigued by the "nontunnel" or mountain features of "John Henry." He suggested that these mountain features might be linked to the white woman sometimes named as John Henry's companion. Barry felt that this white woman might even have composed "John Henry," because he saw the tune of at least one version as nearly note for note identical with a version of the traditional white mountain ballad "Earl Brand." (To me the two tunes sound only vaguely reminiscent of one another, but perhaps Barry had a better ear for gauging their similarity. Norm Cohen notes that in any event that tune might have appeared earlier in Afro-American folksong. Since most early folksong collecting was restricted to white singers, we will never know.) In at least one other of Johnson's ballads, "John Henry" was set to the Hardy tune, which indicated to Barry that even if a white person had not composed it, mountain whites must have sung it frequently enough to confuse the two airs. Barry cited two other pieces of evidence to lodge John Henry in the mountain tradition and thus explain the easy confusion of him with John Hardy. The first verse of "John Henry," and the one most often reappearing in "John Hardy," he found strikingly close to a stanza of the Scottish ballad "Mary Hamilton,"

> "When I was a babe and a very little babe,
>   And stood at my mother's knee,
>   Nae witch nor warlock did unfauld
>   The death I was to dree."[5]

And finally, W. T. Blankenship, the author of the first known broadside of John Henry, was most likely white. The English ballad collector Cecil Sharp had in fact encountered the name Blankenship in the Appalachian mountains.[6] Barry seems to imply that this Blankenship, or a member of his family (his sister, perhaps, who was also John Henry's lover?) may have composed a ballad based on the message of tunnel songs celebrating the hero, but firmly lodged in the musical tradition of white mountaineers with a Scottish air for its tune and a re-created Scottish verse for its first stanza. While wary of Barry's conclusions because there is no way to refute or prove them, Cohen notes three traditional ways to strengthen the argument: he reminds us of the frequent emergence of the Lass of Roch Royal stanzas in the John Henry ballad, and mentions another Anglo-American ballad whose stanzas are faintly reminiscent of the "John Henry" opening stanzas:

> Then Mary took her babe,
> And sat him on her knee,
> Saying, My dear son, tell me
> What this world will be.

> O I shall be as dead, mother,
> As the stones in the wall;
> O the stones in the streets, mother,
> Shall mourn for me all.[7]

Finally Cohen suggests that the sustained narrative of the ballad, rare in black folksong, is perhaps the best evidence of white mountain influence.

While raising and discussing this interesting proposition to account, in part, for the intrusion of John Hardy into John Henry folklore scholarship, both Barry and later Cohen assumed that Cox had been wrong in confusing the two men. Aside from Carpenter's report in 1942, it seemed that the controversy had been laid to rest by 1934. But in 1967 MacEdward Leach revived it in the hope of illuminating some very exciting musical discoveries from Jamaica.

Leach was justifiably critical of evidence purporting to establish John Henry's authenticity. He noted astutely that many of the oral reports obtained by Johnson and Chappell simply duplicated the "John Henry" ballad information, leaving us with inconclusive, unsatisfactory answers about the hero's life. But Leach's caution in evaluating John Henry's authenticity makes his enthusiasm for Cox's work astonishing: he believed that the "sure evidence" missing for John Henry *was* available for John Hardy, and that reliable testimony places him (Hardy) at Big Bend Tunnell under contractors C. R. Mason and Langhorn [sic].[8] By reliable testimony, one can only assume that Leach is referring to Governor McCorkle's report, whose weaknesses have been discussed already. Leach also cited the evidence of the ballads, whose ages he believed to be the same. But for some reason he argued that the oldest songs joining the C & O Railroad, a hero, and a steam drill named that hero as John Hardy. (I believe that here Cox was referring again to McCorkle's version of the song, loaned by Cox to G. L. Kittredge, who printed it in the *Journal of American Folklore* in 1914. He did not mention Combs' ballad, collected in 1911 although unpublished in full until 1925, nor Perrow's versions of 1913.)

Leach resurrected Hardy to account for an intriguing John Henry tradition in Jamaica. While doing research there in the 1950s he had received a map, drawn in 1894, with a song transcribed on the back. The map's owner testified that he had copied the song on the map in 1894 and that it was called the "John Henry Song." This song mentioned a ten-pound hammer and a place called Garden Town. Further investigations of the Garden Town allusion revealed that Walter Jekyll's 1907 collection, *Jamaican Song and Story,* had included a song about the Gar'n Town people with the lines: "A ten pound order him kill me pardner" and "Den number nine tunnel, I would not work de, For somebody dying here ev'ry day."[9] These phrases reappeared in Scarborough's 1925 volume of Negro folksongs, Martha Beckwith's *Black Roadways* of 1929, and in Chappell's 1938 text from North Carolina. Leach noted the story told by Jekyll to explain the song: during the construction of the Garden Town road through the mountains (possibly in a Number Nine Tunnel) a man had been killed. Either his name was in fact John Henry, or the singers commemorating his death borrowed the name from another John Henry killed in the Number Nine Tunnel of the Kingston-Port Antonio Railroad. (Chapter 2 of this volume contains the report of that railroad's chief engineer, who does testify to the latter accident.) Leach found the only rooted knowledge of John Henry in Jamaica to be in the mountain region, where workers' songs frequently referred to him, and was intrigued by the fact that these songs seemed much older than those sung in the United States. (I find this conclusion difficult to accept, as we do not really know when the Jamaican songs first actually mention John Henry.) Leach recognized that the two sets of songs were very different; their stories have little detail in common, and their structures are completely dissimilar. He argued that the hammer songs of Jamaica simply never developed into the more complex and hybrid ballads of the United States.

At this point we see why Leach found John Hardy important to his theory. He suggested three possible hypotheses: that the Jamaican and American stories developed out of similar but different situations; that John Hardy was the original hero of the Big Bend Tunnel but took John Henry from Jamaica's name around 1900; or that the John Henry story traveled to Jamaica via black migrant workers, to be stripped there of all detail other than the hero's name and the fact of his death. It seems to me that either the first or the last of these propositions is well worth exploring: the Jamaican material is indeed compelling. But importing John Hardy as John Henry's stand-in at Big Bend only muddles the matter needlessly.

Until the publication of Norm Cohen's *Long Steel Rail* in 1981, other scholars have not much heeded Leach's argument, except to note in passing that the Jamaican material deserves further consideration. Cohen is cautious of Leach's evidence and suggests that we might consider a modification of the first hypothesis: that the stories are indeed separate, both involving men with the common name "John Henry," that in both places hammer songs were adapted to include the incident, and that in this country a complex group of ballads grew up to commemorate it.

Scholars have been interested in many aspects of the heroic tradition beyond the Hardy question. But as was true of that controversy, their interest lagged between the 1930s and 1960s. The journal *Tracks* printed three brief, local color features during those years: Marion Cooke's "Tracking Down a Ghost" in 1944, Robert Murray's "John Henry and the Steam Drill" in 1952, and James Dickson's "Home Grown Hero" in 1955. In 1952 journalist Forrest Hull contributed "C&O Tunnel is Folk Song Locale" to the *Charleston Daily Mail.* Indicating that popular and journalistic interest in the heroic tradition was still alive, these articles were designed more to increase awareness of John Henry than to discuss critically the man as hero. Dickson's and Cooke's articles are especially appealing in their insistence that John Henry was a real man, and in the local lore they offer to demonstrate his reality. Cooke also describes beliefs that the Big Bend Tunnel is haunted.

It was not until 1961, after a silence in major scholarly publications of almost thirty years, that Marshall Fishwick revived John Henry for an article in *Western Folklore* entitled: "Uncle Remus vs. John Henry: Folk Tension." (This article was reprinted in Fishwick's edited volume *Remus, Rastus, and Revolution* in 1968. Fishwick had been interested in John Henry for a number of years and had submitted a short travel note on the hero to *Ford Times* in 1954.) As the title of the 1961 article suggests, Fishwick was intrigued by the contrasting stances of blacks toward white society that the two kinds of lore expressed. Whereas the trickster tales of Uncle Remus encouraged humor, cunning, and accommodation, John Henry rejected such tactics and instead openly defied his opposition, relying on his own considerable strength in confronting adversity. Fishwick saw this same dichotomy reflected in the political strategies of Booker T. Washington and W.E.B. Du Bois. His article is especially valuable as an early effort to understand John Henry's place in black American consciousness. (It is interesting to note, however, and will become obvious in Chapter 5 that the John Henry of popular culture sometimes appears closer to Washington than to Du Bois. I believe that the story is sparse enough to be twisted either way.) In 1982 Fishwick renewed his exploration of John Henry's heroic appeal in "Where are Uncle Remus and John Henry?" He is concerned here with John Henry's seeming obsolescence in black culture and with discovering another symbolic figure to replace John Henry.

In 1963, Bernard Asbell contributed a general review article, "A Man Ain't Nothin' but a Man," to *American Heritage.* Asbell apparently relied wholly on Johnson's and Chappell's studies in recreating the circumstances of John Henry's life and work. His article primarily summarizes their descriptions, but clearly what interested Asbell most was John Henry's heroic appeal. He marveled at the ballad's popularity and versatility in adapting its message and style to the needs and goals of particular singers. He was especially struck by John Henry as a classic hero who prophesies his own death, pays for victory with his life, and leaves us wondering whether he has won or lost.

Although Asbell never quite answered the question of John Henry's remarkable popularity, he hinted that it had something to do with his appropriateness to modern times: as machines do more and more of our work and in the process threaten to dehumanize us, can we continue to be human and whole? Asbell felt that the answer lies in John Henry's song: "that man, the maker of wondrous mechanical things, is more wondrous than the things he makes; that a man who 'ain't nothin' but a man' is strong and worthy of supreme dignity."[10] Although Asbell's review may not add new information on the John Henry tradition, his tribute to the hero's powerful appeal is well worth reading.

In the mid 1960s Richard Dorson contributed two articles on John Henry. The first, "The Career of John Henry," appeared both in *Western Folklore* and in Dorson's edited collection *Folklore and Fakelore* in 1976. Although not terribly thorough, this is an elegant overview of John Henry's journey through popular culture. Dorson traces early folklorists' concerns for collecting the ballad, assessing John Henry's relationship to John Hardy, and exploring the factual basis for the contest described in song. He felt that with Johnson's and Chappell's convincing studies, such scholarly probes ceased, and John Henry became almost exclusively a creature of popular culture. He astutely noted Roark Bradford's role in transforming John Henry into a stereotypical black Paul Bunyan who would appear in that image in numerous children's books and folklore treasuries. The more traditional hero does not seem to have been commemorated in folktales; at least only very few of those folktales survive. Dorson found John Henry's most powerful impact to have been through recorded music, which gradually has stabilized the ballad and kept it immensely popular.

In 1966 Dorson's "Ballad of John Henry" appeared in *An American Primer*. The second half of this article repeats the 1965 analysis of John Henry's trip through popular culture. The first offers a vivid and concise historical background for the ballad. Finally, Dorson presented an elliptical but provocative explanation of the ballad's formidable appeal: its power, he wrote, comes from the way it combines "dramatic intensity, tragic tension, and simple poetry. . ."[11] For a condensed summary of John Henry's popular career, this article is probably the best there is.

Almost as though Dorson had challenged them to rescue John Henry from a popular Paul Bunyan-like fame worse than obscurity, three writers in the late 1960s and early 1970s contributed articles geared for very different audiences but all designed to reshape public notions of John Henry as a man.[12] In the *Washington Post's Potomac Magazine* in 1969, Hank Burchard vividly recreated the deadly Big Bend Tunnel, its place in railroading and

West Virginia history, its community life, and John Henry's probable skill as a steel driver there. Burchard's article is wonderfully written, though as popular journalism, scantily referenced. He seems to rely mostly on Chappell's work, two tunneling texts, and some interviews of his own with a few elderly residents of Hinton, which he did not find fruitful. (He explained to me in a recent telephone conversation that he had arrived there ten years too late.) Burchard was most concerned with describing the life John Henry might have led, but also found it possible to conclude that John Henry certainly lived, less certainly raced a steam drill, but could very well have defeated it if he did. This article is most valuable because it is so vivid in its evocation of the tunnel community and because it so successfully re-transforms John Henry into a real man whose history belongs to the in-dustrializing south rather than to mythic events.

Virginia Steele was somewhat less concerned with documenting the details of John Henry's life. In her two part series for *Wonderful West Virginia* in 1972, she was most interested in the legend, and particularly in its extra-ordinarily varied claims about who John Henry was, where he came from, and why he raced a steam drill. She found West Virginia especially rich in John Henry lore, quoted extensively from Chappell's interviews in the Big Bend Tunnel area, and visited Talcott herself to question residents about John Henry. I consider one of her interviews especially insightful. Most scholars have assumed that since the C & O records were burned up in the early part of this century, efforts to locate information on John Henry's employment must be doomed to failure. Steele had the foresight to locate contractor Johnson's grandson, now president of a coal company in Smithers, West Virginia, to question him about his grandfather's own records. (As I discovered by talking to Mr. Johnson recently, his grand-father not only left no records, but became a father very late in life and died in 1911 without discussing tunnel stories with his family.) But Steele found the Talcott residents' reminiscences rewarding, and her article is especially valuable for its insights into the West Virginia context for John Henry's life and her portrait of how his legend lives on there.

Jeffrey Miller's 1973 piece "John Henry," written for *The Laborer,* reflects the Laborers' International Union's interest in John Henry as a workingman's hero. Miller had no doubts that John Henry's story is true, and he was especially interested in its appeal to and celebration of the hero as worker. Like most other writers, Miller relied heavily on Chappell's work, though he also cites Burchard. His passionate article contains little news. But it is a masterly, detailed commenoration of grinding and hazardous work, again very important in treating John Henry as a real man whose lot was shared by many others in similar circumstances. (This article was reprinted in the Smithsonian's *Ring Like Silver Shine Like Gold* in 1976.)

In 1978, two brand new and extremely fruitful approaches to the John Henry tradition emerged, both unfortunately recorded in journals which will not be easily available to all interested readers. In her *Kentucky Folk-lore Record* piece, Mary Lou Mulcahy focused on the ballad itself, with a brief discussion of its structure and a more extended exploration of its memorability by testing its contents against her high school students' knowledge of John Henry. Using Leach's version as sample, she commented on the ballad's satisfying use of repetition, which clues the reader to how each stanza will begin and end, its focus upon the man rather than the event, and its flexibility in including several different tales within one version, thus allowing the listener to choose, for example, the ending he or she prefers. She argued also that its lively tune is a significant factor in its longevity. Upon surveying her students, Mulcahy was struck by their ignorance of the ballad's sexual connotations, which she finds significant and dramatic especially in the song's earliest forms. What her students did remember most vividly about John Henry was that he was strong, that he engaged in a contest with a machine, and that he was a steel-driving man. This last I also have found to be a prominent recollection; Mulcahy felt that her students attached little meaning to the term but mentioned it because the ballad repeats it very frequently. Their other two responses she found more meaningful: like today's bionic man and woman, heroes of superhuman strength seem to enjoy a universal and lasting popularity; and the problem of machines which make us feel small can be vicariously resolved by a man who could defeat one with sheer physical strength. Mulcahy offers a novel approach to John Henry lore and packs more original and provocative ideas into four short pages than I have seen in a long while.

Archie Green has begun to explore another new and very promising area of John Henry studies. In what he suggested would be a continuing series with an increasing emphasis on the work of individual artists, Green published the first general piece, "John Henry Depicted" in the *JEMF Quarterly* in 1978. Green's overriding interest is in how commercial artists lift a hero from folk tradition and reshape him to produce a visual image which Americans can widely share. He feels that modern life inspires a celebratory nostalgia for folk tradition—a nostalgia which commonly impels artists to look to folklore for subject material—but that the particular form which each artist assigns that subject can vary a great deal according to the artist's purpose and era. Green was impressed by Johnson's farsightedness in urging poets, playwrights, painters, and sculptors to bring John Henry to life in popular culture; and he feels that in the fifty years since Johnson's charge, artists have accomplished the task, making John Henry "the major hero astride our visual landscape."[13] Green's goal, therefore, is to judge the skill and the sensitivity with which visual artists have depicted the folk hero. He offers the reader an extensive checklist of John Henry depictions and deals with only a few in depth; this carefully limited comparison is eloquently presented and critically insightful. Green discusses and also reproduces the illustrations of Given (for Shay's story), Lankes (for Bradford's novel),

Daugherty (for Shapiro's fiction), Watson (for Felton), and LaGrone (for Bowman). He is intrigued, for example, by Given's placing John Henry in a factory setting far removed from the tunnel to which we link him, by Lankes' juxtaposition of dignified and tender with grotesque, stereotypical portraits, and by the influential role of illustrators in formulating for children a mysterious and awesome or gentle and friendly man, a hero magnified or reduced.

Green's 1979 piece is much shorter and more particular, limited to "Fred Becker's John Henry." Becker was a woodcut engraver and printmaker who produced a John Henry series of wood engravings scratchboard prints while employed by the Federal Art Project in the late 1930s. Because Becker's art is in storage at the National Collection of Fine Arts and unavailable to viewers, Green's reproduction of the nine pieces here is a real service to the John Henry enthusiast. A narrative series including the Black River Country, the Birth of John Henry, John Henry Building a Railroad, John Henry Picking Cotton, John Henry's Hand, and John Henry's Death, Becker's art was inspired in part by the work of Roark Bradford. Green noted, however, the degree to which Becker's "abstractionist bent" has reshaped John Henry: he was "at once young and old, innocent and decadent, naive and grotesque."[14] And Green added that he hoped museums would continue to show Becker's art, as anyone who sees the reproductions would probably agree. I hope that Archie Green will continue his fine series on John Henry in art, for clearly he has discovered an untapped and rich area of investigation.

SCHOLARLY DISCUSSION OF THE JOHN HENRY TRADITION IN LARGER CONTEXTS

In addition to exploring the John Henry tradition on its own, several scholars have drawn him into an examination of larger issues. The studies discussed below vary greatly in length, depth, and subject matter; they have in common their use of some features of the tradition as a case study supporting a more comprehensive argument. Their variety is testimony to the numerous contexts in which John Henry has been influential.

Gordon Hall Gerould's 1932 volume *The Ballad of Tradition* is a study of the origin and diffusion of folk ballads. He draws on the John Henry and John Hardy ballads as case studies for his contention that American ballads are more rough and ready and more likely to deteriorate than improve than their European counterparts, which Gerould felt profited by developing in the context of established community life. He cited the Hardy/Henry complex as evidence of the confusion likely to surround balladry as it moved and mingled with varied traditions across the American landscape. Gerould was also interested in the inevitably significant influence of black music makers on native American song and felt that blacks were bound to improve it, as their composition and dissemination of "John Henry" demonstrated. Gerould reprinted Leon Harris' long and interesting version of "John Henry" (as published by Guy Johnson in 1929) in his appendix.

Several authors have discussed John Henry in general texts on Afro-American music. Sometimes the references are brief and ambiguous: Maud Cuney Hare's *Negro Musicians and Their Music* mentions the song only in passing and appears to confuse it with "John Hardy"; she later praised a CBS radio series based on the legend. Alain Locke mentioned "John Henry" in *The Negro and his Music* of 1936 as part of a larger effort to classify black music by region and type: he categorized it under blues and work songs as a model of the style of the seaboard lower south (primarily the Carolinas and Georgia), whose songs were racier, more realistic, less sentimental. (This reference is repeated in Margaret Butcher's reworking of Locke's materials.) Harold Courlander's *Negro Folk Music USA* offered a remarkable repertoire of black music, including a discussion of John Henry under "Sounds of Work" and a long narrative ballad importing elements from several other songs and describing in great detail John Henry's women, children, and reflections during the contest. (This ballad is reprinted in several other Courlander collections.) Courlander briefly described the legend of John Henry and discussed the versatility of the song. Eileen Southern's *The Music of Black Americans* is, like Courlander's book, an overview, with a greater emphasis on black musical history than song texts. She mentioned John Henry under a section of work songs and reprinted an abbreviated version of Sandburg's sample from *An American Songbag.*

Many blues texts do not include "John Henry," which seems surprising; perhaps blues scholars consider the ballad more of a traditional folksong than a legitimate blues piece. I have found only three. Paul Oliver's *The Meaning of the Blues* is a classic study of blues music's reflection of and commentary on black history. Oliver eloquently described the Reconstruction Era setting, particularly working conditions faced by blacks then, and reprinted Mississippi John Hurt's "Spike Drivin' Blues." Giles Oakley, in his book *The Devil's Music,* also reprinted Hurt's blues ballad, which Oakley felt portrayed John Henry as placid, gentle, and essentially noncompetitive. Oakley noted what he considers an irony to the John Henry tradition: the hero seems to confirm the white stereotype that blacks are only good for hard and mindless labor. Finally, Eric Sackheim's *The Blues Line,* also contains "Spike Driver Blues."

Two texts concerned with the music of particular institutions offer excellent discussions of the John Henry musical tradition. Archie Green's *Only a Miner* is an extensive exploration of miners' songs, where he feels the influence of John Henry is notable. Green considers "John Henry" the best loved of our industrial ballads, symbolizing the pain we all feel about conflict with machines, and easing "the pain of blasting, drilling, loading, and lifting for all workers."[15] Green discussed the ballad in illuminating for his readers the nature of industrial folksong, but he was most interested in the "Nine-Pound Hammer" motif, which appears often in John Henry ballads, emerges as the name of a folksong where it can represent generally the varied functions of the hammer in industrial tasks, and recurs frequently as part of the worksong complex which includes, as examples, "Roll on Buddy" and "Take This Hammer." Green's discussion of the development and diffusion of hammer songs is intriguing, as is his proposal that hammer songs were carried from the tunnels to the coal mines by railroad workers.

In his *Long Steel Rail* of 1981, Norm Cohen expresses an indebtedness to Archie Green, whose volume on miners' songs Cohen sees as a model for his own work. *Long Steel Rail* is a masterful, remarkable study of the railroad in American folksong, with case studies ranging from "John Henry" (and other heroes and badmen) through songs about legendary train wrecks, work songs, hobo songs, and railroad blues pieces, to those ballads which metaphorically link the train ride to a journey to heaven. Cohen's emphasis is on recorded music; his special love is for the hillbilly and race records of the 1920s and 1930s. For each song he offers historical and legendary background, briefly discusses critical scholarship, and presents a thorough, meticulous bibliography and discography.

"John Henry" is Cohen's first case study. He transcribes the versions of Uncle Dave Macon and Fiddlin' John Carson, briefly describes the legend and critiques the folklore scholarship concerning it, reserves special emphasis for the work of Barry and Leach (which I have described above in relation to the John Hardy question), analyzes the structure of the ballad, and offers an overview of John Henry's career on records. Cohen's piece is a superb critical work in which he takes on matters previously often left undiscussed. Most intriguing is his exploration of the influence of whites on the composition and diffusion of the ballad and his provocative, insightful suggestion that we not consider John Henry's protest to be antiindustrial, but rather directed toward our indifference in a capitalist society to those workers who are displaced. (Another case study, "Nine Pound Hammer," presents Mississippi John Hurt's "Spike-Drivin' Blues" once again, and borrows straightforwardly from Green's exploration of John Henry's influence in that complex of songs.)

Other assorted and miscellaneous texts include discussions of John Henry, and again, their variety is surprising. Gosta Sandstrom's *Tunnels* is an informative engineering volume mostly concerned with the history of tunnel construction. He devoted only a few pages to John Henry as part of a tribute to the feats of tunnel laborers. In particular Sandstrom praised the steel-driving man at the front, on whose prowess and endurance the success or failure of the tunnel enterprise rested. He is very impressed by the dignity and power of the John Henry tradition, which he considers "apocryphal," but does not, he feels, stem from an impossible event. Sandstrom described other drilling contests and their heroes, none of whom, as far as he was able to discover, ever broke John Henry's record. According to Sandstrom, hand drilling was a precision sport involving rigorous training and thousands of dollars exchanged through wagers or prize money. Although his account of other champions' records makes John Henry's legendary fourteen feet in thirty-five minutes seem implausible, his evidence that such contests were commonplace and his respect for John Henry lore seems important and convincing.

Hollander's 1970 *Americana* is published in Dutch and includes reports of American folklife and folk heroes based in the southeastern United States. He includes John Henry as a case study, and as far as I can tell the piece is merely an overview of the legend and its popularity, including several representative ballad samples.

Rudolf Haas' book *Theori and Praxis der Interpretation* is an exposition of how to analyze texts using both literary and sociological methods. He offers John Henry as a case study under labor lore. As are many other scholars, Haas is intrigued by the conflict dramatized in the ballad between man and machine; he is also one of several researchers to show an interest in the song's sexual innuendoes.

The last two authors in this section place John Henry in two very different heroic traditions. As a contribution to Luther Luedke's anthology on American Studies methods and theory, Roderick Nash's article "Machines and Americans" explored American's ambivalence about machines and the use of folklore to untangle the significance of those feelings. He thus discussed John Henry in the context of several heroes whose relationships with machines were problematic. John Henry was the only one to directly confront the machine, and "Remembering John Henry was a way of paying homage to every man who found his powers made puny by those of machines."[16] After John Henry, very different heroes emerged. Casey Jones was one who drove or controlled machines, although he self-destructively linked his self-respect and reputation too closely with his locomotive. Paul Bunyan, Joe Magarac (a steelworker who could mold hot lead with his bare hands), and Superman were superheroes who spurned machines; and Charles Lindbergh showed us that we could be the machine's partner. Nash's article is especially interesting in that it places John Henry in a mainstream American heroic tradition of a more general cast than railroading or tunneling.

Lawrence Levine's exploration of John Henry, in *Black Culture and Black Consciousness,* is both crucial and unique. Like other scholars he is concerned with the nature of John Henry's epic heroism and the nearly universal aspects of his story. But Levine's most important contribution to the problem is that he places John Henry clearly in the context of changing black experiences and consciousness. In a rich and well-documented survey of black culture, Levine traces heroic figures from slavery to modern times and finds John Henry pivotal. For slaves, the heroes of the Old Testament promised victory in this world through direct confrontation with evil and misplaced authority. At the same time trickster tales portrayed an irrational and arbitrary world and described a practical morality whereby the weak might outwit the strong but were often quite capable of evil themselves. With freedom, slave spirituals were gradually replaced by the more other-worldly gospel songs and tricksters more and more often faced defeat in the stories former slaves told about them. With freedom came a more individualistic ethos reflected in blues music and in the celebration of heroes like John Henry, Shine, Jack Johnson, and Joe Louis. Like Joe Louis, John Henry was strong, self-contained—he violated no laws or morals, but confronted and triumphed over white society on his own terms. He has much in common with the heroes of the Old Testament and contrasts powerfully with the trickster. Levine thus helps us appreciate John Henry's precise significance in black culture and changing black life.

Finally, researchers can locate information on John Henry in several reference texts, including such general volumes as William Rose Benet's *The Reader's Encyclopedia,* Funk and Wagnall's *Dictionary of Folklore,* edited by Maria Leach, and Compton's *Pictured Encyclopedia,* which featured a brief article by Carl Carmer every year between 1950 and 1977.

Folksong references with bibliography, discography, and ballad samples are Ray Lawless's *Folksingers and Folksongs in America;* Charles Haywood's *A Bibliography of North American Folklore and Folksongs;* Malcolm Laws's *Native American Balladry;* Bruce Rosenberg's *The Folksongs of Virginia: A Checklist of the WPA Holdings;* Kurt Miller's Ph.D. dissertation, "Heroes Found in Song Texts from Folk Music of the United States"; Patricia Porcello's dissertation, "The Railroad in American Literature: Poetry, Folksong, and the Novel"; and two of the Library of Congress' Archive of Folksong's own reference volumes: *Checklist of Recorded Songs in the English Language in the Archive of American Folksong to July 1940* and *A Catalog of American Folk Music on Commercial Recordings at the Library of Congress* (compiled as a Master's thesis in Library Science by Richard Spottswood).

NOTES

1. Lowry Charles Wimberly, "Steel-Drivin' Man," *Folk-Say,* p. 415.
2. D. K. Wilgus, *Anglo-American Folksong Scholarship Since 1898,* p. 398.
3. John Harrington Cox, "The Yew Pine Mountains," p. 227.
4. Gordon Hall Gerould, *The Ballad of Tradition,* p. 266.
5. Phillips Barry, "Reviews," p. 25.
6. Norm Cohen mentions a North Carolina Blankenship family which recorded hillbilly songs throughout the 1920s and "I been working on the railroad" in 1931.
7. Norm Cohen, *Long Steel Rail,* p. 70.
8. MacEdward Leach, "John Henry," p. 95.
9. Walter Jekyll, *Jamaican Song and Story,* pp. 268-69.

10. Bernard Asbell, "A Man Ain't Nothin but a Man," p. 95.

11. Richard Dorson, "The Ballad of John Henry," p. 445.

12. Another popular piece during these years was Albert Scardino's article, distributed by Associated Press Newsfeatures in the fall and winter of 1971.

13. Archie Green, "John Henry Depicted," p. 126. Green's catalog of John Henry art is remarkably thorough and diverse, including wood carvings by folk artists Charlie J. Permelia and S. L. Jones, posters, ceremics, statuettes, a medallion, a decal, a T-shirt, and a salt and pepper shaker souvenir.

14. Archie Green, "Fred Becker's John Henry," p. 31.

15. Archie Green, *Only a Miner,* p. 9.

16. Roderick Nash, "Machines and Americans," p. 104.

5

TRIBUTES TO JOHN HENRY IN LITERATURE AND ART

Although he has lived vividly in American popular song, John Henry has not been commemorated in other popular media as widely as one might expect. His overpowering presence in folk music contrasts starkly with the sparse portraits of John Henry in other media. Nonetheless, the heroic forms he assumes there are instructive. This chapter reviews the work of those authors and artists who have characterized John Henry, beginning with folktales and proceeding through popular fiction, film, poetry, dance and art.

FOLKTALES

Howard Odum and Guy Johnson published the first folktale in their 1925 collection *Negro Workaday Songs*. Although they recorded the story at Chapel Hill, they believed it originated in Stone Mountain, Georgia. Odum and Johnson note the Paul Bunyan-like prowess already demonstrated by this early John Henry. As in later fiction, John Henry exhibits a ravenous appetite, aided in this case by a magical landscape showering him with treats: a "brown baked pig wid sack o' biscuits on this back," a "tree which is full o' flitterjacks," and a "lake o' honey." But although a legendary eater, "Dat nigger could wuk mo'n he could eat."[1] The John Henry of this story was a great steel driver as well, ever demanding bigger hammers and drilling astounding distances, from Rome to Decatur, Georgia, for example, in a single day. And unlike some heroes who are unrealistically chaste, John Henry loved many women, who created quite a spectacle when they all gathered around his grave. This tale is frequently reminiscent of the ballad as when, for instance, John Henry the infant predicts his doom. At other times, this North Carolina story teller's version is both imaginative and quite unique.

Odum and Johnson mention other stories, but unfortunately never collected them for publication. They included only one other fragment, a wishful ending to another North Carolinan's tale in which he describes an imaginary statue at the mouth of Big Bend Tunnel: "No, I ain't ever been dere, but dere he stan', carved in great big solid rock wid de hammer in his han'."

Leon Harris' story, "That Steel-Drivin' Man," has been reprinted three times: in 1925, 1957 and 1973. Harris was a John Henry enthusiast and a sophisticated informant; although he described himself as a rambler, he was also a lifelong railroad employee and secretary of his railway brotherhood. His story is elegantly composed and more complex than the others. Harris claims to have heard it while working with a track-laying gang. One rainy day Shine, the camp clown, was teasing Old Man, a mere temporary who nonetheless commanded a mysterious respect. Old Man silenced Shine by alleging that he had known John Henry and then captured the attention of all the workers (who had admired John Henry for years) with the following story: Because he had once saved his master from drowning, the slave John Henry was made a free man. An unselfish and hard-working person, he drove steel for Captain Walters, an old-school southerner who loved his employees, even though many were slaves hired on contract. John Henry was one of many men attached to various gangs of plow men, wheelers, pick and shovel workers, and skinners, as well as steel drivers. But he was clearly the most proficient. John Henry was in love with Lucy, a woman still a slave, and he wanted to buy her freedom. He named his hammer for her. While his crew was driving through the Virginia mountains, Captain Walters bet a Yankee drummer peddling a steam drill that John Henry could "beat that three-legged steam contraption of yours to a frazzle."[2] He promised John Henry fifty dollars if he won. Although the Yankee cheated by waiting until the hot July sun was high in the sky, John Henry didn't care: "It was steam against muscle; brain against brawn; progress against stagnation; Yankee against Southerner; head against heart."[3] (Including "Progress against Stagnation" in a list which otherwise favors John Henry's stance lends to Harris's tale a curious ambivalence reflected otherwise in the wry affection he shows the Old South). John Henry won and died. At the end of the tale, Shine was cowed and trudged off in the mud singing the song. Although Harris' story has penetrated fictional portraits only occasionally, I find it more remarkable than its limited influence suggests. In setting the scene for the tale to be told, in making it the province of the old man as bearer of cultural tradition, in describing John Henry's life with historical accuracy, and in imputing the noblest of motives to him in his race with the steam drill, it is a gripping and poignant account.

As a project for the Federal Writers' Program, writers in North Carolina gathered folklore for *Bundle of Troubles and Other Tarheel Tales,* edited by W. C. Hendrix. "John Henry and the Cape of Fear" is one of the stories. Unlike the other two tales, this conforms closely to the ballad's narrative, only taking liberties in its description of John Henry's personality.

In the writer's rendition of black North Carolina dialect, as told by a man who was allegedly John Henry's friend, the story unfolds like this: He was thirty pounds at birth and three hundred twelve pounds when he died. Infatuated with a hammer at an early age, he spent his time hammering objects rather than playing with traditional toys. He grew into a strong, quiet, church-going man who worked in a quarry to contribute to his family's finances.

His railroad career began at nineteen when "A white man came to where he lived and asked him, does he want to work for the railroad. They's cuttin' tunnels through the mountings, and they needs good steel drivers. . . . his fame done spread all over the country, and they take him ever'place to show how much steel he can drive and how he handle that big hammer. He was give up to be the strongest man what ever lived—stronger even than Samson, or Goliath, or ennybody. And they say that J. H. is most polite, and he goes to church regular, and he say his prayers ever night, jes like he do when he home."

The narrator describes several heroic incidents: John Henry saved men during a cave-in by holding up the rocks and on another occasion by hoisting up a broken elevator cable, and eventually he confronted the steam drill. During the contest, "The steam hammer gang. . . put two new men on the hammer. I speaks up to the superintendent but he say they is no 'greement that the steam hammer men couldn't change; 'cause it is a race between John Henry and the machine."[4]

With 12 inches left to drive his steel home, John Henry died. He was two inches ahead of the steam hammer. His last words echoed the John 3:16 verse "that whosoever believeth in Him should not perish. . . ."

POPULAR FICTION

Just nine authors have published book length fictional versions of John Henry's life. The first to do so, the only one to write for adults, and by far the most influential in shaping John Henry's popular career was Roark Bradford. Bradford's work emerged in three different formats during the 1930s, and with each reappearance its message was transformed. His 1931 novel *John Henry* received wide circulation when it was distributed by the Literary Guild. More popular probably than it deserved to be, the novel was nonetheless far superior to the serialized version of the story which appeared in *Cosmopolitan*. Finally, in 1939 Bradford rewrote his book as a musical play, also called *John Henry,* that proved to be disastrous.

Bradford had grown up on a southern plantation, where he was exposed to black lore, and he claimed to have developed his book from folk sources. His novel strays dramatically from the John Henry of folk tradition, but a number of its incidents are reminiscent of trickster tales, bad man epics, blues themes, and steamboat lore.[5]

He adapted John Henry to a lower Mississippi setting. The hero is born in the Black River country of northern Louisiana, and appropriate miracles of nature accompany his birth. Weighing forty-four pounds, John Henry enters the world with a cotton hook for a right hand and a river song on his tongue: one easily foresees his destiny. At birth, the obnoxious personality that shapes his destiny is already well-defined: as a newborn, he angrily demands a huge soul food breakfast that he eats before stalking out of his home, presumably forever.

John Henry's absurd and unreal Amos and Andy dialect was popular during the 1930s, but seems rather offensive today, as does Bradford's free and easy use of "nigger" and his hero's jarring braggadocio. However, the episodes that Bradford weaves into the novel are sometimes engaging and humorous, and the story has a certain tragic tension. John Henry's burdens are his work and his woman; he is never able to manage them both, although throughout the novel he tries. In a number of settings, we see him flaunting his skills as a strong and clever laborer: he shows other workers how to roust cotton, pick cotton, load hogs, and lay track by joining the best qualities of brute force, humor, special folk technique—and of course, song—to relieve what might be tedious work. In several cases, John Henry confronts a white supervisor and jives him into concessions for his black employees. In one especially telling episode (grading the Yaller Dog Railroad), John Henry discovers a foreman resting his mules in the shade while driving his men because he has calculated that mules are more expensive than black workers. John Henry argues that "Shade is for white folks and hosses. Sun is made for mules and niggers,"[6] and persuades the boss to give each man two mules and a wheeler to expedite the work. While apparently accepting the man's racial premise, John Henry, through a tongue in cheek, self-abnegating Uncle Tom charade, charms and cons him into offering his workers some relief.

Again and again John Henry meets his adversaary, the "Nigger named Sam." John Henry outwits and outworks Sam in the gambling hall, in the locomotive cab, and in a track-laying contest, but cannot prevent Sam from creeping to his woman Julie Ann while he is gone.

In his relationship with Julie Ann, John Henry's second burden emerges. He is deeply in love with her; although many other women pursue him, he cannot get her off his mind. Nor can he settle down with her, for he is forever lured away by work. Julie Ann loves John Henry too, but finds she cannot wait for him while he is gone. As the witching woman from John Henry's home comments, it is truly a tragic love story for despite their feelings for one another, they cannot get together: he likes to work, and she likes to trifle. Only after death—he dies racing a cotton-hoisting donkey engine and she moments later by trying to carry on his task—are they reunited. At their funeral, the preacher notes that they gave their souls to Jesus Christ because the burden had become too heavy.

Reviewing the book in the *Nation,* Guy Johnson lamented Bradford's tendency toward the burlesque, arguing that his love of tall tale and big talk detracted from the story's occasional vitality and from John Henry's tragic character. Johnson also regretted the extraordinary transformation of the original John Henry into Bradford's vision of the character. But Johnson found much to praise in the novel as well, and it is at times engaging: John Henry is a human, though boastful character: comic, sensible, imperfect and sad. And perhaps just as importantly, the book has a point of view: the vignettes often illuminate the harsh realities of southern life and the creativity with which blacks confront them.

Hearst's International-Cosmopolitan serialized *John Henry* that same year, publishing four fragments of the novel as short stories illustrated with caricatures which today are extremely offensive. Most interesting are the episodes chosen for serialization: John Henry's birth, probably the most popular of Bradford's episodes and reproduced several other places (including Botkin's, Courlander's, and Flanagan and Hudson's folklore treasuries), is foremost. The four installments (*Cosmopolitan* never printed the final one) portray comic moments, impossible exploits, and lovers' quarrels. Readers see John Henry roust cotton, befriend hogs, drive spikes, argue with Julie Ann and trifle with a woman named Ruby, gamble with John Hardy, and fight with Stacker Lee. Lost are the confrontations with unjust employers and law enforcement officials, the social criticism, the moments of reflection, the tragic prophecies, the tension between labor and love, and John Henry's salvation. The story has lost its moral and John Henry is wholly lacking in human integrity.

Eight years later, Bradford adapted his novel for a musical play. His earlier work *Ol' Man Adam an his Chillun* (which sketched a folk version of the Old Testament as lived out by southern blacks) had inspired Mark Connelly's very successful play of the early 1930s, *The Green Pastures.* It lasted five years on Broadway, but like Bradford's *John Henry,* has not fared well with time; when revived in 1951, it was harshly criticized for its stereotypical black characters, dialog and plot.

Bradford's 1939 script bears little resemblance to the novel. A few of the original episodes remain—such as the construction of the Yaller Dog Railroad—but even this event is twisted so that its climax comes when John Henry and Julie Ann switch partners with Ruby and Sam. Here Sam seems to symbolize cunning versus brawn as he persuades Julie Ann to leave for New Orleans while John Henry is at work. Julie Ann's trifling seems mindless and cruel and even nymphomaniacal. In Bradford's earlier work, she is more sympathetic and ambiguous: she does not want to cheat on John Henry, cries as she does so, rejects his replacement before he comes home, and anxiously awaits his return—yet just can't seem to help herself. In the play, she cheats for no better reason than that John Henry is asleep or momentarily preoccupied.

Bradford changes his other characters into prototypes: Sam becomes Stacker Lee, the white steamboat mate, a construction chief. John Henry is not very personable either; one hardly knows him until his rather strange, boastful soliloquy with which the last act comes to a climax. He has just refused salvation and cast off Julie Ann. "As though taking inventory of himself," he rebuilds his own confidence:

> I'm big and bad and six foot tall,
> And I come f'm de Black River country,
> And ain't no work kin bear me down,
> And ain't no man kin shade me.
> My back is iron, my muscles is steel,
> And my name is old John Henry.
> I works my way around dis world,
> And I don't beg no favors.
>
> I works on de river and I works on de land
> And everybody knows I'm a nachal man.
> I wrestles wid de freight all de summer and fall
> And I rolls more cotten den de White kin haul.
>
> I wheel de dirt, and I snake de log,
> And I laid de steel on de Yaller Dog.
> I quits my work cause I want to play,
> And I quits Poor Selma and I wawks away.
>
> When I works I'se happy, and when I plays I'm sad,
> And I kills anybody which do's me bad.
> Cause I'm bawn in de country and I'm raised in de town.
> I'm a workin' poor fool f'm my head on down.
>
> My name is John Henry, and when you calls my name
> Let yo' backbone tremble and bow yo' head in shame.
> I'm gwine back to de Black River country
> Whar de sun don't never shine,
> And hit ain't no womens, and hit's plenty er work,
> And work don't bother my mind.
> Cause my name is old John Henry,
> And God knows, I'm a nachal man![7]

In taking stock of himself, the hero seems equally pleased by his brawn, his love of hard work, and his extraordinary disdain for human relationships. Bradford was particularly fond of the natural man theme, invoking it not only in this self-portrait of John Henry but also in allusions throughout his work, including the subtitle to his earlier *Ol' Man Adam an His Chillun; being the tales they tell about the time when the Lord walked the earth like a natural man.* I find Bradford's meaning unclear; most often in black culture, the label seems to refer to someone who refuses to tolerate abuse or insult, one to whom it comes naturally to be a man. But Bradford employs it as a near synonym for primitive or basic. His massively egotistical hero is in any event uninteresting and unsympathetic.

In addition to dehumanizing its hero, Bradford's play suffers from a transformation in setting. No longer a panorama of black life in the south, the scenes are primarily those of bawdy New Orleans streets and bars. People drink gin and snort cocaine to ease their troubles. Only very occasionally do we see them at work rousting cotton or laying tracks, despite John Henry's recital of his experiences. The play has little unity: its moments seem disjointed, its actions purposeless.

Bradford intended its unity to come from music. To provide background unity, he hired Josh White to play blues singer Blind Lemon, who strolled through the play commenting on its events, setting a mood, or offering the audience musical clues to the message. Blind Lemon's most frequent refrain seemed to be an explanation of John Henry's hopeless entanglement with Julie Ann: "You love your woman, but you hate her lowdown ways."

Otherwise, Roark Bradford expected that Jacques Wolfe's score would give the play an aura of southern black culture within which its plot would seem to make sense. In a short piece for *Collier's* just before *John Henry* opened, Bradford described Wolfe's problems in transcribing traditional Negro music. Finally they journeyed to New Orleans where Bradford guided Wolfe through back streets, churches, cotton fields, and river front settings, until at last a group of convicts singing "Ol' Stewball" at Parchman State Penal Farm inspired Wolfe to race for a piano on which to transpose their song. From there his work went smoothly and even Paul Robeson, whose greatest reservation to starring in the play was that its music might not be authentic, was pleased with the score.

Both Wolfe and Bradford assumed from the start that the title role was meant for Robeson. Bradford's *Colliers* piece was entitled, in fact: "Paul Robeson is John Henry and John Henry is Paul Robeson." Equating the men so unequivocally seems to overlook their unique qualities, but Bradford explained he did so because they were both first in their social arenas: Robeson was America's most popular Negro entertainer, and John Henry sprang to life whenever older Negroes gathered "to spin simple, moving tales about him."[8] Robeson had actually returned from a lengthy, self-imposed exile in England just to take the part, which Bradford found only natural—after all, John Henry had always been in the right place at the right time as well.

In retrospect, Robeson's decision to star in a play which seems at worst racist and at best a travesty of the life and lore it purported to celebrate is unfathomable. By the late 1930s he was an outspoken radical, a Spanish Civil War partisan, and a very moral and committed man. He had refused many roles offered by major studios, finally agreeing in 1938 to appear in

Proud Valley, a film produced by a small independent company dramatizing the plight of Welsh miners. Otherwise, in the late 1930s he had restricted himself to such London productions as *Stevedore,* where he played a labor organizer, *Song of Freedom,* in which he was a longshoreman, *Toussaint L'Ouverture,* (in which he starred), and *Plantation in the Sun,* produced by the London trade unionists' own Equity Theatre. He had established himself as a staunch friend of international laborers and was most comfortable portraying working men. Moreover, after earlier appearances in *Showboat, Othello,* and *All God's Chillun,* Robeson was enjoying international fame.[9] Why would he agree to participate in a play which seemed to degrade black workers and proved to be a dismal failure as well?

Robeson thought it an actor's moral duty to evaluate his part and determine whether or not it was demeaning or uplifting. He often spoke in the thirties of his desire to enact black culture in a way that portrayed the true spirit of the Negro people. He was very proud of black culture and especially of its traditional music, which he felt spoke to the soul of his race, reflecting an emotionalism, a relationship between art and life and work which white society lacked. He was also proud of John Henry, citing him in his introduction to *Favorite Songs of the Red Army and Navy* as representative of the music which sprang directly from black people's working lives, and referring to him later when reflecting on the oppression of southern blacks in the 1950s: ". . . we all should and must feel powerful strong, that we should and must feel some of the mountain-moving strength of our legendary John Henry."[10]

By the time Robeson returned home from his ten year exile, he believed himself an internationalist who felt close to oppressed peoples all over the world and also closer than ever to his own country. He had been inspired by the international appeal of traditional black songs, and in an interview with Julia Dorn for *TAC,* likened John Henry to Peer Gynt.[11] He must have found John Henry a man of both national and worldwide appeal, and he must have thought Bradford's portrait authentic. During the 1930s many other progressives were enchanted with "the folk" as not only the truest Americans but as inherently political. In this climate, perhaps Robeson's decision to appear as Bradford's John Henry is not so mysterious after all.

In any case the play, with its nearly all-black cast of fifty, was a miserable flop, lasting only a few performances in Philadelphia and a few more at the 44th Street Theatre on Broadway. The critics were devastating; some simply ignored it. The *New Yorker's* "Goings on about Town" never recommended it; *Theatre Arts* limited publicity to two photographs; many journals never bothered to review it at all. Of those who did, *Time* termed it "an elaborate bore. . . . A rambling, rag-picaresque tale of a black giant toting 800 pound bales of cotton, laying rails with his bare hands, groaning with woman trouble and at last, cracking down while trying to perform a Black River labor of Hercules." *Time's* reviewer further complained that the play lacked dramatic excitement or heroic force, that Robeson's feats seemed like vaude-ville acts, that the music was heartless, that Robeson "could not carry on his back 800 pounds of bad play."[12] Both *Time* and the *New Yorker* labelled John Henry a Negro Paul Bunyan, a label which Richard Dorson argues would taint his image from then on. The *New Yorker* praised Robeson's voice, but lamented both the plot—"a maladjusted series of montage shots"—and the score, which to the reviewer epitomized the dismal state of what "passed for Negro music" at the time: "In Negro music, there comes a point when everything sounds like 'Water Boy.' "[13] In some ways, a more devastating critique of the reviewer's notion of black music (as rendered by Jacques Wolfe) than of Bradford's play, these comments nonetheless fairly reflected the critics' reactions. Like the others, Brooks Atkinson of the *New York Times* complimented Robeson, but thought the play lacking the tremendous vitality of the John Henry tradition.

In addition to Bradford, several other writers have thought the John Henry story worthwhile drama; two composed radio programs for school children which will be discussed under the section on school curricula. The other two dramas were based on Bradford's earlier novel, rather than on his play. In 1933, CBS presented a weekly radio series starring Juan Hernandez who took the part of John Henry and adapted and sang an original score stemming from traditional work and religious songs. I have not heard this series, but Maud Cuney Hare claims that it was well received by critics.[14]

In 1951, Eileen Burrer submitted her Master's thesis "John Henry: A Negro Folk Play Based on the Novel by Roark Bradford" to Ohio University's Department of English. As far as I know, her play went no further, which is regrettable, for it is far more interesting than Bradford's. Although Bradford's novel had inspired Burrer to transform the ballad into a play, she is forth-right about her modifications of Bradford's thrust. She tempers what she considers "pure fancy" with a spirit of realism and tries to clarify the motiva-tions of Julie Ann and John Henry so that they appear more human.[15] All of Burrer's action takes place in the area of a West Virginia railroad con-struction camp. She poses three dramatic conflicts: between John Henry and Sam, Julie Ann and Ruby, and the religious Aunt Dinah and the Witch-ing Woman. John Henry and Sam compete at work and for women, and Sam persuades Julie Ann to desert John Henry for the cheap thrills she enjoys when her man is preoccupied. At these moments, Ruby tries to tempt John Henry. But John Henry is not interested in other women; Julie Ann's rival for his affections is his love for work, which often leaves her at loose ends in the dreary camp. Much of the play's action takes place in a nearby town, where John Henry searches for the missing Julie Ann, and the Witch-ing Woman and Aunt Dinah offer conflicting bits of comfort and advice. Finally, Julie Ann convinces John Henry that they cannot sustain a relation-ship unless they move to the city. But just as they prepare to depart, Sam tempts John Henry with the new steam drill. John Henry cannot resist the race; Julie Ann, betrayed, abandons him but returns in time to inspire him to win and then to beat the steam drill until it explodes after John Henry has died. She is killed by the explosion, leaving Aunt Dinah to comment that the lovers have not really died, but just laid down their burden.

Other than inspiring drama, Bradford's work has been influential in shaping other popular fictional portraits of John Henry. I cannot agree with Richard Dorson's assessment that Bradford reshaped John Henry into a version of Paul Bunyan, which was to overshadow his unique heroic qualities and dominate his popular career. Nonetheless, as we examine the remaining novels about John Henry's life, we will see bits of Bradford's characterization reemerge.

Between 1942 to 1950, three authors wrote books for teenagers based on the John Henry legend. James Cloyd Bowman was a folklorist of sorts who had written of other American heroes and claimed to base his *John Henry: The Rambling Black Ulysses* on authentic records, as well as on songs and stories from "colored folk." Bowman cited as his source seven people he interviewed, who ranged from a South Carolina steel driver to his own golf caddy. He was very impressed with the story's appeal to black people, finding that they made up a taller tale about John Henry for each new and threatening machine invented, and when tired or discontented about white people's social and educational advantages, John Henry's "diploma written on his calloused hands" inspired and calmed them. Bowman's story is difficult for me to place in black culture; it seems more a moral tale designed to pacify blacks. It offers an excellent illustration of the ambiguity of the legend. Bowman's twists transform John Henry into a hero who celebrates the antebellum preindustrial south.

Bowman devotes much attention to John Henry's birth, which is a magico-spiritual Moses-like event. John Henry's mother desires a "boy-chile" because she already has seven daughters and her master is complaining. She conjures up a baby from a Sambo doll, which she perfects with ingredients from John the Conquer, Brer Rabbit, a mockingbird, and iron filings from an old drill. Setting the doll afloat in a boat on the bayou, she returns the next morning to find a forty-pound bragging and ravenous baby, reminiscent of Bradford's infant and something of a family calamity until his father returns and tricks him out of his big appetite.

John Henry quickly becomes his master's son's favorite companion slave. When they grow up, Master Jimmy and John Henry fall in love, respectively, with Miss Margery Jane and her maid Polly Ann who live on a neighboring plantation. They fight side by side in the Civil War, when Master Jimmy is killed dashing suicidally into battle. John Henry risks his life to ensure proper burial, then journeys home to find his beloved plantation in ruins. John Henry's master frees him in gratitude for his faithful service, after which he sets off to find Polly Ann, also freed; a search which occupies most of the book and accounts for, I believe, Bowman's likening John

Henry to Ulysses in his subtitle. John Henry's search is problematic because the very provincial blacks he asks for directions to Alabama have no idea how to help him. The book becomes a formulaic series of encounters in which John Henry comes upon disgruntled crowds of ex-slaves—beset by carpetbaggers and agitators urging them not to work for southern whites anymore—and southern white employers from coal mines, cornfields, tobacco and cotton plantations, and steamboats—begging them to come earn an honest living. In each case, John Henry persuades his people of the joys of honest work and teaches them how laughter and song can make work less tedious. He is anxious to show the whites how well freedmen can work, but never stays long because his search for Polly Ann must continue. After his departure, the workers are dismayed. But a new leader soon emerges and sings of John Henry to inspire the others. Thus, the ballad and John Henry's fame are born.

John Henry's travels climax at Big Bend Tunnel, where he meets "Breezy Manners," a fast talking steam-drill salesman who proclaims the New Age, where steam, machinery and the head will replace hand labor. As in Bradford's play, John Henry symbolizes brute strength. Ever the champion of the Old South, he races the steam drill and wins only because it is still new and very primitive. In the middle of the two-day race, he marries Polly Ann, who has appeared at Big Bend. No one knows for sure whether or not John Henry dies, but Bowman seems to favor the second of his endings, in which Polly Ann nurses him back to health and they return to a cabin on a small farm to raise their own food and pickaninnies. Thus they accept the wise and ancient commentator's warning that progress is inevitable and that a better machine will eventually replace the hammer man, choosing an honest life on the soil for themselves.

Irwin Shapiro's book *John Henry and the Double-Jointed Steam Drill* is most intriguing for its title (which borrows from blacks' labeling John Henry double-jointed to account for his strength) and for its frontispiece, which as Archie Green notes is a tribute to the spirit of national unity pervading America during World War II. This illustration joins a defense worker, Joe Louis, George Washington Carver, Paul Robeson, Marian Anderson, Booker T. Washington, Richard Wright and John Henry in a pantheon of patriotic heroes. Unfortunately, Shapiro's text does not do justice to this initial celebration of black culture, remaining very close to Bradford's work in its presentation of black dialect and in many of its episodes. We first meet John Henry, dressed as a country bumpkin, during Mardi Gras. In New Orleans, he encounters his adversary John Hardy, whom he bests rousting cotton, and his future wife Polly Ann, whose heart he wins at this first of many contests. The book's unity comes from the recurring encounters where John Henry meets and defeats Hardy at laying track and when Hardy operates the steam drill at Big Bend. (Placing the machine in the hands of another black man—a personal rival—is reminiscent

of both Bradford's and Burrer's presentations and a peculiar twisting of
the ballad, which almost always portrays that person as a white man and a
Yankee at that.) Throughout the book, Polly Ann encourages John Henry,
waits for him to summon her to each new job site, and cooks him wonderful
snacks of hog jowls, chittlin's, cracklin's, corn pone, side meat and greens
to fortify him for his various matches. After his final contest with the steam
drill, everyone believes John Henry to be dead. Too big for a coffin, he is
laid out in a box car and left alone with Polly Ann who nurses or feeds him
back to health.

Ashamed of his weakness, John Henry and Polly Ann plan to keep his
resurrection a secret. Finding no jobs left because the steam drills have
taken them and because no one seems to recognize him, John Henry and
Polly Ann ramble about until John Hardy discovers them and turns their
lives around for the better. Arguing that the steam drill has a unique and
worthwhile beat all its own, Hardy persuades John Henry to return to Big
Bend. There he practices secretly with the steam drill and one day emerges
from obscurity to blast through the last part of the tunnel and defeat the
steam drill once again by driving it until "Every nut, bolt and screw flew
off the steam drill. While the folks laughed and cheered, it buckled up and
fell down—because John Henry had run the steam drill right into the
ground."[16] Thus the hero achieves his final revenge, and Shapiro's book
ends on this perversely comic note. Shapiro's book was reissued in 1962
as part of an anthology, *Heroes of American Folklore,* in which John Henry
is joined by Old Stormalong, Casey Jones, Steamboat Bill and Joe Magarac.

In 1950 Harold Felton, a lawyer by profession and folklorist on the side
who has chronicled other heroes such as Pecos Bill, Paul Bunyan, Jim Beck-
wourth and James Weldon Johnson, published his creative, entertaining
and beautifully illustrated *John Henry and His Hammer.* Like Bowman,
Felton gives his readers vivid background on his personal interest in the
subject. He finds the ballad intriguing, with its detailed portrait of the
beginning and end of John Henry's life, and its elliptical middle which
leaves most of the life subject to conjecture. But Felton is even more powerfully drawn by the subject of railroading and its meaning to men of John
Henry's day. Because railroading transformed stubborn raw materials and
natural barriers into the industrial-age qualities of speed and strength, Felton
finds it an inevitably heroic enterprise—and those men who built the railroads heroic men. Therefore, although Felton researched his story through
the studies of Johnson and Chappell, his enthusiastic vision of railroading
much more profoundly shapes his message.

Like Bradford, Felton links John Henry's birth to miracles of nature,
but in his story the miracles are omens which reappear as tragic motifs
throughout the novel. The night John Henry is born is as black as the inside
of a coal mine, the moon red as hero's blood, the stars white as an angel's
wing, the wind and river possessed of unreal powers. The great, beautiful

baby is born with a hammer in his hand, appropriately interpreted by those who witness the birth as a meaningful sign.

Indeed, Felton's John Henry is driven all his life by a need and desire to hammer which he can barely articulate. Even as a child on his parents' farm (Felton avoids the issue of slavery), John Henry never feels quite right without a hammer in his hand: "Time was," John Henry went on, "when I was a young 'un, I wanted to touch a star. I wanted to reach up an' see what's behind a star. But not for long. It was only an idea. It came an' it went, an' always when I stopped thinkin' and dreamin' about stars, I thought 'bout my hamma, a' I picked up my hamma an' went back to drivin' hard, black oak sticks into the groun', and then I was happy and content."[17]

The story details his various jobs as rouster, steamboat fireman, and locomotive fireman for Casey Jones. He works with hoes, saws, and mules, but nothing "fits" except working with his hammer. John Henry's journeys take him closer and closer to his destiny: from the "life-giving river" he discovers railroading and with Casey Jones' sponsorship secures a prestigious track-laying job which eventually lands him a well-paying, dangerous but exciting position at Big Bend. There his prowess as a steel driver and his heroism on behalf of other men bring him fame: like Atlas, he supports a caved-in roof with his bare hands; on another occasion, he hurls his hammer at an explosive to douse the fuse before it blows up a group of entrapped workers. He dies from a busted head after persuading his Captain to let him test the steam drill, which did not fare well either. Its gears gave way, hose crumbled, valves blew out, gauges dropped, and its boiler split wide open.

Although the Captain offers to call a doctor, John Henry dissuades him with his last words: "I done all I's supposed to do. I started this here Big Bend Tunnel and I finished it. I had me a contest with the steam drill. An' I drove more steel than the steam drill. An' now I's done."[18]

Despite the awkward dialect, Felton is a lyrical and imaginative writer, unabashedly patriotic in his evocation of the southern landscape and his celebration of the nation-building enterprises of steamboating and railroading. Yet his descriptions of the hazards and horrors of tunnel life are poignant and realistic.

His John Henry is unusual. He has no woman. His family is not very important. He performs many heroic feats, such as rousting hundreds of pounds of cotton and rice, two snarling river cats, and his own shadow all at once; pushing the Diamond Joe freight steamer off a sandbar; and firing Casey Jones' engine so expertly that he meets an impossible deadline. But unlike the hero created by Shapiro and Bradford, he never brags. Felton recruits a sidekick/trickster, Li'l Bill, for that purpose. John Henry does not complain when laid off work, humbles himself before his white employers, and does not consider his heroic deeds acts of protest. Some may agree with Archie Green's assessment that Felton has reduced John Henry to non-heroic proportions: he may be too bland, too gentle, too friendly for some tastes.[19] I cannot help but believe, however, that Felton's hero is appealing for his modesty, his courage, his enthusiasm for railroading, the joy he takes in his work, and his stoicism in living out his fate.

After Felton's book, popular fiction neglected John Henry until the mid-1960s when a sudden spurt of four young children's books between 1965-1971 reflected America's changing race relations and a greater tolerance for black consciousness. The first, in 1965, was Ezra Keats' *John Henry: An American Legend*. Filled with giant-sized, colorful illustrations, this book is quite similar to Felton's in its emphasis on John Henry's miraculous birth, his hammering destiny which he embraces even as a child, his heroic feats and the way he joins his life course to industrial progress until, ultimately, he discovers railroading and Big Bend Tunnel. Again he has no woman. Again Li'l Bill is his loyal companion until the final moment when John Henry breaks through the tunnel, defeats the steam drill, and dies with his hammer in his hand. Keats' work is most notable for its excellent, realistic emphasis on the horrors of Big Bend Tunnel, and its beautiful illustrations. More appropriate to a later decade but just as appealing as Felton's story, it is by far the best available for younger readers.

Adele DeLeeuw is a prolific writer of children's books, which her jacket covers note she was inspired to write because of her love for storytelling. Like Felton, she has written of many American heroes, often in a light-hearted vein exemplified by her *Casey Jones Drives an Ice Cream Truck*. She wrote *John Henry: Steel-Drivin' Man* for Garrard's Tall Tale series, "happy rollicking stories based upon America's great treasury of folklore."[20] Her John Henry harks back to Bradford's—he is loud and obnoxious at birth, big as a boxcar at eighteen, ravenous and musical throughout his life. Upon leaving home, he rips open a tree for its honey and performs several other heroic feats—loading cotton and laying tracks—before arriving at Big Bend where he dies. DeLeeuw's illustrations are surprising for the mid-1960s: John Henry's huge feet, loud clothes, and extraordinary lips are reminiscent of old stereotypes. Her book is very cheerful; her John Henry truly a rollicking black Paul Bunyan.

R. Conrad Stein's *Steel Driving Man: The Legend of John Henry* is unorthodox except in his emphasis on the place of music in John Henry's life, a quality upon which all authors agree. Otherwise, Stein's John Henry is a home-owning family man laying track in Georgia. The captain of a work gang, he challenges the steam drill out of loyalty to his crew. The confrontation opens on a note of racial consciousness, as a nervous little white man drives the tireless, heartless machine against John Henry who is big, black and proud. But as the race proceeds, victory seems to become more of an affair of the ego to John Henry, who stops to cry that no man or machine ever made by God can drive steel like he can. Although he wins and dies as does the traditional hero, the reader is left unconvinced of his purpose and suspecting that his motives were rather shallow. Otherwise,

Stein's illustrations are large and lovely, and the book a gripping personal account.

Wyatt Blassingame's *John Henry and Paul Bunyan Play Baseball*, written in 1971, is the most recent of the children's books, and it explicitly likens John Henry to Paul Bunyan. This is a cheerful, friendly tale of a meeting between two heroes. Coming from the North, Paul Bunyan loves to play baseball. But because he uses an oak limb for a bat, with which he continually slams balls over the mountains, he has trouble finding people willing to play with him. John Henry, laying track in the South (with a fifty-pound hammer in each hand), takes time off to join Bunyan for a legendary game halfway between the North and the South. Using cotton bales for balls and a pine tree for a bat, they play a friendly game. The match ends in a tie when, after two strikes, both bat and ball burn up. Blassingame's book is similar to other works of this era in its presentation of a very well-groomed John Henry. It is the only work of fiction to ignore the John Henry of folk tradition in constructing a twentieth century adventure for him.

To say John Oliver Killens' *A Man Ain't Nothin' but a Man* is the best of the popular fiction is perhaps only to admit that Killens' book best suits contemporary tastes. A sensitive novel for teenagers, it was published in 1975. Like several other authors, Killens links John Henry's birth to miracles of nature, grounded in this case on Chittling Switch, an Alabama slave plantation: the chickens stopped cacklin', the dogs stopped barking, and the cotton pickers stopped pickin' cotton. Killens warns us that his hero will live out a tragic tension between his daddy and his mama. The novel opens by quoting two stanzas of the ballad: one where John Henry's father urges him to "be a steel drivin' man like me," the other where, from his mother's knee, John Henry predicts: "Hammer be the Death of Me."[21] John Henry's childhood is marked by this tension. He enjoys hearing his daddy's tales of railroad work, when his father says, he felt like a man, "Like the Power and the Glory was flowing all thru me like the Mississippi River."[22] However, his mother had encouraged his father to settle down and hopes that John Henry also will choose a settled life. He knows that she is right, but his daddy's dreams set his soul on fire. Finally he leaves home, motivated to do so by the realization that after years of hard work nothing belongs to him. "I'm sick and tired of picking the white man's cotton," he declares. His mother, heartbroken, tries to warn him to be wary of the various captains he will encounter, but he replies with the claim by which we will learn to identify him: "All I ask anyplace is to be treated like a man. Cause a man ain't nothin' but a man. Don't care if he be a great big cap'n or a little ol' water boy."[23]

Intimidating the plantation overseer who tries to prevent him from leaving (in a confrontation testifying to Killens' belief that sharecropping is much like slavery), John Henry makes his way to Mobile where his prowess lands him a job rousting cotton; but he refuses to displace another worker who turns out to be a lifelong family friend. "Mr. Buddy" will be Killens' version of Felton's trickster/sidekick for John Henry; throughout the book he boasts of John Henry's strength and attracts many bullies and competitors who hope to outdo the hero.

John Henry and Mr. Buddy lead an adventurous life in Mobile, and John Henry is popular with many women with whom he "makes awkward, loveless love."[24] But he is anxious for his true love Polly Ann to join him. She hesitates, fearful that they will replay his mother's and father's relationship. She feels that he is not ready to settle down, and links his restlessness to history: "You just too busy enjoying the freedom we just won. Ain't none of us got used to it yet."[25] Finally, John Henry returns to Chittling Switch and insists that she marry him, but much of their story will involve the tension she foresaw between his love for her and his inability to settle down.

Killens describes their marriage tenderly and frankly; sometimes his descriptions seem so sentimental as to be trite, but they are probably appropriate for his teenage audience. Their home is filled with love, but John Henry cannot resist leaving to work on the railroad. For Polly Ann, the last straw is his decision to travel to Big Bend. Although he tries to convince her that his motives are to earn and save enough money to buy their own land, she knows very well that he is truly enthusiastic about working in the tunnel and warns him that this is the last time he will ever leave her.

Nonetheless, John Henry leaves, accompanied by Mr. Buddy and two more friends they have collected—one white and the other Chinese-American. In spite of a white foreman who is as demanding and rude as the others he has encountered, John Henry finds Big Bend the challenge he'd sought all his life. His prowess is awesome, and he frequently races other workers in contests encouraged by the Captain for free overtime. At one point racist remarks from the sideline inspire him to beat Robin O'Flannagan because "he felt like he carried all the dark-skinned races of the world on his broad shoulders."[26]

Just after Polly Ann arrives, pregnant and therefore resigned to try once more, terrible trouble comes to Big Bend. With the coming of winter, the men grow more and more fearful of a machine they hear will displace them. The Captain tries to persuade the workers to labor fourteen and a half hours a day rather than twelve, and stirs up trouble between John Henry and his friends when John Henry refuses to cooperate in convincing the men to agree. Determined to bring John Henry down for his resistance, the Captain imports the steam drill to humiliate him. He argues that if the men had agreed to work longer hours, they would not face obsolescence.

Although Polly Ann pleads with him not to go, John Henry insists for he believes that if man does not control the machine, it will roll right over him. He beats the steam drill by ten inches, but tells his unborn baby: "Man can't outdo no machine . . . machine gon' be here and man gon' be here.

Machine gon' multiply like man gon' multiply . . . the only thin' left for man to do is learn and plan how to live with the machine.'' Resigned to the industrial revolution but stressing its social costs and human responsibilities, John Henry dies. Polly Ann lifts his hammer, feels his strength, and realizes, ''John Henry lives.''[27] Like John Henry's mother, she turns her thoughts to her unborn child as an embodiment of her own future. She knows that she must be strong for its sake.

Killens' interpretation of the legend is compelling. He treats the story as a family saga, as do many versions of the ballad. Generational destinies frame the book. Like all other writers, he creates for John Henry a life that is heroic on the novelist's terms. Killens' John Henry is clearly a black hero and a laboring hero. He does not represent dumb brute strength, but rather links his contest with the machine drill to human dignity. Although he wins, he recognizes the wisdom of coming to terms with the machine and controlling it so that it does not overpower humanity. Uncannily, Killens' approach is similar to Bowman's: both show how an elliptical legendary moment can be shaped and transformed so that the hero speaks to a particular vision of human life. Their visions, of course, are completely different.

All these writers have drawn on oral tradition, especially ballad texts, and occasionally the work of Johnson and Chappell. Bradford and Bowman claim to have used folktales as well. Most faced the creative dilemma which Felton makes explicit: the ballad is sparse, it frames a life and treats one moment within it, but it does not detail that life for us. Writers of fiction must thus create a life, a vision for John Henry. That the ballad is elliptical gives them great license in creating the sort of biography appropriate to the times in which they wrote and to their own purposes in reshaping folk lore for popular—usually juvenile—audiences. Their purposes range from drawing on a traditional hero's life to inspire nationalist sentiments to awakening black pride and protest. John Henry can be gentle and friendly, as in Felton's work, or boastful and pugnacious as in Bradford's. Sometimes a man of simple dignity, at other times he seems a parody of himself. Some writers, such as Killens, stress his place in a family; others, the situation he shared with all Reconstruction Era blacks; still others, the details of his work life. His motives for challenging the steam drill range from nostalgia through personal loyalty to real protest against technological displacement. Every book, appropriately, stresses the role of music in his life. Otherwise, the variety of the popular literature is reminiscent of the energetic folk-song tradition.

TALL TALE ANTHOLOGIES

That several tall tale anthologies present the John Henry story is interesting in itself, for collections in other genre, such as books about heroes, do not. He appears, to the best of my knowledge, in only two such volumes: the collected children's stories of Irwin Shapiro, *Heroes in American Folklore,* and Tristram Coffin and Hennig Cohen's *The Parade of Heroes,* issued in 1978. In the latter volume, John Henry is represented only by a few hammer songs and a ballad which has been transformed to eulogize Moe Stanley. Otherwise, authors and editors have found him a more appropriate subject for fantastic tales, where his most frequent companions are Paul Bunyan, Pecos Bill, Old Stormalong, Casey Jones and the like.

John Henry has appeared in ten such collections between 1930 and 1966. Frank Shay was the first to present him in a tall tale in his 1930 book *Here's Audacity!* Shay had earlier published a collection of sea shanties and was no stranger to the field of folklore. In the same year that he issued *Here's Audacity!,* he contributed "The Tall Tale in America" to Benjamin Botkin's annual volume *Folk-Say.* In considering the American tall tale, Shay characterized American heroes as "audacious industrialists," ourselves as we wish we could be.[28] He felt that each of our heroes was but a regional version of Paul Bunyan and that traveling laborers and especially modern communications systems would eventually dissipate each one's local individuality. The folklorist's task, therefore, even when writing for a popular medium, is to capture that local lore before it is too late.

Shay's tall tale is true to this sense of his mission. He recruits an elderly East Virginia man, who worked as John Henry's shaker and knew him "lak ah knowed mah ol' pappy," to describe the hero.[29] Strumming a banjo and interspersing his story with verses from the John Henry ballad, the shaker tells Shay's readers how he and John Henry grew up in slavery together. John Henry's pappy used to sing to him that he would be a steel-drivin' man. After the Civil War, both John Henry and the narrator worked as itinerants, "toting stones on road wuk."[30] Eventually they landed at Cruzee Mountain, where John Henry distinguished himself by his dexterity with a twelve-pound hammer. He wielded it so vigorously that he wore down two handles during each shift and had to have buckets of water splashed on his hammer to cool it. Shay's hero dies a traditional death, with his Captain ironically winning a free steam drill as a result of the hero's victory.

Carl Carmer's story, *The Hurricane's Children,* printed in 1937 and slightly modified for reissue in 1942, is less true to local lore. His John Henry is a hero from Georgia and the "biggest and blackest black man that ever lived."[31] A sometime roustabout, he sits on the safety valve of the steamer "City of Natchez" in an effort to send her pressure soaring high enough to break the steamboat's speed record. Exploding, the boiler sends John Henry sailing ten miles into the air to land on a wagonload of cotton bound for Savannah, where he lands a job on the Central of Georgia Railroad. From here on, Carmer's story is more traditional; like Shay, he dramatizes John Henry's extraordinary prowess by claiming that the steel driver breaks or burns up the hammers he uses. Carmer poignantly describes John Henry's family: his wife fortifies him for the final match with corn pone and collard greens, and his son watches with pride from the sidelines. In the end, while sitting in his father's palm, the little boy hears John Henry's last words: "Son, you're goin' to be a steel drivin' man."[32] Carmer's second version of the tale is very similar except that he deletes the more fanciful steamboating episode.

In 1934, Olive Miller included "John Henry's Contest with the Steam Drill" in her collection, *Heroes, Outlaws, and Funny Fellows of American Popular Tales.* In no way a stereotypical tall tale, Miller's piece is extraordinary. She joins John Henry's life story to the drama of railroading and enriches her description of his job by focusing on the life of the shanty-town housing workers at Big Bend. Like other men there, John Henry brings his wife and children to live with him; through song, he makes his parents' presence felt as well. When the men hear of the steam drill, their first response is to worry for their families:

> "Sorrowfully, they watched their boys and girls at play in the street of Shanty Town. What would happen to these merry children if the steam engine took the places of their fathers in the tunnel? The steam drill at that moment seemed to these steelmen like a cruel and heartless giant, taking away their jobs."[33]

Thus, John Henry's heroic act is linked to a Depression Era family saga. The tragic conflict is one which must face any man who martyrs himself for principle: though John Henry thinks he is acting on behalf of laborers concerned for their families, his own family does not want him to die. His son pleads with him not to let the hammer kill him; his mother travels to Shanty Town from Tennessee to try to persuade her son to think of his own family first. Nonetheless, John Henry martyrs himself. After he dies, he is buried near the White House and commemorated by the workers of Shanty Town through a song they compose in his honor. The appeal of Miller's story rests on her refusal to portray John Henry as simply a southern offshoot of Paul Bunyan. She insists that he is an individual human hero who acts in a context of conflicting human sentiments and motivations. His feat is heroic but not impossible; and most importantly, we are left wondering how we would feel if this abstract deed were personalized—if John Henry were our husband, or father, or son.

Anne Malcolmson's post-Depression piece of 1941, *Yankee Doodle's Cousins,* was inspired by her desire to tap the nationalist sentiments accompanying World War II, and to encourage children to feel affectionate pride toward their country through exploring its folklore. Her collection includes a pantheon of American heroes such as Mike Fink, Daniel Boone, Johnny Appleseed and Paul Bunyan. Her John Henry's life is very much a railroad life: he secures a job at Big Bend through his heroism in unfurling coils of track and then securing them by "spitting spikes through his teeth and smashing them into place."[34] He thus miraculously lays the track just in time to save the 5:15 express that is roaring past flags signalling it to stop, and threatening to fly off the end of the freshly laid track it has been travelling on. At Big Bend, John Henry's fame rests on the familiar motif: "He worked so fast that his helper, Li'l Bill, had to have a bucket of ice water on hand to keep the handles of his sledges from catching fire."[35] His Captain seems to be of the old school, and somewhat reminiscent of the foreman portrayed in Leon Harris' folktale: he persuades John Henry to race the steam drill in exchange for a promise to love him like a father, to buy him a new suit of clothes, and to pay him fifty dollars. Like Carmer, Malcolmson places John Henry's son in the palm of his hand to hear his father's last words: "Son, yo're gonna be a steel-drivin' man. But the Big Bend Tunnel is the end o' me."[36]

Walter Blair singles out John Henry from others in the cast of his *Tall Tale America* (1944) as the American hero who finally was forced to challenge the machine. Like Roark Bradford's hero, Blair's John Henry is a ravenous and boastful man (termed "uppity" by whites) and a legendary cotton and corn picker, roustabout and deckman. But Blair adds several imaginative twists to his drama, including John Henry's fascination with the number nine, and a coal black preacher (a motif borrowed from Harold Felton, perhaps) to preside over the hero's birth and death. The tale's special strength is in its vivid portrait of what John Henry's life at Big Bend might have been like; this description rescues John Henry from the Paul Bunyan-like oblivion to which Blair's story might otherwise consign him.

Alice Schneider's 1946 version in *Tales of Many Lands* is a repetition of the Mardi Gras episode recounted in Irwin Shapiro's book, while the stories of Franklin Folsom [Michael Gorham] in 1952 and Maria Leach in 1958 straightforwardly elaborate the ballad's typical narrative, describing John Henry's work and his contest elegantly and attributing to him a tragic purpose and a foresight of the significance of his heroic act. Folsom is especially interested in John Henry's lifelong fascination with hammering and in his intimate relationship with his shaker Little Bill. The real surprise in the 1950s is the tale of Irwin Shapiro, appearing in his collection *Tall Tales of America* along with Paul Bunyan, Old Stormalong, Johnny Appleseed, Davy Crockett, Pecos Bill and Joe Magarac. In this third rendition of the John Henry legend, Shapiro offers an altogether different sort of hero, and one who is much more appealing than his earlier character.

Shapiro's John Henry had predicted his fate as a little baby, declaring that he was a natural man and would die with his hammer in his hand. His mama spent many years trying to prevent him from hammering and had successfully encouraged him in a musical career, but he outgrew all available instruments and insisted on picking cotton. From cotton picking, he turns to rousting, to laying track, to driving steel in Big Bend. His race with the steam drill is an egotistical matter of proving that he is indeed a natural man, and he is deaf to the pleas of his mother and his wife Polly Ann that he forego the race. As he dies, he lifts his little son in the palm of his hand,

and we see that his son will be like his father, as the little boy reaches for the sky. "You got a power of strength in you," John Henry said.[37] Unlike Shapiro's earlier character, this John Henry is rooted in a family and community of people who care about him. Although Shapiro avoids the larger issues, preferring to weave a drama about an individual living out his fate on his own, his John Henry strikes the reader as a man of quiet integrity who simply does what he has to do.

Adrien Stoutenberg is the last author to include John Henry in an anthology of fantastic tales, where he is juxtaposed to High John the Conqueror. In *American Tall Tales* she portrays a very realistic John Henry, who purposefully takes on the steam drill to prove that "A man ain't nothin but a man." Much of her tale concerns the hero's premonitions of his own death, and she offers great detail on the contest.

On the whole, these writers of so-called tall tales have tended to portray John Henry as quite human. They rarely follow the lead of Roark Bradford in constructing a boastful larger-than-life man performing unbelievable heroic deeds. Although several epic feats recur—his spitting out spikes to lay track, or burning up hammers when driving steel—these tales are invariably riveted around the climax of the contest with the steam drill. Their John Henry appears in many contexts, with some stressing his life as a railroader, others his membership in a community, still others his place within a family. These writers seem to prefer the clues of the ballad to the grotesque portrait of Roark Bradford. Given the wide diffusion of Bradford's novel, one can only wonder that his influence was not more profound. Although influential in launching John Henry's career in popular culture, Bradford did not shape his image there.

PROGRAMS DESIGNED FOR SCHOOL CHILDREN

In 1940, Florida's Statewide Recreation Project suggested a series of recreational programs based on black American music entitled *The Negro Sings.* This thoughtful and creative collection includes "The Saga of John Henry, Working Man," with a sampling of ballads and hammer songs from *Negro Workaday Songs* arranged for children to perform in groups and (for storytelling hour) the North Carolina folktale collected by Odum and Johnson.

In 1951, *Junior Scholastic* presented a feature article on John Henry for its audience of school children. The presentation was unfortunate, a composite of mythical deeds which leaves John Henry without personality or purpose. *Junior Scholastic* portrayed John Henry as a wanderer who picked 4,500 pounds of cotton in one day in Alabama, stripped a whole field of tobacco in just one hour in North Carolina, and fired a steamboat with a half a ton of coal in less than three hours in Mississippi. In many cities he worked as a roustabout, digging ditches, mining coal, building houses, or paving roads. Inspiring him to work as hard as he did were thoughts of

Polly Ann, who had promised to marry him as soon as he found a job to satisfy him well enough so that he could settle down. His job at Big Bend seems to be the right one for him. Polly Ann joins him there to get married. However, Captain Tommy asks his star steel driver for a favor that changes their lives. He has been challenged by a stranger to the contest. The Captain will receive two free steam drills if John Henry wins the match. If he loses, the Captain will have to buy one. (Either way, it appears, the steel drivers would lose.) The newly married John Henry wins and then dies. This portrait reached many school children who read of a John Henry whose most distinguishing attribute is his power, whose toil reads like a lark, and whose life is sacrificed so that his employer might win a bet.

The other general curriculum resource is *Tall Tales and Tunes,* prepared by New York State's Department of Education for secondary school curricula. This resource booklet is now dated, having been released in 1959, but it is still a useful model for introducing heroes to the classroom. John Henry is only one of many legendary heroes included, with suggested themes and activities, records, texts, written assignments and discussion topics. The approach seems both provocative and fair, as teachers are encouraged to help their students explore the meaning of heroic acts.

Two authors have proposed a series of radio programs based on American folk heroes, and both feature John Henry. Eloise Johnson's *Stout Hearts a-Singin' with Freedom"* was submitted as a Master's thesis to Ohio State University in 1947. It consisted of eight programs, all but John Henry provided with original music. (She felt that Guy Johnson had collected such excellent ballad texts that it would be foolish of her to write her own "John Henry" song.) The programs project the heroes' tales, and she adds an analysis of the reaction of young listeners. Her John Henry is boastful but good natured. Emphasizing his work at Big Bend, she tries to make him visually alive. I think listeners would enjoy joining their imaginations to such phrases as "a hammer that rings like silver and shines like gold," or "Faster and faster he swung until his hammer of gold looked like a rainbow swinging round his shoulder."[38] Johnson also stresses his relationship with Polly Ann, who cooks him large sumptuous meals. For example, when John Henry first hears of the steam drill, he loses his appetite: "Polly Ann thought maybe he was just tired of ham and cabbage, corn pone and molasses every day, so she hurried up and fixed some cowpeas and a piece of fresh side, cooked some turnip greens, made fresh corn bread and pot likker."[39] Johnson attributes a purpose to John Henry: he faces the steam drill because he is fearful for his job and the life in what she calls "the pretty little cabin" he shares with Polly Ann.[40] Although she omits the grislier features of life at Big Bend, she does treat John Henry as a hero with a sense of his own destiny. The greatest flaw in Johnson's program is her total reliance on just two parts, John Henry's and the narrator's, with the narrator bearing the largest dramatic burden.

Nellie McCaslin's radio play "John Henry" is also designed for school children and is one of a group of twelve plays in her book *Tall Tales and Tall Men* (1956). All the plays treat America's legendary heroes, ranging from St. Nicholas to Paul Bunyan. Unlike Johnson's program, McCaslin's play has more than twelve parts, including two story tellers, John Henry's family, his shaker, five workmen, the steam drill salesman and many townsfolk. Beginning with John Henry's birth and legendary first meal, the storytellers then summarize for their listeners the era in which John Henry lived. "It was right after the Civil War and a good time for a strong man to be living. Everywhere they were chopping down trees, blasting out tunnels, digging ditches and raising up farms, making places for people to live. John Henry, he did his share. . . . "[41] This is a very cheerful portrait of the Reconstruction South, and sets the tone for the play. John Henry receives a job at Big Bend as a reward for rapidly laying track in time to save the 5:15 express. The climax comes with the detailed contest, accompanied by vivid sound effects and the death of John Henry, as the whole cast gathers to sing his ballad. The play seems to be exceptionally well dramatized and should be a real treat for children to participate in.

Several texts include the John Henry ballad arranged for school children. These are *America Reads: Good Times Through Literature,* edited by Pooley, et al.; Wagenheim's *This is America; Proudly We Sing,* edited by Wolfe, et al. (in their *Together We Sing Series, Grade 8*); Mursell's *Music for Living, Grade 5* in his *Music Around the World* series; and the *American Songs for American Children,* compiled by the Music Educators' National Conference. In 1974, the *American Red Cross Youth News* offered the John Henry ballad in a special folklore edition.

Finally, two school readers present John Henry to children. Lee and Robertson's 1963 *Lore of Our Land* unfortunately offers a reprint of the *Junior Scholastic* feature article as part of a general reader on American folklore. *Open Highways* (1966) cites Odum and Johnson as source for its piece "The Legend of John Henry" for fifth graders. This piece includes two ballads and almost wholly concerns the contest, deleting details about life in Big Bend.

Introducing John Henry into the classroom is obviously problematic unless teachers want to involve children in a serious discussion of the meaning of his heroic act in the context of the era in which he lived. It is unfortunate that the materials available for interested teachers are so sparse and, in most cases, seriously flawed by a superficial treatment which robs John Henry of integrity or purpose.

ARTISTS' TRIBUTES

As early as 1927, Guy Johnson suggested that John Henry deserved the attention of fine artists who should paint or sculpt him and commemorate him in poetry or music. I conclude this chapter with a discussion of the tributes of those artists who have done so.

Only two poems commemorate John Henry: Margaret Walker's "Big John Henry" of 1942 in *For My People,* and Sterling Brown's "Strange Legacies" published in his *Collected Poems* of 1980. Walker's poem is in tall tale style, written as though the narrator were enthusiastically reciting for us John Henry's feats. Roark Bradford's influence is evident in Walker's re-creation of John Henry's birth in Mississippi and his epic first meal of buttermilk and sorghum. The poem enumerates, without apologies, a folk hero's legendary acts. John Henry skins mules, catches barracuda, boxes, rides the thunder, and befriends hogs. Walker's hero has no family life, no railroading career, and dies without elaboration when a ten-pound hammer "Bust him open, wide Lawd."[42]

Sterling Brown's piece is quite different, with a quiet, poignant dignity testifying to a more contemporary mood. "Strange Legacies" offers us heroes who might inspire black Americans. Brown suggests three: Jack Johnson, "You used to stand there like a man, taking punishment"; John Henry, "You taught us that a man could go down like a man"; and an elderly farming couple suffering terribly while trying to eke out a living, but "muttering," beneath an unfriendly sky, "guess we'll give it one mo' try."[43] These legacies are strange because all of the heroes are defeated. What they seem to offer, however, is dignity in defeat, spirits which will not suffer that defeat and therefore, the extraordinary possibility that against impossible odds the heroes are victorious after all:

> You had what we need now, John Henry,
> Help us get it.[44]

Brown's portrait of John Henry in this context is especially wrenching, for he suggests a novel heroic image. The particulars of John Henry's life do not matter; more significant and inspiring are his courage and determination as he goes down. Nonetheless, it is strange and sad that blacks must look to such a tragic hero for encouragement. As we have seen many times, in these two poems—both by popular black writers—the vitality and variety of John Henry's heroic tradition reemerge.

Visual artists depicting John Henry include Charles O. Cooper who sculpted the hero's statue at the mouth of Big Bend Tunnel. The statue was commissioned by the Talcott-Hilldale Ruritan Club in 1972, and can be seen in photographs accompanying newspaper articles reporting its arrival. These include pieces in the *Hinton Daily News,* the *Charleston Gazette* (by George Steele), the *Morgantown Sunday Dominion Post,* and the magazine *Wonderful West Virginia* (by O. D. Tony Hylton). Jeffrey Miller also reproduces a photograph of the statue in his piece in *The Laborer.* The other sculptor portraying John Henry is Holland Foster, whose figure is described in his

University of Iowa Master's thesis of 1959. Artist Fred Becker's wood engravings are reproduced in the 1979 article by Archie Green; Green's 1978 piece cites twelve oil paintings of John Henry completed by Palmer Hayden between 1944-1954, a color lithograph of him included in William Gropper's 1953 portfolio "American Folklore," and a number of works by lesser known commercial and folk artists.

Other than the playwrights cited earlier in this chapter, two artists have celebrated John Henry in the performing arts. Robert Eley's "Ballad Set in Five Movements for Full Orchestra" was submitted as a Master's thesis to Ohio State University in 1954. In June of 1980, the Mary Anthony Dance Studio performed its "John Henry," choreographed by Daniel Maloney, at New York's Riverside Church. Although the company has no immediate plans to present the piece again, a videotape of the original is available at the main branch of New York City's Public Library.

Maloney's score was inspired by the work of Cannonball Adderly, whose unfinished piece, "Big Man," was issued after his death. Maloney refined the piece as backdrop to the dance. He purposefully avoided portraying a stereotypical black man unable to cope with the industrial revolution. His John Henry is only coincidentally black, but above all a very sensitive person concerned about such universal problems as the nature of love, unemployment and technological displacement, and the coexistence of humanity with the machine.

Central characters in the dance are John Henry, his friend Josiah, and two women, representing the good and the bad sides of love, who compete for the hero's affections. As the piece opens, Josiah sings an old Yiddish melody and John Henry, knowing he is needed on earth, descends from the sky. The story traces the legend fairly closely, with an additional tension stemming from the roles of the two women. John Henry's contest is explicitly motivated by the threat of technological displacement; after he dies, the men symbolically hoist him up to heaven. I have not seen this dance, but find Maloney's conceptualization compelling. He includes segments such as a Men's Dance and a Whores' Dance and freely uses metaphor throughout. He hopes to add a duet in which John Henry asks the river questions about life and a climax in which the men's hammers lock together to lift John Henry to heaven.

Of all the tributes to John Henry, I cannot help but feel that he would be most pleased by the John Henry Memorial Foundation, organized by Ed Cabbell of Princeton, West Virginia, and dedicated to celebrating what he sees as the unappreciated but rich culture of the more than one million black residents of Appalachia. Cabbell believes that John Henry is an appropriate symbol of the contributions of black Appalachians, whose identities have suffered from mainstream stereotyping along with the white mountaineer. Hoping to make black Appalachians more aware of their own cultural heritage as well as to promote understanding and sharing among highlanders of all cultures, the Foundation sponsors workshops, exhibits year round, and plans to develop a permanent collection of documents and artifacts and to publish a journal, *Black Diamonds*. Its most exciting project for the last six years has been the John Henry Memorial Festival, featuring multiethnic Appalachian musicians (black, white and Cherokee) and such well known performers as Odetta, Sleepy John Estes, and Johnny Shines. The festival is held at different locations each year. In 1978, it was located in Summers County and inaugurated an annual spike-driving contest in addition to the music. For the last two years, the festival has been recorded for Steve Rathe's Folk Festival USA on National Public Radio. Tapes of the festival are available in National Public Radio's Washington, D.C., office. The Foundation and Festival are described in Cabbell's article in *Long Journey Home: Folklife in the South* and Karen Mitchell's piece in the *Charleston Sunday Gazette-Mail*. The Foundation's address is Box 135, Princeton, West Virginia 24740.

NOTES

1. Howard Odum and Guy Johnson, *Negro Workaday Songs,* pp. 238-39.

2. Leon Harris, "That Steel-Drivin' Man," in *Phylon Quarterly*, p. 405 and in Alan Dundes, ed., *Mother Wit from the Laughing Barrel,* p. 566.

3. Harris, in *Phylon,* p. 406 and in Dundes, *Mother Wit,* p. 567.

4. "John Henry and the Cape of Fear," as told by Glasgow McLeod to T. Pat Matthews, in W. C. Hendricks, ed., *Bundle of Trouble and Other Tarheel Tales,* pp. 42, 49.

5. Bradford's John Henry at times resembles tricksters such as B'rer Rabbit as he outwits more powerful adversaries; the bad man motifs are seen in Bradford's mobilization of such legendary desperadoes as John Hardy and Stacker Lee. At times the relationship between John Henry and Julie Ann reads like a blues piece, with a classic blues lament on the no-good ways of women. In *Steamboatin' Days,* Mary Wheeler describes the legendary rouster Stavin' Chain (whose exploits are similar to Bradford's John Henry) and an epic steamboat race between the *James Lee* and the *Kate Adams.*

6. Roark Bradford, *John Henry,* p. 36.

7. Roark Bradford, *John Henry: A Play,* pp. 75-76.

8. Roark Bradford, "Paul Robeson is John Henry, and John Henry is Paul Robeson," p. 15.

9. Charles H. Wright, *Robeson: Labor's Forgotten Champion,* pp. 8-10.

10. Philip Foner, *Paul Robeson Speaks: Writings, Speeches, Interviews, 1918-1974,* pp. 269-70.

11. Ibid., pp. 130-32.

12. *Time,* 22 January 1940, p. 49.

13. *New Yorker,* 20 January 1940, p. 30.

14. Maud Cuney Hare, *Negro Musicians and their Music,* p. 155.

15. Eileen Burrer, "John Henry: A Negro Folk Play Based on the Novel by Roark Bradford," p. vi.

16. Irwin Shapiro, *John Henry and the Double-Jointed Steam Drill* (on last page, no page numbers shown in book).

17. Harold Felton, *John Henry and His Hammer,* p. 11.

18. Ibid., p. 80.

19. Archie Green, in "John Henry Depicted," argues that Felton offers children a hero reduced. He points particularly to the illustrations which portray, for example, a tidy little cabin with freshly washed clothes hanging out to dry and a friendly bird singing in a nearby tree.

20. Adele DeLeeuw, *John Henry: Steel-Drivin' Man,* frontispiece.

21. John Oliver Killens, *A Man Ain't Nothin but a Man.* Prologue.

22. Ibid., p. 12.

23. Ibid., p. 13.

24. Ibid., p. 49.

25. Ibid., p. 37.

26. Ibid., p. 117.

27. Ibid., pp. 173, 176.

28. Frank Shay, "The Tall Tale in America," p. 382.

29. Frank Shay, *Here's Audacity!,* p. 247.

30. Ibid., p. 248.

31. Carl Carmer, *The Hurricane's Children,* p. 122.

32. Ibid., p. 128.

33. Olive B. Miller, *Heroes, Outlaws and Funny Fellows of American Popular Tales,* pp. 152-153.

34. Anne Malcolmson, *Yankee Doodle's Cousins,* p. 102.

35. Ibid., p. 104.

36. Ibid., p. 107.

37. Irwin Shapiro, *Tall Tales of America,* p. 109.

38. Eloise Johnson, *Stout Hearts A-Singin' with Freedom,* pp. 86 87

39. Ibid., p. 89.

40. Ibid., p. 90.

41. Nellie McCaslin, *Tall Tales and Tall Men,* p. 44.

42. Margaret Walker, *For My People,* p. 49.

43. Sterling Brown, *The Collected Poems of Sterling Brown,* pp. 86-87.

44. Ibid., p. 86.

JOHN HENRY, THE STEEL DRIVING MAN

John Henry was a railroad man,
He worked from six 'till five,
"Raise 'em up bullies and let 'em drop down,
I'll beat you to the bottom or die."

John Henry said to his captain:
"You are nothing but a common man,
Before that steam drill shall beat me down,
I'll die with my hammer in my ha...

John Henry said to the Shakers:
"You must listen to my call,
Before that steam drill shall beat me down,
I'll jar these mountains till they fall."

John Henry's captain said to him:
"I believe these mountains are caving in."
John Henry said to his captain: "Oh Lord!"
"That's my hammer you hear in the wind."

John Henry he said to his captain:
"Your money is getting mighty slim,
When I hammer through this old mountain,
Oh Captain will you walk in?"

John Henry's captain came to him
With fifty dollars in his hand,
He laid his hand on his shoulder and said,
"This belongs to a steel driving man."

John Henry was hammering on the right side,
The big steam drill on the left,
Before that steam drill could beat him down,
He hammered his fool self to death.

They carried John Henry to the mountains,
From his shoulder his hammer would ring,
She caught on fire by a little blue blaze
I believe these old mountains are caving in.

John Henry was lying on his death bed,
He turned over on his side,
And these were the last words John Henry said
"Bring me a cool drink of water before I die."

John Henry had a little woman,
Her name was Pollie Ann,
He hugged and kissed her just before he died,
Saying, "Pollie, do the very best you can."

John Henry's woman heard he was dead,
She could not rest on her bed,
She got up at midnight, caught that No. 4 train,
"I am going where John Henry fell dead."

They carried John Henry to that new burying ground
His wife all dressed in blue,
She laid her hand on John Henry's cold face,
"John Henry I've been true to you."

Price 5 Cents   W. T. BLANKENSHIP.

1. The Blankenship Broadside. First known published sheet music of the
"John Henry" Ballad. Date unknown.

2. John Henry rousting cotton. Frontspiece by J. J. Lankes for
Roark Bradford's novel *John Henry,* 1930.

3. A Chessie (C & O Railroad) Steam Special emerging from Big Bend Tunnel. Photograph by Curt Messer of Hinton, West Virginia.

4. "The Ghost of John Henry" by Curt Messer of Hinton, West Virginia.
The statue of John Henry commissioned by the Talcott-Hinton Ruritan Club
superimposed against the old and new Big Bend Tunnels dramatically
captures the sense that many local people share: Big Bend has long been haunted
by the steeldriver who died there.

6
THE HEROIC APPEAL
OF JOHN HENRY

Most compelling about John Henry's heroic legacy is its versatility in speaking to the vastly different needs of particular Americans in varied times, places, and life situations. Our sparse knowledge of the details of his life and of the purpose motivating his stand against the steam drill has made him most amenable to flights of creative fancy, as we make of John Henry almost whatever we wish. He has been a hero of several traditions in evolving community contexts: his spirit has been invoked by laborers and by railroad buffs as well as those passionately opposed to the railroad as an institution; he has symbolized evolving black consciousness and the celebration of southern culture. To appreciate John Henry's impact on American culture is to trace his life as hero in these several heroic traditions at the times when he has been appropriate to them. In this chapter, I explore each in turn and finally examine the possibility that he may be a universal hero, whose saga is best understood as a family tragedy. As we shall see, this last possibility may explain why John Henry's most powerful and lasting influence on American society has been through song.

Chapter 1 described the grim working conditions of Big Bend Tunnel, which most people believe to have been the source of the John Henry story. This story emerged as both a ballad whose authorship remains a mystery and in hammer songs, which almost certainly were composed, improvised, or adapted right in Big Bend. All of the earliest fragments of songs in the "Nine-Pound Hammer" complex (except the "Roll on Buddy" phrases) mention John Henry, which indicate that he was integral to the hammer motif from the very beginning.[1]

We can easily imagine why John Henry was a hero to the workers at Big Bend, especially when we recall the nature of their work, the role of music in that work, and the message of the John Henry hammer songs. The men at Big Bend were invisible, unsung laborers, toiling at some of the most grinding, unpleasant, dangerous jobs imaginable. Those who were steel drivers found that singing made that work tolerable by relieving the tedium and helping them find a rhythm by which to pace their strokes. John Henry might have been any one of hundreds of workers who died a gruesome, ugly death at the tunnel and experienced the most casual of burials. To speak of his death was to invite dismissal or harassment; to sing obliquely of him was to comment on both the hardships of the work and one's own determination not to suffer John Henry's fate. "This Nine-Pound Hammer, just a little too heavy for my size, for my size," may not summon up especially vivid images today, but for workers wielding hammers, it may have captured symbolically all that was arduous about their labor. "This old hammer, killed John Henry, But it won't kill me, it won't kill me," similarly invokes the hazards of work, but at the same time comments on an unmentionable death and avows the singers' determination not to suffer the same fate. It is a life affirming refrain in a tunnel filled with death. "Take this hammer, and carry it to the captain, tell him I'm gone, tell him I'm gone," is more fanciful, allowing singers to imagine that they could walk away from their work, leaving the captain to ponder the tool which spoke to the reasons why they would want to do so.

These hammer songs were very close to protest songs, although, like the John Henry ballad, they do not detail the grisly aspects of tunnel life; but they do evoke images that all workers in John Henry's situation could relate to. John Henry, in this community, was a very different hero from the one we think of today. Many of the workers may have been his intimates; some may have seen him die. They sing of him to dramatize their own pain, yet they call on his example as one they have no intention of following. He is much more a martyr than a leader.

Throughout the Reconstruction Era South—indeed, wherever there was rock to be driven—workers employed hammers. Laborers on canals, turnpikes, and dams, in tunnels, quarries, and mines also found music integral to their work; and like the men in Big Bend they shared the imagery evoked by songs of the deadly, heavy hammer. Because many of the black workers were itinerants, they probably carried the hammer songs to many job sites. Archie Green notes that railroad workers would have brought them into the mines, as they laid spurs into the coal-rich Allegheny Mountains or drove track into the mines for coal cars to travel on. In West Virginia, railroading and coal mining were always closely linked; her wealth of coal resources had been a major incentive for the C & O to build there. And the Nine-Pound Hammer songs have been significant pieces of the coal miners' repertoire for many years.[2] As underground workers, they had the most in common with the laborers at Big Bend; that the two sorts of jobs are quite similar is reflected in the fact that tunneling workers were often termed "miners."

However, the hammering motif had an appeal far beyond the tunnels and coal mines as it embodied the fears and hopes of hammering everywhere. And the songs have endured, sung on chain gangs and in prisons at least into the 1960s, as long as laboring conditions were reminiscent of the primitive manual tasks of the late nineteenth century.

The ballad is more difficult to place in a laboring tradition because we do not know who composed it. It also may have emerged from Big Bend Tunnel, although such scholars as Barry and Cohen argue convincingly for the influence of white mountain narrative tradition.[3] Editors of folksong anthologies frequently classify the ballad as a workingman's song, and folklorists such as Archie Green see it as speaking to the needs of all workers.[4] Its message is quite different from the hammer songs; for in the ballad, as in many fictional accounts which elaborate it, John Henry is a hero to the displaced worker. He takes a stand against a machine which will take away his job and in so doing, he testifies to the ultimate dignity of humanity. In most versions of the ballad, this confrontation is not explicit, however. If the hammer songs comment obliquely on the horrors of underground work, the ballads avoid the issue altogether. Much is left unsaid, and we do not know if workers summon up the same images that popular storytellers and novelists do. Indeed, it is possible to argue, as does Roderick Nash, that the confrontation between man and machine transcends work altogether, that we should more appropriately see John Henry in a long line of folk heroes who, according to the times, controlled, spurned or befriended machines.[5]

But if the John Henry of balladry is problematic, his place in the hammer song tradition is irrefutable. Unlike would-be workers' heroes such as Joe Hill who may never have appealed broadly to those they sought to represent, or others such as Mother Jones whose following was more local and short-lived, John Henry through his life in work song had a universal appeal transcending the particular situation of Big Bend Tunnel. His life as a laborers' hero cannot be separated from his place in the songs which were rooted in communities of workers, guiding them in joining their work and providing relief by "underlining the truth that the individual worker did not suffer an individual fate."[6] Because he lived vividly through the communal process of making music in the workplace, and because he came to stand for the needs and fears of many in circumstances similar to his, John Henry may be our most authentic working people's hero.

Most often scholars and popular collectors have considered "John Henry" a railroad song, and the man a railroad hero. Objectively, this designation may seem inappropriate, as the man we can trace to Big Bend was an underground laborer under contract to a construction chief, rather than to the C & O itself. Hammer songs commemorating him must have been carried all over the country by railroad workers, but often these workers performed other kinds of tasks as well, for the hammering theme was appropriate to many different jobs. The ballad barely mentions the railroad, and offers no details on railroading life or work, or John Henry's feelings about the institution. Most often the first stanza simply begins:

When John Henry was a little baby,
Sittin' on his mama's knee
He said, 'The Big Bend Tunnel
On the C & O Line
Is gonna be the death of me'

or with words to that effect. The reference is much more casual than in most songs we consider truly railroad songs, such as those celebrating Casey Jones and numerous other fatal wrecks; those praising the great trains such as the Wabash Cannonball or the Orange Blossom Special; others describing railroad work such as "I've Been Workin' on the Railroad," and "Brakeman's Blues"; or even those which summon the railroad as metaphor, including such gospel/blues pieces as "This Train is Bound for Glory." How, then, can we understand John Henry's heroic place in the railroading tradition?

Once again we must return to the period of John Henry's emergence. Today when we bother to think of trains at all, we are most likely to do so nostalgically—it is difficult to remember the passion with which Americans greeted them in the nineteenth century. The railroad was the quintessential machine, embodying, as Leo Marx has noted, all that was best and worst of the Industrial Revolution as it entered the pristine American landscape. The train dramatized the qualities of speed, power, smoke and noise which were to change our lives forever.[7] Railroads unified the continent, imported thousands of immigrants as laborers and homesteaders, revolutionized the distribution of agricultural and manufacturing goods, linked forsaken prairie towns to the economies of growing cities, and imposed on us the constraints of Standard Time. Even before America's first railroad (the Baltimore & Ohio) had begun to lay track, two songs celebrated that feat, hinting at a relationship between railroads and musicians which was to last well into the twentieth century.[8]

Railroad song, disregarding for the moment such big band pieces of the 1940s as "Chattanooga Choo Choo" and nostalgic contemporary works like "City of New Orleans," has stemmed almost exclusively from the black and white musicians of the South. It was first recorded commercially by the country and blues singers of the 1920s and 1930s. Setting their songs to the rhythms of the wheels on the tracks, reproducing with their instruments the sounds of the train (the harmonica as whistle, for example), these musicians captured much of the nineteenth century enthusiasm for railroading in a remarkable repertoire of song.

When we consider the role of railroading in southern small town life, this celebration of trains in southern expressive culture makes sense. While artists and writers saw them as harbingers of the industrial revolution, trains seem to have evoked a variety of other symbols for musicians of the south. They spoke of freedom and mobility, the departure or homecoming of loved ones, and restlessness or a longing to be home. Southern musicians captured, in short, many of the familiar sentiments inspired by riding on the train, awaiting its arrival and hearing it pass. Some pieces, such as the bluegrass band Seldom Scene's recent "On the Railroad Line" speak to all the affection and lore that might surround trains in a small town, as children befriended the regular engineers and laid pennies on the tracks to be miraculously flattened.[9]

But celebratory and friendly as railroad music may seem, this affection for trains is far from the whole story, especially during the years when Big Bend Tunnel was constructed. Popular enthusiasm for railroading may have peaked with the completion of the first transcontinental route in 1869, but in the 1870s many Americans grew to loathe and fear them. These years were the heyday of the great rail barons, who grew wealthy and powerful through often unconscionable acts of corruption and exploitation. Homesteaders had been lured to remote and desolate areas of the country by deceptive advertisements promising them they could grow rich there. Stockholders had lost small fortunes through owners' manipulation of railroad stocks. Farmers felt crushed by the monopolistic weight of railway companies in setting the prices and terms for shipping produce and stock. Finally the railroad workers, laboring long hours under hazardous conditions, with little pay and many arbitrary wage cuts, fueled a populist reaction against the institution which many had welcomed as one which would benefit all Americans.

Except perhaps for Chicago, West Virginia (more than any other place in the country) was a hotbed of antirailroad sentiments. We have seen how, even in tiny Hinton and Talcott, the Chesapeake & Ohio's overbearing presence created in the townspeople conflicting feelings of dependence and resentment. Almost all the residents owed their livings to the railroad, but its high-handed politics, lackadaisical safety measures and hasty, shoddy construction of bridges, trestles and tunnels were bound to anger them.[10]

The C & O Railroad had opened up West Virginia's great lumber and coal resources for exploitation, but had behaved rather willfully in doing so. The railroad had swallowed up a number of small local lines in the process of consolidation and had then insisted on the same tax-exempt privileges granted its predecessors. When ordered by the Supreme Court to pay West Virginia several years' worth of back taxes, the railroad declared bankruptcy, dissolved, then reorganized itself—ownership intact—as the C & O *Railway*.[11]

Statewide resentment was evidenced by the popularity of the Grange, often a hotbed of railroad opposition, which organized its first lodge in 1873 and was active throughout the seventies and eighties in lobbying for regulatory legislation and promoting Populist political candidates. Also, our first nationwide strikes were initiated by West Virginia railroad men, angered by a slash in wages and harboring years of hostility due to the hazards encountered on their jobs. Before that time, the railway brotherhoods had been quiescent craft organizations whose main concerns were improved safety precautions and widows' insurance, which indicated how dangerous their work was. Norm Cohen notes that the pages of the early brotherhoods' journals often featured advertisements for artificial limbs (by such companies as the Veteran and Railroad Men's Artificial Limb Manufacturing Company) and "homiletic pieces about the tragic deaths and disfigurements of railroad employees."[12] Engineers and brakemen were more articulate, probably because they were less powerless, than the tunnel workers in voicing grievances about the hazards of their work; and the rapid mobilization of strikers in 1877 and again in 1893 testifies to a hostility toward their employers which transcended the immediate indignity of wage cuts.

Some of these sentiments did emerge in folksong, blatantly in such pieces as R. J. Harrison's "The Anti-Monopoly War Song," which begins: "Lo the car of Juggernaut, lo the ruin it had wrought." A more subtle manifestation of working people's concerns was the trend in subjects for folksong: before the 1870s, most had treated the affairs of travelers; but during the 1870s, many of the Irish melodies commemorating construction tasks ("Drill ye Tarriers, Drill," for example) emerged—songs which, unlike the longer-lived hammer songs, were about work rather than to work by. In the 1880s, the many ballads celebrating heroic engineers and brakemen who lost their lives in legendary wrecks began to appear: some of the more familiar of these include "The Wreck of the Old 97" and "Ben Dewberry's Final Run."[13] In part, this latter type of folksong still reflected an enthusiasm for railroading and in particular, the whole new cast of American heroic characters called forth by the often romanticized drama and danger of railroad work. Yet these songs also realistically reflect the concerns of the engineers and brakemen themselves, who must have known that during these years fatal wrecks actually occurred almost every day.

These legendary engineers lost their lives when their trains flew off the trestle, exploded from too much steam, or like Casey Jones', flew into the back of another train because the overzealous driver hoped to secure his reputation by meeting an approaching deadline. They constituted one of several heroic types inspired by American railroading. It is in this pantheon of heroes that we can best see folk hostility to the institution. The engineers are perhaps the least ambiguous of the lot; most are loyal railroaders, sometimes careless but always dedicated to their work. The songs and stories rarely blame their employers for their deaths which are more likely considered due to individual oversight or excessive enthusiasm for the job. They are true occupational heroes who embrace their work and their destinies. Occasionally, as seems to have been Casey Jones' fate on Tin Pan Alley, they become either comic or pathetic characters whose deaths are absurd; perhaps because they have linked their own egos too closely to the machines which they are supposed to control. Interestingly, all of the occupational heroes we associate with railroading were white, skilled laborers. The only exception is the black sleeping car porter Daddy Joe, who allegedly could make up two berths simultaneously, but seems to be a barely familiar character—even to lifelong sleeping car porters.[14]

Another heroic type is more accurately an antihero: in the outlaws who enjoyed extraordinary popularity, including commemoration in song, we can very clearly see Americans' growing hostility toward the rail barons. Probably the two best known are Jesse James, train robber of the 1870s and Railroad Bill, a black outlaw of the 1890s. Both were almost unfathomably admired, with Railroad Bill in particular transformed, probably mythically, into a sort of Robin Hood because he robbed the rich white railroaders and then shared his booty with poor blacks. The contrast between these outlaws and the loyal engineers seems clear enough and polarizes very well our contrasting sentiments toward railroading in the nineteenth century. John Henry's place in this heroic tradition, however, is quite ambiguous.

His very era probably makes John Henry a railroad hero, for his destiny was linked to the nation-building enterprise capturing the attention of most Americans during those years. That music was integral to the rhythms of railroad work and that itinerant railroad laborers carried his song to the farthest reaches of the country indelibly fixed him as a railroad man. Folksong collectors probably found trackliners among the most accessible of workers singing at work, and may have been especially likely to term the song a railroad song. But the association has lasted: with the exception of Roark Bradford, every writer who has memorialized John Henry in fiction has portrayed him as a railroad man. Even the wide publicity of Bradford's work did not dislodge John Henry from an institutional role that novelists such as Harold Felton and John Oliver Killens, who recreated a compelling attraction between John Henry and the drama of railroad life, saw as a near sacred association.

Is John Henry an occupational hero like Casey Jones, or do we love him because he protests what railroading has come to mean, as did Railroad Bill? Through hammer songs, workers incorporated him into a medium of discreet and indirect protest but, again, the ballads are unclear. They do not speak to us of railroading, except to link John Henry's destiny to the C & O. I believe that this very ambiguity endears John Henry to both train buffs and those whose passions run the other way. He could be either kind of hero. He could care so much about his job that he would die to preserve it; like Casey Jones perhaps, his sense of self is tied too closely to his occupational prowess. On the other hand, in combating the steam drill he may be battling the machine as an abstraction, epitomized by the trains and the powerful images they evoke in bringing the industrial revolution to life. Or he may be protesting, not industrialization per se, bu the railroad magnates' casual disregard for human life—be it a steel driver's whose duties are hazardous, or the worker's whose job is becoming obsolete, and who sees that no one will take responsibility for the problem of his obsolescence. There can be no one answer to these questions, nor can we ever explain why John Henry would have wanted to preserve his right to such an unpleasant job as the one he held in Big Bend. It is the sparseness of John Henry's story that allows him to embody each individual's vision of railroading and of humanity.

Does it matter that he was black? Does he have a special heroic place in black culture? To understand John Henry as a hero to black Americans, we must trace the changing contexts of black experience in which heroes emerged.

Those who presented heroic possibilities to slaves were of two very different types. Slaves created a very sacred universe, not to escape the realities of the secular world, but rather to expand it. Through religion, slaves looked to Old Testament precedents which promised confrontation and deliverance in this world, not the next. The heroes celebrated in spirituals were men who took on a more powerful but overbearing authority and defeated it, thus liberating a people chosen by God as special. Old Testament heroes included little David (whose pretechnological victory, notes Lawrence Levine, is reminiscent of John Henry's), Moses and Joshua. Not only does this selection of heroes belie any notion that slaves looked forward to a better life only after death, but it also demonstrates that slaves had not internalized their masters' conception of them as less than human. They identified with the Israelites as a chosen people.[15]

Complementing these more sacred heroes in Afro-American culture under slavery was a more pragmatic figure, commonly referred to as the trickster and manifested in the forms of B'rer Rabbit and the slave John. Both operated in an amoral, arbitrary universe where the weak might defeat the strong through cunning and guile: John steals chickens from his master, when discovered cooking them claims they are possum, and when the master wants to share the possum, discourages him by relating how family members have spit into the pot to make the meat tender. When Wolf and Rabbit court the same women, Rabbit hints to her that Wolf is only his riding horse. Responding to Wolf's demand that he go to the woman and set the story straight, Rabbit convinces him that he is too ill to travel unless Wolf will carry him on his back. Often the trickster (especially in animal form, for John suffers the real life constraints of slavery) is every bit as ruthless and merciless as his adversary. The trickster's victories can be seen as the victories of the slave; but even more importantly, the climate of the trickster tales recreated the everyday evil of slavery. While the sacred world of slaves helped to explain the present by drawing on the past to promise a better future, the world of the secular heroes offered guidelines to a practical morality for negotiating the senseless world of the plantation.[16]

With freedom Afro-Americans found these heroes increasingly inappropriate, and they turned to others who reflected the marginal, bicultural place of former slaves. In religion, gospel music replaced the old spirituals and Christ grew more important than the heroes of the Old Testament. The trickster, although he lasted many years in oral tradition, won fewer and fewer of his confrontations. As slaves, blacks had had little use for the individualist heroes of white culture—men like Davy Crockett—who grew to heroic, larger than life proportions when faced with a problem which required that they be more than an ordinary man. As free citizens, and in spite of continuing discrimination and segregation, blacks were bound to absorb some of the individualist ethos of mainstream white culture. It is in this climate that John Henry emerged.

Cunning and guile remained important as long as blacks were vulnerable to the greater power of whites, and trickster tales and heroes lasted well into this century. But other kinds of heroes gradually grew more important: slave ancestors who had directly confronted their masters, with much courage and at great personal risk, bad men/bandits who seemed to act out a kind of nihilistic rage against white society—men like Railroad Bill, Stackolee and John Hardy—and those Levine labels moral hard men, strong self-contained heroes who for the most part acted within the rules of white society, but violated its preordained roles and stereotypes for blacks. Like the heroes of the Old Testament, these heroes met adversity through direct confrontation, but, reflecting the changing experience of black Americans, they operated on a secular level. Levine identifies four who emerged during Reconstruction and through the 1930s: John Henry, Jack Johnson, Shine, and Joe Louis.[17]

Johnson and Louis were verifiably real men, differing from one another in that Johnson's flashier life style and associations with white women were often interpreted as a deliberate flaunting of society's moral code. Louis was a quieter hero and easier for whites to accept as well. Similarly Shine and John Henry, both possibly mythical, differed in that Shine mocked white society by mercilessly swimming away from the Titanic and the remaining passengers who had not heeded his warnings that the ship would sink. What all share is a willingness to stand on their own, to confront the adversary on his own terms, and to demonstrate that individuals can succeed by relying on themselves alone. It is in this pantheon of heroes that some scholars argue John Henry belongs. He has undeniably been a hero to black Americans, who sang of him in the nineteenth century and knew of his prowess at least through the 1920s.[18] John Henry is less a hero to black Americans today, but understanding his contemporary fate requires a brief digression on his place in the evolution of black musical styles.

With freedom, black Americans gradually developed and recognized distinctive sacred and secular styles of music. Although as slaves they had punctuated their work with song, these work songs often incorporated religious themes. The expanded sacred world of slaves was one in which music, as well as other media of oral expression, was crucial to transmitting, sharing and recreating beliefs. But the demise of the sacred world after

Emancipation meant that black music reflected more and more the marginal position of blacks in American society, incorporating purely secular themes and concerns.

As we have seen, wherever black laborers worked at tasks which were tedious or required a certain harmony of effort, they sang to relieve the boredom through lyrics which carried them beyond the present time, or to release hostility by graphically, realistically detailing the features of the task at hand. Work songs suffered a long, gradual decline with the changes in American labor wrought by urbanization and mechanization, surviving longest on the railroads and in prison settings.

The music which was to parallel John Henry's heroic career in black culture was the blues. The blues' roots lay in the same worksongs which had so appropriately memorialized John Henry for black workers. Both musical styles rely on improvisation, and both are profoundly concerned with the troubles, the thoughts, the sentiments of the singers. The blues was originally a cultural product of rural black musicians of the nineteenth century who, after Emancipation, could travel through the South building a repertoire of song. Unlike work songs, it was refined by men at leisure, and unlike spirituals it became a music of pure self. Realistically portraying the experiences of the individual musician, its message is that a person's experiences are worthy of consideration and that the individual black's problems are significant. Not a music of self pity, blues songs often express pride, philosophical acceptance, even hope. A worldly musical style, blues themes rarely treat higher spiritual values or emotions. Often a song may be a specific response to a specific situation; through singing about that situation the singer appears to have achieved a kind of catharsis.

The blues was rooted in black history to the extent that it treated many of the themes more telegraphically expressed in work songs—problems with work or with women. Although often performed by an individual for an audience, it retained the communal spirit of the spirituals and work songs, in that the audience was generally a participatory one that responded to the singer's lyrics. The music remained communal as well in the musicians' evocation of themes with which the audience could identify; often the catharsis was one in which others shared.

Blues remained important to black historical experiences until the 1950s. The country blues of the Carolinas, Mississippi, and Texas, in which one man accompanied himself with a guitar, was succeeded by the classic blues of the 1920s and 1930s. The classic blues was characterized by female singers backed by piano or sometimes full orchestra, and was in turn succeeded by the even more sophisticated urban blues of Chicago, Memphis, and New York of the 1940s. The blues was integrally linked to the migration of southern blacks to northern cities, and its demise seems to have been an inevitable result of the pressures migrants suffered in urban contexts, as well as the aspirations that grew there. Many blacks came to see it as backward, as overly accommodative, as a tribute to all that was wrong with their lives in the old south. Its decline in popularity among blacks accompanied the civil rights movement, the ideology of soul, the rise of the more urban rhythm and blues style, and the more forthright and urbane soul music.[19]

John Henry's career traces the history of the blues. Because blues music relied so heavily on improvisation, it was not an especially appropriate medium for narrative ballads. The lyrical thread of a blues piece often involves a slow, tortuous opening in which a singer slowly works his way into the song through spoken narratives and fragments of tunes, carefully sets a mood, and then digresses frequently as the song progresses. Thus a blues song often takes on its shape and style in the course of the performance itself. In many situations, especially more relaxed settings in the rural south, a musician found it desirable to stretch out his songs as long as possible. Moreover, the subjective content of the blues makes it an unlikely medium for the celebration of folk heroes. As Paul Oliver puts it:

> Whilst the ballad singer projected on his heroes the successes that he could not believe could be his own, the blues singer considers his own ability to achieve them. The ballad hero of noble proportions has little relevance to modern life but the blues is realistic enough for the singer to declare his successes and failures with equal impartiality. Far from extolling the virtues of the folk hero, the blues singer is so brutally determined to deny them as to be markedly ungenerous toward the achievements of others even of his own race.[20]

Blues singers themselves were often heroes to other blacks, and the very nature of the medium indicates a problematic relationship to John Henry. That he was commemorated by blues singers at all testifies to the fact they shared a place in history: both arose from the turmoil of the industrializing south and the movement of blacks into a secular society in which they were still vulnerable and discriminated against. John Henry's ambiguous act seemed to speak to the hopes and fears of blacks at that time; and the sparseness of the ballad, which does allow for individual interpretation and flexibility, inspired a number of blues singers to include it in their repertoires.

John Henry's demise may also be rooted in the same circumstances which have led to the increasing unpopularity of blues music among blacks. We know that as late as the 1920s, his was a familiar and respected name among blacks interviewed by Johnson and Chappell in many different parts of the country. Since then we have no evidence; for example, if we look to popular culture we find that he has most often been commemorated there by whites.

Although we cannot say for sure why John Henry became more an embarrassment than a hero to urban blacks, we can speculate that the roots of his decline lie in the dilemma of the urban situation. This situation varies by particular cities, but in those cities where circumstances of work and travel require black residents to interact in an urban milieu, they may find their southern heritage becomes something of a burden.

I base this claim on three years of research in a Washington, D.C., neighborhood, which is becoming increasingly multiethnic, international and multiclass, but whose core of residents are rural blacks from North Carolina. They have created in this neighborhood a community rooted in southern black lore, with a personalistic style much like that one expects to find in a very small town. Intimate, face to face relations characterize the life of the streets, the shops and the taverns; persons cement relationships by sharing the stories, the foods, the whiskeys, and the remedies of the rural South.

Yet this neighborhood, like many others in our cities, cannot exist as a self-contained community, for residents must commute long distances to work, to visit kin and friends, or for shopping and diversion. The urban rhythms are reflected in the life of the community as residents do not rely wholly on the rural south in constructing identities, but must testify to one another that they can successfully negotiate urban situations. In particular, mainstream popular culture intrudes in the worlds of music, fashion, and sports, as residents adopt, modify and ground popular styles to the small-town southern world of the neighborhood. Traditional southern music has been displaced by popular urban forms such as disco, and those people who do not dress appropriately to the city are often termed "Bamas."[21]

I found this neighborhood a fruitful place to test the John Henry tradition, for in it residents selectively draw on, revise or abandon southern lore in constructing their community. In the neighborhood are almost a dozen men bearing the name "John Henry," most of them coming from families with many members also bearing that name. It seemed a likely place for his story to thrive. However, the very opposite is true. Those men named John Henry have no sense of being named for a hero—as has been true traditionally for black Americans, they feel that they were called after relatives with that name. Their older kin substantiate this feeling. In no case have I found a family in which the hero's story lives.

Interviewing others in the community, I have found only one older man who knows the story.[22] Most are familiar with the name's referent and may, for example, tease a man named "John Henry" by calling him "Steel Drivin' Man." Their knowledge of the tradition seems to go no further, however, with two exceptions: some children have learned the story in the District of Columbia public schools (which self-consciously transmit black history and culture to their students, ninety percent of whom are black), and one man (other than the elderly person just mentioned) knows the story from reading it in a magazine in his doctor's office a year ago. Although his brother is named John Henry, he had no inkling of the legend before then.

Those men named John Henry seem to consider the name a somewhat embarrassing allusion to the old-fashioned South rather than a reference to be proud of. All call themselves "John" in contexts outside the neighborhood, and most sign their names "John H. _____." Like blues music, the name is inappropriate to the urban situation.

Blues musicians today perform for largely white audiences, many of whom appreciate and can afford to celebrate its traditional folk qualities. I believe that in the urban situation, John Henry is experiencing the same fate. A new designer label, "John Henry," can be found today in Washington's finest stores; this is a classy, masculine brand somewhat reminiscent of L. L. Bean. Washington Bullets' football forward Mitch Kupchak, who is white, sometimes advertises this designer brand. A representative advertisement reads: "Action men appreciate the body-contoured comfort fit of tall John Henry shirts in *French poplin.* (emphasis is mine). . . . Solids, checks, stripes, designer collars and the legendary John Henry tall fit . . . 6' 10" Mitch Kupchak . . . The Fashion Forward."[23] The John Henry design seems to sport the same appeal as much of the back to nature paraphernalia of the last decade. But the John Henry shirts are a far cry from the world of the Big Bend Tunnel, and their appeal to fashion-conscious urban men at the same time that the hero seems to have lost his clout for black men is telling. In taking a stand against the machine, he also tried to resist an inevitably more modern life; and he seems to have lost his appeal to those who must testify that they can cope with it. Stripped of rebellious implications, he has entered the mainstream.

The crux of the matter is that, because of his legendary ambiguities, John Henry personifies many diverse notions about who blacks are and what kind of people they should be. We do not know what kind of person he was, but we do know that certain of his most obvious attributes, his individualism and his willingness to compete against a machine, seemed to be singularly appropriate to a particular time and place. He probably could not have been a hero to blacks before that time, and he has again become inappropriate in the years since. John Henry is too vulnerable to misinterpretation, as the various fictional portraits of him (often constructed by white authors) demonstrate. His story is easily twisted so that he symbolizes all the most demeaning white stereotypes of black Americans: dumb, brute strength, unrepressed sexuality, retrograde Uncle Tomism, the comic naiveté of Amos and Andy. Even the natural man motif, which to many of my informants evokes a still valued set of characteristics embodying a "man who don't take *no* shit from *nobody,*" is easily distorted in mainstream culture to represent primitivism. Thus, as he has moved out of the era which called him forth because it needed him, and been subjected to both celebration and parody in a century when his heroic act is ambiguous, John Henry seems to have become a less potent figure for many black Americans.

The final heroic tradition to claim and memorialize John Henry has been the expressive culture of the South—in particular, the world of southern music. He seems to have appealed to southern white musicians almost immediately for, as Norm Cohen notes, our earliest collected, printed and recorded versions of the ballad are by whites.

The influence of mountain white narrative tradition on the shape of the John Henry ballad has been discussed in Chapter 3, so I will recapitulate only the major points here. In the first place, the very narrative strength of the John Henry ballad is closer to white tradition; from what we know of the nineteenth century black folksong, such structured ballads were rare. Further, stanzas from well known Anglo and Scottish ballads frequently intrude into the John Henry sequence, most noticeable among these being the ''Who's gonna shoe your pretty little foot?'' verses from ''The Lass of Roch Royal.'' We know that white folksingers actually sang the ballad because the first reported stanzas (those of Bascom, Combs, Perrow and Lomax) came from white singers. In part, this bias reflects the focus of early collectors who tended to concentrate their efforts among whites. That the ballad was truly a part of white mountain tradition is suggested by Bradley's report from Berea College in 1915.

The first broadside to emerge—that of Blankenship—was printed anywhere between 1900 and 1920 and was surely of white authorship. And through the years, white hillbilly and country singers have recorded the ballad frequently, beginning with Fiddlin' John Carson's Okeh disc in 1924 and including hundreds since.[24]

It is easy to see how white singers might have learned the song, for often blacks and whites in the south lived and worked very closely, the music of each group coming from the sounds of the field, the railyard, the lumber camp and mine, as well as from the repertoires of family and friends and the music broadcast by commercial media. Southern blacks and whites shared a large common stock of folksong, including the ballads of Jesse James, Casey Jones, Railroad Bill, and Frankie and Johnnie, as well as John Henry.[25]

One can argue that a singer might find a ballad aesthetically pleasing without necessarily admiring its hero. Mulcahy argues that the song's singable tune and good lively story contribute equally to its phenomenal popularity.[26] Singers can make of the story and the man almost what they wish; the ballad is flexible enough to allow for several different emphases. Race is not an issue; the only way one knows from the song that John Henry is black is that he often speaks in dialect. Some of Johnson's and Chappell's informants in the 1920s, in fact, claimed that John Henry was a white man. So it is possible to argue that southern whites have enjoyed the ballad without necessarily honoring its hero as a black man.

On the other hand, one can imagine that he was a most appropriate hero for the late nineteenth century south. John Henry speaks to all the turmoil of industrialization; he captures all the anxieties of the time. The song, like the hero, grew from the meeting of Anglo-American ballad tradition and Afro-American worksongs in a labor-intensive integrated workplace unique to the southern experience. Thus, both speak to the southern cultural renaissance through which blacks and whites responded to a very difficult set of circumstances. Perhaps this is why sometimes songs and often stories portray the steam drill salesman as a cool Yankee; the conflict becomes a confrontation between the impersonal North and the more humane South. John Henry speaks to the terrible bitterness dividing the two regions long after the Civil War had ended, and to the special humiliation and populist rage directed against northern capitalists who swallowed up the railroads and industries of the south, and reaped the benefits of her revitalization.

One might have expected John Henry to emerge as a true southern hero during the 1930s, a decade in which many Americans turned to the lore of their own regions as a source of patriotic pride. As far as I can tell, this did not happen.[27] Perhaps race relations were still too raw. However, in the last ten years, with the awakening of the New South, he has become a hero to southerners. In 1972, the Hillsdale-Talcott Ruritan Club erected his statue at the mouth of Big Bend. The grandson of his employer, also named W. R. Johnson, boasts a cast statuette of the hero on his desk at the Johnson Coal Company of Smithers, West Virginia. A 1966 issue of the journal the *Appalachian South* includes an anonymous article hailing John Henry as a hero who protested the same crass materialism "that grinds the poor and lays the mountains of a whole region waste by strip and sugar mining."[28] This author thus invokes John Henry to speak to contemporary concerns about the impact of industrialization. And finally, the John Henry Memorial Foundation's success testifies that John Henry can inspire those of very different ethnic backgrounds. He has at last become a local hero, preserved by nearly a century's worth of song, and celebrated through several additional media today.

These are the heroic traditions which have claimed John Henry: labor lore, the world of railroading, black culture, southern musical expression, and most recently, the New South. He has been appropriate and compelling to each in different ways and eras. Part of John Henry's appeal lies in his versatility at fitting the needs and goals of each; but to account for the phenomenal popularity of the John Henry ballad, American's most beloved folksong and the medium through which most of us know John Henry, I believe that we must look beyond particular historical and cultural contexts. We must look to the universal message of the song.

"John Henry" has been transcribed, recorded, performed and rearranged countless times and with remarkable variety, so it may be fruitless to try to analyze its contents. Any attempt to do so will not do justice to its rich and appealing permutations in the hands of individual musicians and editors. With this caveat in mind, we can at least begin by considering what is *not* there. The ballad does not describe railroading or Big Bend Tunnel, it does not detail the conditions of work, it rarely (only once to my knowledge) elaborates on matters of race, and it does not report chronologically on an event. As Cohen notes, it is more like an editorial than a news article—it comments on an episode the listeners presumably already know about.[29]

(It would be interesting to know how many listeners really do know the story, and if so, how? I suspect that many do not.)

Norm Cohen classified the ballad's elements as these five:

1. an infantile premonition,

2. preparation for the contest (including the challenge, a financial incentive, John Henry's request for hammers of a specific weight, and the like),

3. the contest itself (usually limited to such information as who stood where, how rapidly each contestant drove, John Henry's comments as the contest proceeded, and praise for John Henry's powerful strokes),

4. the hero's last words, death and burial, and

5. much editorializing on his woman (the clothes she wore, her behavior at his funeral, sometimes her own steel-driving prowess).[30]

This classification seems accurate, but I am most struck by the ballad's fairly consistent frame. We first meet John Henry as a baby, sitting on the knee of either his mother or father or sometimes both, in sequence. As many other scholars have noted, he is a classic hero, born fully conscious of his fate, which he predicts from the lap of his parents and then stoically acts out. Although the middle of the song tells us nearly nothing of his workplace, it devotes a great deal of attention to his personal relationships: his wife or woman, or sometimes several women and his child, usually a son to whom he passes on the tragic burden. Often he addresses his last words to this child, and often he warns the boy that he too will die a steel-driving man. The ballad impresses us with a sense of an heroic legacy.

Thus, John Henry's infancy and death frame the ballad. He predicts his own death, does what he must and passes on the heroic burden to his son. The story is a family tragedy. It explores life and death and human purpose, generational continuity, parents and children, hopes and prophecies. It is this family context that gives John Henry his human dignity and complexity, renders his most profound statement, "A man ain't nothin' but a man," so proud and sad, and makes fictional parodies of him so often offensive. The song is a wonderful reaffirmation of the worth of a human life—a worker's in a workplace which denies it, a black man's in a context reminiscent of slavery, a southerner's during a time of bitter humiliation and drastic change—and, ultimately, of every ordinary person who through dignity and strength of will can be great. The ballad not only praises John Henry's courage and skill, but it also reminds us that the details of his personal life matter. Like all of us, he is a member of a family.

Anyone who has heard the John Henry ballad performed well can perhaps understand why his heroic life has been largely known through song and why, on the other hand, fictional efforts to pin down or elaborate the legend often do not quite work. The power of his appeal lies in the sketchiness of the story. The fluidity of the ballad, as well as the detail which it leaves to our imagination, allows individual musicians to interpret his heroic act in ways most appropriate to the moment. But even more importantly, the song's emphasis on John Henry's ordinary humanity enables the singer to stir us, though we may not be sure why, with profound empathy. That he combines heroic strength and courage with the simplest, commonest human emotions makes John Henry great.

NOTES

1. Norm Cohen, *Long Steel Rail*, pp. 575-76.
2. Archie Green, *Only a Miner*, p. 356.
3. Phillips Barry, "Reviews," pp. 24-26; Norm Cohen, *Long Steel Rail*, p. 70.
4. Archie Green, *Only a Miner*, p. 9.
5. Roderick Nash, "Machines and Americans," p. 104.
6. Lawrence Levine, *Black Culture and Black Consciousness*, p. 214.
7. For extensive discussion of this theme, see Leo Marx's *The Machine in the Garden*.
8. For discussion and texts of the B & O Songs, see Norm Cohen, *Long Steel Rail*, pp. 39-42.
9. See Lee Cooper, "Oral History and the Railroad: Examining Shifting Images of Transportation Technology through Popular Music, 1920-1980," as well as Norm Cohen's *Long Steel Rail* for excellent discussions of railroad songs' themes.
10. James H. Miller, *History of Summers County, West Virginia*, pp. 164, 181, 190.
11. Charles Henry Ambler, *History of West Virginia*, pp. 393, 398, 399; Miller, *History of Summers County*, pp. 175-76.
12. Cohen, *Long Steel Rail*, p. 53.
13. Ibid., pp. 39-55, offers a much expanded discussion of the trends in subjects for railroad songs.
14. Folklorist Jack Santino, who with his colleague Steve Zeitlin is interviewing many former sleeping car porters for a film on the Brotherhood of Sleeping Car Porters, communicated this information to me. Santino briefly discusses John Henry in his "The Folk Heroes of Occupational Groups."
15. Lawrence Levine devotes a whole chapter of his book *Black Culture and Black Consciousness* (pp. 3-55) to the sacred world of black slaves.
16. Again the best most recent discussion of trickster themes is Levine's *Black Culture and Black Consciousness*, pp. 90-133.
17. Ibid., pp. 367-420.
18. For a very different analysis, see Fred Weldon's "Negro Folktale Heroes," where he argues that John Henry, as more than a passive trickster, is unique among black heroes, but is not perceived racially.
19. In this brief discussion of blues music, I have relied heavily on Paul Oliver's *The Meaning of the Blues* and Eileen Southern's *The Music of Black Americans*. Michael Haralambos in *Right On: From Blues to Soul in Black America* convincingly discusses the demise of blues music in the city.

20. Oliver, *Meaning of the Blues,* p. 326.

21. For a more elaborate ethnography of this neighborhood, see Brett Williams, "The South in the City," *Journal of Popular Culture,* 16:2 Winter 1982.

22. See the Appendix for a telling interview with this man.

23. *Washington Post,* 1 November 1979, p. A29.

24. Norm Cohen reproduces Fiddlin' John Carson's text and tune on pp. 61-62 of *Long Steel Rail.*

25. Tony Russell, *Blacks, Whites, and Blues,* pp. 9, 10, 28.

26. Mary Lou Mulcahy, "John Henry," p. 9.

27. Although Bradford's novel and play appeared in the 1930s, as well as several tall tale collections, individual compositions and folksong anthologies, for the most part these were not self-consciously southern works. Nor was there a great surge in John Henry lore as in the 1960s. Of the Federal Writers' Project *American Guides,* dedicated to collecting and preserving local lore, none so much as mentions John Henry.

28. "Folk Heroes and Protest," *Appalachian South,* p. 26.

29. Cohen, *Long Steel Rail,* p. 72.

30. Ibid.

7
CHECKLIST OF PRINTED JOHN HENRY MATERIALS AND FILMS

This chapter assembles the written sources on John Henry, all of which have been explored more fully in previous chapters. I have also included a brief list of films, some of which have printed material accompanying them. For quick reference here, I have organized them into four categories: (1) *Cultural and Historical Background,* which includes materials ranging from discussions of the heroic tradition through musical criticism to historical and ethnographic works; (2) *Ballad Texts,* which includes all ballads except those appearing with very elaborate discussions of background information; (3) *Fiction, Poetry, and Drama,* which includes all examples of these literary works, as well as criticism and background on them; (4) *Films* and (5) *Sheet Music,* which is self-explanatory.

CULTURAL AND HISTORICAL BACKGROUND

Ambler, Charles Henry. *History of West Virginia.* New York: Prentice-Hall, 1933.

Asbell, Bernard. "A Man Ain't Nothin' but a Man." *American Heritage* 14 (1963): 34-37, 95.

Barry, Phillips. "Reviews." *Bulletin of the Folk Song Society of the Northeast* 8 (1934): 24-26.

Barton, William E. "Recent Negro Melodies." *New England Magazine* 19 (Feb. 1899). Reprinted as *Old Plantation Hymns.* Boston and New York: Lanson, Wolffe, 1899. Also reprinted in *The Negro and his Folklore in Nineteenth-Century Periodicals,* ed. by Bruce Jackson. Austin: University of Texas Press, 1967.

Benet, William Rose. *The Reader's Encyclopedia.* New York: Thomas Crowell Co., 1948. p. 495.

Botkin, Benjamin A. *Folk-Say: A Regional Miscellany.* Norman: University of Oklahoma Press, 1930.

———, ed. *A Treasury of American Folklore.* New York: Crown Publishers, 1944. pp. 230-40.

Bradford, Roark. *Ol' Man Adam an his Chillun; being the tales they tell about the time when the Lord walked the earth like a natural man.* New York and London: Harper and Bros., 1928.

———. "Paul Robeson is John Henry, and John Henry is Paul Robeson." *Colliers,* 13 January 1940, p. 15.

Bradley, William A. "Song-Ballets and Devil's Ditties." *Berea Quarterly* 18 (1915): 5-20.

Burchard, Hank. "In Quest of the Historical John Henry." *Washington Post Potomac Magazine,* 24 August 1969, pp. 11-16, 22-24.

Butcher, Margaret Just. *The Negro in American Culture.* New York: Alfred A. Knopf, 1972. p. 60.

Cabbell, Edward. "John Henry Memorial Foundation." *Long Journey Home: Folklife in the South. Southern Exposure* 5, nos. 2 and 3 (1977): 192.

Carmer, Carl. "American Folklore and Its Old-World Background." *Compton's Pictured Encyclopedia.* Chicago: F. E. Compton, 1950-1977.

Carpenter, Charles. "Folk-Song Gleanings Along the C & O." *West Virginia Review* 8 (1941): 368, 369, 382.

Center for Southern Folklore. *American Folklore Films and Videotapes: An Index.* Memphis: Center for Southern Folklore, 1976.

Chappell, Louis. *John Henry: A Folk-Lore Study.* 1933. Reprint. Port Washington, N.Y.: Kennikat Press, 1968.

———. "Review." *American Speech* 6 (1930): 144-46.

Clear Track. "John Henry: Muscle vs. Machine." Volume 5:9 (September 1981): 192, 201.

Coffin, Tristram, and Cohen, Hennig. *The Parade of Heroes.* Garden City, N.Y.: Anchor/Doubleday, 1978.

Cohen, Norm. *Long Steel Rail.* Urbana, Chicago and London: University of Illinois Press, 1981. pp. 61-89.

Connelly, Mark. *The Green Pastures.* New York: Farrar and Rinehart, 1929.

Cooke, Marion. "Tracking Down a Ghost." *Tracks* 29 (1944): 24-27.

Courlander, Harold. *Negro Folk Music USA.* New York: Columbia University Press, 1963.

Cox, John Harrington. "John Hardy." *Journal of American Folklore* 32 (Oct.-Dec. 1919): 505-20.

———. *Folk-Songs of the South.* Rpt., Hatboro, Pa.: Folklore Associates, 1963.

———. "The Yew-Pine Mountains." *American Speech* 2 (1927): 227.

Daniel, Pete. *The Shadow of Slavery: Peonage in the South, 1901-1969.* Urbana: University of Illinois Press, 1972.

Dickson, James. "Home Grown Hero." *Tracks* 40 (1955): 60-62.

Dorson, Richard. "The Career of John Henry." *Western Folklore* 24 (1965): 155-63. Reprinted in *Folklore and Fakelore,* edited by Richard Dorson. Cambridge: Harvard University Press, 1976.

———. "The Ballad of John Henry." In *An American Primer,* edited by Daniel Boorstin. Chicago: University of Chicago Press, 1966.

Drinker, Henry S. *Tunneling, Explosive Compounds and Rock Drills.* New York: John Wiley 1878.

Dundes, Alan, ed. *Mother Wit from the Laughing Barrel.* Englewood Cliffs, N.J.: Prentice-Hall, 1972.

Engineering Magazine, September 1892, p. 886.

Ferris, Bill. *Blues from the Delta.* Garden City, N. Y.: Anchor/Doubleday, 1978.

Fishwick, Marshall. "The John Henry Country." *Ford Times* 46 (1954): 50-51.

————· "Uncle Remus vs. John Henry: Folk Tension." *Western Folklore* 20 (1961): 77-85.

————, ed. *Remus, Rastus, and Revolution.* Bowling Green, Ohio: Popular Press, 1968.

————· "Where are Uncle Remus and John Henry?" *Journal of Regional Cultures* 1 (2): 117-22.

"Folk Heroes and Protest." *Appalachian South* 1 (1966): 26-27.

Foner, Philip. *Paul Robeson Speaks: Writings, Speeches, Interviews, 1918-1974.* Larchmont, N.Y.: Brunner/Mazel, 1978.

Foster, Holland. "A Sculptured Figure of John Henry, An American Legendary Character." Master's thesis, State University of Iowa, 1939.

Gerould, Gordon Hall. *The Ballad of Tradition.* Oxford, Eng.: Oxford University Press, 1932.

Glass, Paul. *Songs and Stories of Afro-Americans.* New York: Grosset and Dunlap, 1971.

Green, Archie. "Fred Becker's John Henry." *John Edwards Memorial Foundation Quarterly* 15 (1979): 30-37.

————· "John Henry Depicted." *John Edwards Memorial Foundation Quarterly* 14 (1978): 126-43.

————· *Only a Miner.* Urbana: University of Illinois Press, 1972.

Gutman, Herbert G. *The Black Family in Slavery and Freedom, 1750-1925.* New York: Pantheon Books, 1976.

Guthrie, Woody. "State Line to Skid Row." *Common Ground* (Autumn 1942): 35-44.

Haralambos, Michael. *Right On: From Blues to Soul in Black America.* London: Eddison Press, 1974.

Hare, Maud Cuney. *Negro Musicians and their Music.* 1936. Reprint. New York: DaCapo Press, 1974.

Haywood, Charles. *A Bibliography of North American Folklore and Folksongs.* New York: Dover Publications, 1951.

Hinton Daily News, 28 December 1972. "The Long Awaited John Henry Statue is Finally Erected."

Hollander, A.N.J. den. *Americana: studies uber mensen, dieren en een kaktus tussen Rio Grande den Potomac.* Amsterdam: J. A. Boom en Zoon Meppel Verzorging amslagheendeert Stotbergen, 1970.

Hull, Forrest. "C & O Tunnel is Folk Song Locale." *Charleston Daily Mail,* 9 November 1952.

Hurston, Zora Neale. "High John de Conquer." In *Mother Wit from the Laughing Barrel.* Edited by Alan Dundes. Englewood Cliffs, N.J.: Prentice-Hall, 1973.

Hylton, D. C. "Tony." "Medallion to Honor John Henry . . . The Steel Driving Man." *Wonderful West Virginia,* May 1976.

130   John Henry: A Bio-Bibliography

Johnson, Guy B. "John Henry: A Negro Legend." In *Ebony and Topaz, A Collectanea.* Edited by Charles S. Johnson. New York: National Urban League, 1927.

———. "John Henry: A Negro Legend." *Southern Workman* 56 (April 1927): 158-60.

———. *John Henry: Tracking Down a Negro Legend.* 1929. Reprint. New York: AMS Press, 1969.

Kilham, Elizabeth. "Sketches in Color." *Putnam's Magazine* 5 (1870): 31-38.

Langhorne, Orra. *Southern Sketches from Virginia.* Edited by Charles E. Wynes. Charlottesville: University Press of Virginia, 1964.

Lawless, Ray M. *Folksingers and Folksongs in America.* New York: Duell, Sloan and Pearce, 1960.

Laws, G. Malcolm, Jr. *Native American Balladry: A Descriptive Study and a Bibliographic Syllabus.* Rev. ed., Vol. 1. Philadelphia: Publications of the American Folklore Society, Bibliographical and Special Services. 1964. p. 246.

Leach, MacEdward. "John Henry." In *Folklore and Society.* Edited by Bruce Johnson. Hatboro, Pa.: Folklore Associates, 1966.

Leach, Maria, ed. *Funk and Wagnall's Standard Dictionary of Folklore, Mythology and Legend.* New York: Funk and Wagnalls, 3d ed. 1972.

Levine, Lawrence. *Black Culture and Black Consciousess.* New York: Oxford University Press, 1977.

Lewis, Ronald L. *Coal, Iron and Slaves.* Westport, Conn.: Greenwood Press, 1979.

Library of Congress Music Division. *Check-list of Recorded Songs in the English Language in the Archive of American Folksong to July 1940.* Washington, D.C., 1942.

Lloyd, A. L. "The Anatomy of John Henry." *Keynote* 2 (1947): 12-15.

Locke, Alain. *The Negro and his Music.* 1936. Reprint. New York: Arno Press and the New York Times, 1969.

Marx, Leo. *The Machine in the Garden.* New York: Oxford University Press, 1967.

Miller, James H. *History of Summers County, West Virginia.* Hinton, W.Va., 1908.

Miller, Jeffrey. "John Henry." *The Laborer* 27 (1973): 9-14. Reprinted in *Ring Like Silver, Shine Like Gold.* Washington, D.C.: Smithsonian, 1976.

Miller, Kurt. "Heroes Found in Song Texts from the Music of the United States." Ph.D. dissertation, University of Southern California, 1963.

Mitchell, Karen. "A Festival to Share Talents and Cultures." *Charleston Sunday Gazette-Mail,* 20 August 1978.

Morgantown (West Virginia) *Sunday Dominion Post Panorama Magazine.* "His Hammer Is Still But the Legend Goes On." 24 August 1974.

Mulcahy, Mary Lou. "John Henry." *Kentucky Folklore Record* 24 (1978): 6-9.

Murray, Robert. "John Henry and the Steam Drill." *Tracks* 37 (September 1952): 36-40.

Nash, Roderick. "Machines and Americans." In the *Study of American Culture: Contemporary Conflicts,* edited by Luther S. Luedke. Deland, Fla.: Everett/Edwards, 1977.

Nelson, James Poyntz. *The Chesapeake and Ohio Railway.* Richmond: Lewis Printing Co., 1927.

New York State Education Department, Bureau of Secondary Curriculum Development. *Tall Tales and Tunes: A Resource Unit for Junior High School English.* Albany, 1959.

Nordhoff, Charles. *New York Weekly Tribune,* 1 November 1871.

Oakley, Giles. *The Devil's Music.* New York: Taplinger Publishing Co., 1977.

Oliver, Paul. *The Meaning of the Blues.* New York: Collier Books, 1960. pp. 49-50, 246-47.

Porcello, Patricia. "The Railroad in American Literature: Poetry, Folk Song and Novel." Ph.D. dissertation, University of Michigan, 1968.

Pound, Louise. "Review." *Journal of American Folklore* 43 (1930): 126-27.

Puckett, Newbell Niles. "Names of American Negro Slaves." In *Mother Wit from the Laughing Barrel.* Edited by Alan Dundes. Englewood Cliffs, N.J.: Prentice-Hall, 1972.

Railroad Gazette. 2 April 1870; 15 June 1872; October 1872; 2 November 1872. p. 478.

Ray, Emrick. "John Henry: The Steel Drivin' Man." *Pathway Magazine* 2 (March 1971): 15-17.

Rosenberg, Bruce. *The Folksongs of Virginia: A Checklist of the WPA Holdings.* Alderman Library. University of Virginia. Charlottesville: University of Virginia Press, 1976.

Richmond Dispatch. 21 January 1871; 18 November 1871; 30 April 1872.

Russell, Tony. *Blacks, Whites and Blues.* New York: Stein and Day, 1970.

Sandstrom, Gosta. *Tunnels.* New York: Holt, Rinehart and Winston, 1963.

Santino, Jack. "The Folk Heroes of Occupational Groups." *1976 Festival of American Folklife.* Washington, D.C.: Smithsonian., 1976, pp. 35-38.

Sapp, Jane W. "A Bluesman and his Music: L. C. (Bunk) Pippens—Eutaw, Alabama." Montgomery: *Alabama Folklife Association Newsletter* 1 (July 1980): 15.

Scharnewski, Inge. "wer war eigentlich . . . John Henry?" *Country Corner* 8 (December 1973): 21-22.

Scardino, Albert. "Folk Hero's Memory Lives On. (John Henry)." Columbus, Ohio, *Dispatch,* 3 October 1971; "John Henry." Milwaukee *Journal,* Insight, 26 December 1971.

Southern, Eileen. *The Music of Black Americans.* New York: W. W. Norton, 1971.

Spottswood, Richard Keith. "A Catalog of American Folk Music on Commercial Recordings at the Library of Congress, 1925-1940." Master's thesis, Catholic University, 1962.

Steele, George. "John Henry Tall on Park Pedestal." Charleston *Gazette,* 29 December 1972.

Steele, Virginia. "Legends of John Henry." *Wonderful West Virginia,* October 1972, pp. 10, 11, 14; November 1972, pp. 18-19, 21, 29.

Washington Post, 1 November 1971. p. A29.

Weldon, Fred O. "Negro Folktale Heroes." In *And Horns on the Toad.* Edited by Mody Boatright. Publications of the Texas Folklore Society no. 29. Dallas: SMU Press [1959].

Wheeler, Mary. *Steamboatin' Days.* Freeport, N.Y.: Books for Libraries Press, 1969.

Wilgus, D. K. *Anglo-American Folksong Scholarship Since 1898.* New Brunswick: Rutgers University Press, 1959.

Williams, Brett: "The South in the City." *Journal of Popular Culture,* 16:2 Winter 1982.

Wimberly, Lowry Charles. "Steel-Drivin' Man. In *Folk-Say: A Regional Miscellany.* Edited by Benjamin A. Botkin. Norman: University of Oklahoma Press, 1930.

Wright, Charles H. *Robeson: Labor's Forgotten Champion.* Detroit: Belamp Publishing Co., 1975.

BALLAD TEXTS

Abrahams, Roger. *Deep Down in the Jungle.* Chicago: Aldine, 1963. pp. 74-75.
American Red Cross Youth News, February 1974, pp. 7-9.
America's Story in Song. Warner Bros. Publications, 1975. p. 80.
Ames, Russell. *The Story of American Folk Song.* New York: Grosset and Dunlap, 1960.
An Anthology of Ballads. Kansas City: Black, Sivalls and Bryson [1949], pp. 68-69.
Arnett, Hazel. *I Hear America Singing.* New York: Praeger Publishers, 1975. p. 111.
Asch, Moses and Lomax, Alan, eds. *The Leadbelly Songbook.* New York: Oak Publications, 1962.
Bascom, Louise Rand. "Ballads and Songs of Western North Carolina." *Journal of American Folklore* 22 (1909): 247-49.
Beckwith, Martha. *Black Roadways.* 1929. Reprint. New York: Negro Universities Press, 1969. p. 208.
Belafonte, Harold. *Songs Belafonte Sings.* New York: Duell, Sloan and Pearce, 1962. pp. 51-53.
Boette, Maria. *Singa Hipsy Doodle and Other Folk Songs of West Virginia.* Parsons, W.Va.: McClain Printing, 1971.
Boni, Margaret. *The Fireside Book of Folksongs.* New York: Simon and Schuster, 1952. pp. 170-71.
Botkin, Benjamin A. *A Treasury of Southern Folklore.* New York: Crown Publishers, 1949.
————, and Harlow, Alvin F. *A Treasury of Railroad Folklore.* New York: Bonanza Books, 1953. p. 402.
Brannon, Peter. *Railway Maintenance of Way Employees' Journal* 40 (September 1931): 13.
Brewer, Mason. *American Negro Folklore.* Chicago: Quadrangle Books, 1968. p. 202.
Brown, Frank C. *The Frank C. Brown Collection of North Carolina Folklore.* Edited by Newman I. White. Vol. 2, *Folk Ballads.* Edited by Henry M. Benden and Arthur P. Hudson, 1952. pp. 622, 624. Vol. 5, *The Music of the Songs.* Edited by Jan Philip Schinhan, 1962. p. 298. Durham, N.C.: Duke University Press.
Buckley, Bruce R. "Uncle Ira Cephas—A Negro Folk Singer in Ohio." *Midwest Folklore* 3 (1953): 5-18.
Burton, Thomas G., and Manning, Ambrose N. *Collection of Folklore: Folksongs.* Two volumes. Johnson City: East Tennessee State University, 1967, 1969.
Bush, Michael E. "Jim." *Folk Songs of Central West Virginia.* Ravenswood, W. Va.: Custom Printing, 1969. p. 53.
Carmer, Carl. *America Sings.* New York: Alfred A. Knopf, 1942. pp. 172-79.
————. *Stars Fell on Alabama.* 1934. Reprint. New York: Hill and Wang, 1961. p. 225.
Cazden, Norman. *American Folksongs for Piano.* Stamford, Conn.: Jack Spratt Music Co., 1962. p. 54.
Chappell, Louis. *Folksongs of Roanoke and the Albemarle.* Morgantown, W. Va.: Ballad Press, 1939. pp. 170-81.
Clark, Edgar Rogie. *Copper Sun.* Bryn Mawr, Pa.: Theodore Presser Co., 1957.

Clifton, Bill. *Old Time Folk and Gospel Songs.* North Wilkesboro, N.C.: Adams Printing and Calendar, 1956.

Combs, Josiah. *Folk Songs du Midi des Etats-Unis.* Paris: Les Presses Universitaires de France, 1925.

———· *Folk Songs of the Southern United States.* Edited by D. K. Wilgus. Austin: University of Texas Press, 1967. pp. 164-66.

Courlander, Harold. *Negro Songs from Alabama.* New York: Oak Publications, 1960.

———· *A Treasury of Afro-American Folklore.* New York: Crown Publishers, 1976.

Curtis-Burlin, Natalie. *Negro Folk Songs.* Hampton Series, Book 4. New York: G. Schirmer, 1919. pp. 22-27.

Davis, Arthur K. *Folk-Songs of Virginia.* Durham, N.C.: Duke University Press, 1949.

Davis, Henry. "Negro Folk-Lore in South Carolina." *Journal of American Folklore* 27 (1914): 241-54.

Downes, Olin, and Siegmeister, Elie. *A Treasury of American Song.* Rev. Ed. New York: Alfred A. Knopf, 1943. p. 312.

Duncan, Ruby. "Ballads and Folk Songs Collected in Northern Hamilton County." Master's thesis, University of Tennessee, 1939.

Eley, Robert M. "Ballad Set in Five Movements for Full Orchestra Based on Folk Songs of Ohio." Master's thesis, Ohio State University, 1954.

Emrich, Duncan. *American Folk Poetry.* Boston: Little, Brown and Co., 1974. pp. 657-59.

Ewen, David. *Songs of America.* Westport, Conn.: Greenwood Press, 1978. pp. 139-40.

(Florida) Statewide Recreation Project. *The Negro Sings.* Jacksonville, Fla.: 1940. pp. 11-16.

Fowke, Edith, and Glazer, Joe. *Songs of Work and Freedom.* 1960. Reprint. Garden City, N.Y.: Dolphin Books, 1961. p. 82.

Friedman, Albert B. *The Viking Book of Folk Ballads.* New York: The Viking Press, 1956. pp. 383-92.

Gainer, Patrick. *Folksongs from the West Virginia Hills.* Grantsville, W. Va.: Seneca Books, 1975. pp. 13, 112.

Glazer, Tom. *A New Treasury of Folk Songs.* New York: Bantam Books, 1964.

Gordon, Robert W. "Old Songs that Men Have Sung." *Adventure Magazine,* 20 April 1923, p. 191.

Grafman, Howard and Manning, B. T. *Folk Music USA.* New York: Citadel Press, 1962. pp. 106-7.

Greenell, Horace. *Young People's Records Folk Song Book.* New York: Young People's Records, 1949. p. 11.

Greenway, John. *American Folksongs of Protest.* New York: Octagon Books, 1970.

Handy, W. C. *Blues: An Anthology.* New York: Albert and Charles Boni, 1926. pp. 135-38.

———· *Treasury of the Blues.* New York: Charles Boni, 1949. pp. 203-6.

Haufrecht, Herbert. *Folk Sing.* New York: Hollis Music, 1959.

Haun, Mildred. "Cocke County Ballads and Songs." Master's thesis, Vanderbilt University, 1937.

Henry, Mellenger Edward. *Folk Songs from the Southern Highlands.* New York: J. J. Augustin, 1938. pp. 441-43.

Hille, Waldemar. *The People's Song Book.* New York: Boni and Geer, 1948. p. 8.

Hodgart, Matthew. *The Faber Book of Ballads.* 1965. Reprint. London: Faber and Faber, 1971. pp. 243-46.

Hubbard, Freeman. *Railroad Avenue.* New York: McGraw-Hill Book Co., 1945. pp. 58-64.

Hudson, Arthur P. *Specimens of Mississippi Folk-Lore.* Ann Arbor: Mississippi Folklore Society, 1928. p. 99.

Hurston, Zora Neale. *Mules and Men.* Philadelphia: J. B. Lippincott Co., 1935.

Ives, Burl. *Burl Ives Song Book.* New York: Ballentine Books, 1953.

————. *More Burl Ives Songs.* New York: Ballantine Books, 1966. pp. 112-15.

————. *Song in America.* New York: Duell, Sloan and Pearce, 1962. pp. 228-30.

Jackson, Bruce. *Wake Up Dead Man.* Cambridge: Harvard University Press, 1972. pp. 233-40.

Jahn, Jahnheinz. *Blues und Work Songs.* Hamburg: Fischer Bychere, 1964. pp. 81-83.

Jekyll, Walter. *Jamaican Song and Story.* New York: Dover Publications, 1966. pp. 199, 268-69.

Johnson, Charles S. *Ebony and Topaz, A Collectanea.* New York: National Urban League, 1927.

Johnson, John Rosamund. *Rolling Along in Song.* New York: Viking Press, 1937. pp. 180-82.

Kittredge, G. L. "Various Ballads." *Journal of American Folklore* 26 (1913): 174-82.

Kolb, Sylvia, and Kolb, John. *A Treasury of Folk Songs.* New York: Bantam Books, 1948. p. 46.

Krehbiel, Henry. *Afro-American Folk Songs.* New York: F. Ungar Publishing Co., 1962.

Landeck, Beatrice. *Git on Board.* Rev. Ed. New York: E. B. Marks, 1950. pp. 46-47.

Leach, MacEdward. *The Ballad Book.* New York: A. S. Barnes, 1955.

————, and Beck, Horace P. "Songs from Rappahannock County, Virginia." *Journal of American Folklore* 63 (1950): 257.

Leisy, James. *The Folk Song Abecedary.* New York: Hawthorne Books, 1966. pp. 189-91.

Life Treasury of American Folklore. New York: Time, 1961.

Lomax, Alan. *The Folk Songs of North America.* London: Cassell & Co., 1960. pp. 551-53, 560-64.

Lomax, John A. "Some Types of American Folk Song." *Journal of American Folklore* 28 (1915): 1-17.

————, and Lomax, Alan. *American Ballads and Folk Songs.* New York: Macmillan Co., 1934. pp. 3-10.

————. *Best Loved American Folk Songs.* New York: Grosset and Dunlap, 1955.

————. *Folksong USA.* New York: New American Library, 1947. pp. 330-35.

————. *Our Singing Country.* New York: Macmillan Co., 1941. pp. 258-61.

Longini, Muriel. "Folk Songs of Chicago Negroes." *Journal of American Folklore* 52 (1939): 96-111.

Luboff, Norman, and Strache, William. *Songs of Man.* Englewood Cliffs, N.J.: Prentice-Hall, 1965. p. 208.

Lumsford, Bascom, and Stringfield, Lamar. *Thirty-One Songs.* New York: Carl Fisher, 1929. p. 32.

McPherson, James Alan, and Williams, Miller. *Railroad.* New York: Random House, 1976. p. 75.

Mason, Robert. "Folk Songs and Folk Tales of Cannon County Tennessee." Master's thesis, George Peabody College for Teachers, 1939. pp. 104-5.

Maurer, B. B. *Mountain Heritage.* Morgantown, W. Va.: Morgantown Printing and Binding Co., 1974. p. 242.

Moore, Dash. *John Henry and Some Other Stuff.* Mimeographed pamphlet. Avon Park, Fla., 1965.

Morehead, James. *Best Loved Songs.* Cleveland: World Publishing Co., 1965. pp. 172-73.

Morris, Alton. *Folksongs of Florida.* University of Florida Press, 1950. p. 182.

Morse, Jim. *The Dell Book of Great American Folk Songs.* New York: Dell, 1963. pp. 147-49.

Mursell, J. L. *Music Around the World. Music for Living, Grade 5.* Morristown, N.J.: Silver Burdett, 1956. p. 144.

Music Educators' National Conference. *American Songs for American Children.* Chicago, 1942. pp. 13-15.

Odell, Mac. *Radio Song Book.* N.P. [1949].

Odum, Howard, and Johnson, Guy B. *The Negro and His Songs.* 1935. Reprint. New York: Negro Universities Press, 1968.

——. *Negro Workaday Songs.* 1926. Reprint. New York: Negro Universities Press, 1969.

Okun, Milt. *Something to Sing About.* New York: Macmillan, 1968. pp. 78-79.

Perrow, E. C. "Songs and Rhymes from the South." *Journal of American Folklore* 26 (1913): 123-73.

Pooley, Robert; Pooley, Irwin; Leyda, Jean Cravens; Zellhoffer, Lillian; and Gray, William S. *America Reads: Good Times Through Literature.* Chicago: Scott, Foresman and Co., 1951. p. 532.

Poulakis, Peter. *American Folklore.* New York: Charles Scribner's Sons, 1969. pp. 200-4.

Ritchie, Jean. *Singing Family of the Cumberlands.* New York: Oxford University Press, 1955.

Sackheim, Eric. *The Blues Line.* New York: Grossman Publishers, 1969, p. 226.

Sandburg, Carl. *An American Songbag.* New York: Harcourt, Brace & Co., 1927. pp. 24, 362, 376.

——. "Songs of Old Frontiers," *Country Gentlemen,* April 1927, p. 134.

Scarborough, Dorothy. *On the Trail of Negro Folk-Song.* 1925. Reprint. Hatboro, Pa.: Folklore Associates, 1965. pp. 218-22.

Scott, Tom. *Sing of America.* New York: Thomas Y. Crowell, 1947. p. 16.

Seeger, Pete. *American Favorite Ballads: Tunes and Songs Sung by Pete Seeger.* Edited by Ethel Raim and Irwin Silber. New York: Oak Publications, 1961. p. 82.

Seeger, Ruth Crawford. *American Folk Songs for Children.* Garden City, N.Y.: Doubleday and Co., 1948.

Shearin, Hubert, and Combs, Josiah. *A Syllabus of Kentucky Folk-Songs.* Lexington: Transylvania Printing Co., 1911.

Sherwin, Sterling, and McClintock, Harry. *Railroad Songs of Yesterday.* New York: Shapiro-Bernstein, 1933. p. 12.

Siegmeister, Elie. *Work and Sing.* New York: William R. Scott, 1944.

Silber, Fred, and Silber, Irwin. *Folksinger's Workbook.* New York: Oak Publications, 1973. p. 123.

    rwin. *Folksong Festival.* New York: Scholastic Book Services, 1967. p. 22.

_____. *This Singing Land.* New York: Amsco Music Publishing Company, 1965. p. 79.

Silverman, Jerry. *The Back Packer's Song Book.* New York: G. Schirmer, 1977. p. 13.

_____. *Folk Harmonica.* Chappell Music, 1974. p. 58.

_____. *The Folksinger's Guitar Guide.* New York: Oak Publications, 1964.

_____. *Folk Song Encyclopedia.* Vol. 2. New York: Chappell Music, 1975. p. 414-15.

Spalding, Henry D. *Encyclopedia of Black Folklore and Humor.* Middle Village, N.Y.: Jonathan David Publishers, 1972.

Stuart, Forbes. *A Medley of Folk-Songs.* London: Longman Young Books, 1971. pp. 53-57.

Talley, Thomas W. *Negro Folk Rhymes.* New York: Macmillan Co., 1922. p. 105.

Their Weight in Wildcats: Tales of the Frontier. Boston: Houghton Mifflin, 1936. p. 136.

von Schmidt, Eric. *Come for to Sing.* Boston: Houghton Mifflin; Cambridge: Riverside Press, 1963. p. 16.

Wagenheim, Harold; Dolkey, Matthew; and Kobler, Donald. *Our Reading Heritage. Volume 5. This is America.* New York: Holt, Rinehart and Winston, 1963. p. 477.

White, Josh. *The Josh White Song Book.* Chicago: Quadrangle Books, 1963.

White, Newman I. *American Negro Folk-Songs.* 1928. Reprint. Hatboro, Pa.: Folklore Associates, 1965. pp. 189-91.

Whitman, Wanda. *Songs that Changed the World.* New York: Crown Publishers, 1970. p. 65-66.

Williams, Cratis. *Ballads and Songs.* Lexington, Ky.: Southern Atlantic Modern Language Association, 1937. p. 327.

Wolfe, Irving; Krone, Beatrice; and Fullerton, Margaret. *Proudly We Sing. Together We Sing Series, Grade 8.* Chicago: Follett Publishing, 1956. p. 62.

Work, John W. *American Negro Songs and Spirituals.* New York: Bonanza Books, 1940. p. 242.

FICTION, POETRY, AND DRAMA

Blair, Walter. *Tall Tale America.* New York: Coward-McCann & Geoghegan, 1944.

Blassingame, Wyatt. *John Henry and Paul Bunyan Play Baseball.* Champaign, Ill.: Garrard, 1971.

Bowman, James Cloyd. *John Henry: The Rambling Black Ulysses.* Chicago: Albert Whitman Co., 1942.

Bradford, Roark. "The Adventures of John Henry." *Hearsts International-Cosmopolitan* 39, no. 12 (December 1930): 32; 90, no. 1 (January 1931): 72; 90, no. 3 (March 1931): 56; 90, no. 4 (April 1931): 82.

_____. *John Henry.* New York: Harper and Bros., 1931.

_____. *John Henry* (The play). New York and London: Harper and Bros., 1939.

Brown, Sterling Allen. *The Collected Poems of Sterling Brown.* Selected by Michael S. Harper. New York: Harper & Row, 1980. pp. 86-87.

Burrer, Eileen. "John Henry: A Negro Folk Play Based on the Novel by Roark Bradford." Master's thesis, Ohio University, 1951.

Carmer, Carl. *The Hurricane's Children.* New York: Farrar and Rinehart, 1937. pp. 122-28.

DeLeeuw, Adele. *John Henry: Steel-Drivin' Man.* Champaign, Ill.: Garrard, 1966.

Felton, Harold W. *John Henry and His Hammer.* New York: Alfred A. Knopf, 1950.

Flanagan, John T., and Hudson, Arthur P. *Folklore in American Literature.* Evanston, Ill.: Row, Peterson, 1958. pp. 354-55.

Folsom, Franklin [Michael Gorham]. *The Real Book of American Tall Tales.* Garden City, N.Y.: Garden City Books, 1952. pp. 106-17.

Harris, Leon. "That Steel Drivin' Man." *The Phylon Quarterly* 18 (1957).

Harris, Leon. "The Steel-Drivin' Man." In *Mother Wit from the Laughing Barrel.* Edited by Alan Dundes. Englewood Cliffs, N.J.: Prentice-Hall, 1973.

Hendricks, W. C., ed. *Bundle of Troubles and Other Tarheel Tales.* "John Henry and the Cape of Fear" (as told by Glasgow McLeod to T. Pat Matthews). Durham, N.C.: Duke University Press, 1943. pp. 37-51.

Johnson, Eloise Lisle. "Stout Hearts A-Singin' with Freedom." Master's thesis, Ohio State University, 1947.

Johnson, Guy B. "A Mighty Legend." *The Nation.* 7 October 1931. p. 367.

Junior Scholastic 29 (17 October 1951): 28-29.

Keats, Ezra. *John Henry: An American Legend.* New York: Pantheon Books, 1965.

Killens, John Oliver. *A Man Ain't Nothin' but a Man.* Boston: Little, Brown and Co., 1975.

Leach, Maria. *The Rainbow Book of American Folktales and Legends.* Cleveland and New York: World Publishing, 1958.

Lee, Hector, and Robertson, Donald. *Lore of Our Land.* Evanston, Ill.: Harper & Row, 1963. pp. 62-65.

McCaslin, Nellie. *Tall Tales and Tall Men.* Philadelphia: Macrae Smith Co., 1956.

Malcolmson, Anne. *Yankee Doodle's Cousins.* Boston: Houghton Mifflin, 1941. pp. 101-8.

Miller, Olive B. *Heroes, Outlaws and Funny Fellows of American Popular Tales.* New York: Doubleday Doran, 1939.

New Yorker. 20 January 1940. p. 30.

Open Highways, Book 5. Chicago: Scott, Foresman and Co., 1966.

Schneider, Alice. *Tales of Many Lands.* New York: Citadel, 1946.

Shapiro, Irwin. *Heroes in American Folklore.* New York: Julian Messner, 1962.

———. *John Henry and the Double-Jointed Steam Drill.* New York: Julian Messner, 1945.

———. *Tall Tales of America.* Poughkeepsie, N.Y.: Guild Press, 1958. pp. 97-110.

Shay, Frank. *Here's Audacity!* Freeport, N.Y.: Books for Libraries Press, 1930. pp. 247-53.

———. "The Tall Tale in America." In *Folk-Say: A Regional Miscellany.* Edited by Benjamin A. Botkin. Norman: University of Oklahoma Press, 1930. pp. 182-85.

Stein, R. Conrad. *Steel Driving Man: The Legend of John Henry.* Chicago: Children's Press, 1969.

Stoutenberg, Adrien. *American Tall Tales.* New York: Viking Press, 1966. pp. 88-100.

Theatre Arts 24 (January 1940): 166-67.

Time. 22 January 1940. p. 49.

Walker, Margaret. *For My People.* New Haven: Yale University Press, 1942. p. 49.

FILMS

There are a number of excellent films and filmstrips available, most of them intended for classroom use. I have not seen any of those listed below, but I have provided information from the distributors. I am also indebted to resource materials published by the New York State Department of Education, the Center for Southern Folklore (*American Folklore Films and Videotapes: An Index*), and Archie Green, for many of the titles and descriptions I was able to gather.

(no date)   *Three American Ballads.* 8 minutes, color. Humorous sketches illustrate the singing of "Acres of Clams," "Old Dan Tucker," and "John Henry." Distributed by UCLA. Educational Film Sales Department; Los Angeles, California 90007 (213-825-4321).

(no date)   American Folklore Heroes Series filmstrips, including Paul Bunyan, Joe Magarac, Johnny Inkslinger, Febold Feboldson, Mose Humphreys, Pecos Bill, Johnny Appleseed, Hiawatha, Davy Crockett and John Henry. Distributed by Visual Education Consultants, 2066 Helena Street, Middleton, Wisconsin 53562 (608-831-6565).

1941.   *Tall Tales.* 10 minutes, black and white. Singers Burl Ives, Winston O'Keefe, and Josh White present "Grey Goose," "Strawberry Roan," and "John Henry." Will Geer narrates. Setting is farmhouse yard just after the noonday meal. Singers play horseshoes and sing ballads before returning to work. Produced by Willard Van Dyke and Irving Lerner. Distributed by Audio Brandon Films, Inc., 34 MacQuesten Parkway S., Mt. Vernon, New York 10550 (914-664-5051).

1946.   *John Henry and the Inky-Foo.* Directed by George Pol with Latham Owens and Robert Monroe. One reel. Paramount Pictures. Distributed by Paramount Oxford Films, 5451 Marathon Street, Hollywood, California 90038 (213-463-0100).

1967.   *John Henry: An American Legend.* 35 mm filmstrip, part of ten feature multimedia kit "Folktales Around the World." With one 33 rpm mound disc or one cassette. Distributed by Guidance Associates, Communications Park, Box 3000, Mt. Kisco, New York 10549 (914-666-4100). Order # 2-7246.

1969.   *American Folklore: John Henry.* 35 mm filmstrip, 11 minutes, 47 frames in color. One 12″ 33 rpm sound disc. Distributed by Coronet Instructional Media, 65 E. South Water Street,

Chicago, Illinois 60601 (312-332-7676). Order # 3102 with user's guide. For elementary grades.

1969.   *Tall Tales of America, Look, Listen and Learn: John Henry.* 35 mm filmstrip, 51 frames in color. Distributed by Joshua Tree Productions.

1970.   *John Henry and his Mighty Hammer.* 35 mm filmstrip, 42 frames. Distributed by Troll Associates, Mahwah, New Jersey 07430 (201-529-4000). Available only to teachers and librarians.

1970.   *Children's Folk Tales: John Henry.* 35 mm filmstrip, 42 frames in color. Distributed by Milliken Publishing Company, 1100 Research Blvd., St. Louis, Missouri 63132 (314-991-4220). Order # FSC 30 (with cassette); FSR 30 (with record). With teacher's guide.

1972.   *John Henry.* 16 mm, 11 minutes, color. Produced by Jerry Weiss/BFA Educational Media, from the American Folklore Series. Distributed by BFA Educational Media, 2211 Michigan Avenue, P.O. Box 1795, Santa Monica, California 90406 (213-829-2901). Order # 11478.

1974.   *American Tall Tale Heroes.* 16 mm, 15 minutes in color. Animamation brings to life legendary deeds of four heroes: Old Stormalong, Paul Bunyan, John Henry, and Pecos Bill. Produced and distributed by Coronet Instructional Media. Order #3671. Purchase only.

1974.   *The Legend of John Henry.* 16 mm, 11 minutes, color. Animation. Narrated and sung by Roberta Flack. Produced by Pyramid Films and Stephen Bosustow. Distributed by Pyramid Films, P.O. Box 1048, Santa Monica, California 90406 (213-828-7579).

1974.   *The Legend of John Henry.* 35 mm filmstrip, 113 frames in color. 2 phonodiscs (2 sides each) 12", 33 rpm. 21 minutes. Adapted from Pyramid Film by Stephen Bosustow. Stephen Bosustow Productions. Directed by Sam Weiss. Music by Tom McIntosh. With teacher's guide.

SHEET MUSIC

Atkins, Chet. "John Henry." Nashville: Athens Music Co., 1962.
Bradford, Roark and Wolfe, Jacques. "Careless Love." New York: Chappell, 1939.
——— · "Got a Head like a Rock." New York: Chappell, 1939.
———. "I've Trampled All Over." New York: Chappell, 1939.
———. "Sundown in my Soul." New York: Chappell, 1940.

Brookhart, Edward. "John Henry." East Stroudsburg, Pa.: Shawnee Press, 1950.

Cavella, Joe, and McIntosh, Tom. "John Henry." ToMac Music, 1973.

Copland, Aaron. "John Henry." London: Boosey and Hawkes, 1953.

Dudley, Dave. "John Henry." Circle Dot Publishing Co., 1963.

Donnegan, Lonnie. "John Henry." Essex Music, 1956.

Ehret, Walter. "John Henry." Richmond, Ind.: Richmond Music Press, 1974.

Gordon, Philip. "John Henry (Folksong Fantasy for Band)." Bryn Mawr, Pa.: Theodore Presser Co., 1957.

Kerr, Anita. "John Henry." Hollywood: Poker Music, 1963.

Kubick, Gail. "John Henry: American Folk Song Sketch." New York: G. Ricordi and Co., 1960.

Lee, Jeanie. "John Henry's Woman." Afton Music Publishing Co., 1962.

McLin, Edward. "John Henry." Melville, New York: Pro Art Publications, 1966.

Miller, Carl. "John Henry." New York: Chappell and Co., 1973.

Mosley, Snub; Jaffee, Moe; and Drezners, Henry. "John Henry." New York: David Gornston, 1952.

Musser, Benjamin, and Cohen, Charlie. "The Ballad of John Henry." New York: Galaxy Music Corporation, 1935.

O'Neil, Mattie. "John Henry Blues." New York: Mills Music, 1950.

Ostrus, Merrill, and Leyden, James. "John Henry." New York: Carl Fischer, Inc., 1959.

Seeger, Charles. "Three American Folksongs: John Riley, Wayfaring Stranger, John Henry for Solo Voice and Orchestra." Washington, D.C., 1937.

Siegmeister, Elie. "John Henry: An American Saga." New York: Carl Fischer, 1938.

Singleton, Margie. "John Henry's Surf." Nashville: Raleigh Music, 1963.

Stone, Leonard. "John Henry." Rockville Center, N.Y.: Belvin, 1965.

Triplett, Jack. "John Henry, Junior." Nashville: Blalon Music, 1965.

Winkler, Ray, and Hathcock, John. "John Henry's Girl." New York: Painted Desert Music Corp., 1964.

Wood, Sue, and Wood, Lionel. "John Henry." Winona, Minn.: Hal Leonard Music, 1959.

Work, John. "This Ol' Hammer (Killed John Henry)." New York: Galaxy Music Corp., 1933.

8

DISCOGRAPHY

The rich and extensive recorded versions of the John Henry ballad and hammer songs appear in this last chapter. The Discography has been divided into two parts. The first section contains the commercially recorded songs; the second section catalogs the collection of tape recordings available in the Archive of Folk Song at the Library of Congress. The selections in Part I are listed alphabetically by artist. Immediately following the artist's name is the name of the record company producing the record, then the record's release number. Two release numbers indicate that the record was issued twice, most often in mono and stereo versions. Some albums do not have titles, but most do: these titles are italicized and follow the release numbers. A further title appearing in quotes indicates that the John Henry song appears under a unique title which sometimes disguises it. Some artists have recorded many John Henry songs, and these appear as indented lists under those artists' names. All records are 33 rpm unless otherwise indicated.

The selections in Part 2 are also listed alphabetically by artist. Following the artist's name is information concerning where the song was recorded and the date of the recording session. The numbers appearing under each selection are the Archive's catalog numbers. Occasionally additional information appears where special remarks about the accompanying instruments or unique features such as extended commentary may be of interest.

COMMERCIAL RECORDINGS

Amerson, Rich. Folkways FE 4471: *Negro Folk Music of Alabama: Rich Amerson Volume I.*
Ames, Ed. RCA Victor LSP 3460: *It's a Man's World.*
Anderson, Pink. Riverside RLP 12-611: *American Street Songs.*
Atkins, Chet. RCA Victor LPM/LSP-2025: *Hum and Strum Along with Chet Atkins.*

RCA Victor EPA 4343 (45 rpm).

Atkins, Chet, and Reed, Jerry. RCA Victor CPL2-1014: *In Concert.*
Axton, Hoyt. Vee-Jay 1601: *Greenback Dollar.*

Bailey, Bill. Mercury 70080.
Bailey, De Ford. Victor 23336.

Victor 23831.

Herwin 201: *Sic em Dogs on me.*

Bailey Brothers. Rich-R-Tone 449.

Rounder 1018: *Have you Forgotten the Bailey Brothers?*

Baker, Etta. Tradition TLP 1007: *Instrumental Music of the Southern Appalachians.*
Baker, James "Ironhead." Library of Congress Archive of Folksong L53: *The Ballad Hunter,* Part X, "Little John Henry."
Baker, Kenny and Graves, Josh. Puritan 5005: *Bucktime!*
Barber, Chris. Everest 224: *Chris Barber.*
Barber, Chris, and his Jazz Band. Decca (England) ACL 1037: *The Best of Chris Barber.*
Belafonte, Harry. RCA Victor LPM/LSP 1022: *Mark Twain and Other Folk Favorites.*

RCA Victor LPC/LSO 6006: *Belafonte at Carnegie Hall.*

Bell, Arthur. Library of Congress Archive of Folksong L3: *Afro-American Spirituals, Work Songs, and Ballads.*

Library of Congress Archive of Folksong L50: *The Ballad Hunter, Part IV.*

Bibb, Leon. Vanguard VRS 9058: "Tol' My Captain. 'This is the Hammer that Killed John Henry.'"
Birmingham Jug Band. OKeh 8895.

RBF RF6: *The Jug Band's Bill Wilson*

Blind Thomas. Fonotone 611. (78 rpm).
Bluegrass Pals. Shawnee LPS3: *Best of Bluegrass.*
Blue Haze Folk Band. Ranwood 8132: *The Blue Haze Folk Band.*
Blueridge Mountain Boys. Time 52083/2083: *Hootenanny and Bluegrass.*
Blueridge Partners. GHP (West Germany) 901: *Mountain Folks.*
Boggs, Dock. Folkways FA 2392: *Dock Boggs, Volume II.*
Border Mountain Boys. Homestead 101: *Bluegrass on the Mountain.*
Bray Brothers and Red Cravens. Rounder 0053: *Prairie Bluegrass.*
Brazos Valley Boys. Dot 10004: *The Brazos Valley Boys.*
Bridges, Lucius, Eaglin, Blind Snooks, and Randolph, Percy. Folk Lyric FL 107: *Possum up a Simmon Tree.*
Brill, Marty. Mercury MG 20178: *The Roving Balladeer.*

Broonzy, Big Bill. Mercury MG 20822/SR60822: *Big Bill Broonzy Memorial.*

> Emarcy MG26034: *Folk Blues.*
>
> Emarcy EM 36052: *Jazz Giants,* Volume 4, *Folk Blues.*
>
> Folkways FS 3864 (FP 86/4): *Folksongs and Blues with Pete Seeger and Big Bill Broonzy.*
>
> Folkways SA 2328: *Big Bill Broonzy Sings Folksongs.*
>
> Verve MGV-3000-5: *The Big Bill Broonzy Story.*
>
> Verve MGV-3003: *Big Bill Broonzy's Last Session.* Storyville (Denmark) SLP 154: *Portraits in Blues,* Volume 2.
>
> Storyville SEP 383.
>
> Vogue (France) 118 (45 rpm).
>
> Vogue LDM 30037: *Big Bill Blues.*
>
> Vogue LD 524.
>
> Vogue CLVX 272: *Big Bill Broonzy.*
>
> Crescendo GNPS 10009: *Lonesome Road Blues.*
>
> Scepter M/S 529: *The Blues.*
>
> Joker SM 3608: *Blues/Folk Songs/Ballads.*
>
> DJM DJLMD 8009: *All Them Blues.*

Brown, Buster. Fire 1020. (45 and 78 rpm).

> Fire FLP 102.

Brown, Don, and the Ozark Mountain Trio. K-Ark 6027: *Don Brown Live.*
Brown, Fleming. Folk Legacy FSI-4: *Fleming Brown.*
Brown, Gabriel, French, Rochelle, and French, John. *Fly Right Match Box* SDM 257: *Out in the Cold Again:* Library of Congress series, Volume 3 (from LCAFS 335).
Brown, Hylo. Rural Rhythm RR176: *Hylo Brown.*

> Capitol F4035. (45 rpm).
>
> CMH (West Germany) 301: *Four Sessions.*
>
> Jessup, Michigan Bluegrass MB134: *Hylo Brown Sings his Bluegrass Hits.*

Brown, Walt. Warner Brothers W/WS 1568: *Walt Brown Show.*
Buckley, Bruce. Folkways FA 2025 (FP23-2): *Ohio Valley Band Ballads.*

Caffrey Family. TCAF 1075: *Country Thoughts.*
Callahan Brothers. Decca 5998.

> MCA (Japan) 3013-17: *The Fifty Year History of Country Music.*
>
> Old Homestead OHM 90031: *The Callahan Brothers.*

Campbell, James, and his Nashville Street Band. Arhoolie F 1015: *Blind James Campbell.*
Carson, Fiddlin' John. OKeh 7004. "John Henry Blues." (12" 78 rpm).
Cash, Johnny. Columbia CL-1930/CS-8370: *Blood Sweat and Tears.*

    Philips (England) CBS-BPG-62015: *Blood Sweat and Tears.*

    Columbia GP 29: *The World of Johnny Cash.*

Chapman, Bob. Scholastic CC-0630: *Train Ballads.* (7" LP).
Chicago String Band. Testament T-2220: *The Chicago String Band.*
Clauson, William. Capitol T-10159: A William Clauson Concert.

    RCA Victor LPM 1286: *Folk Songs.*

Clayton, Paul. Folkways FG 3571: *Dulcimer Songs and Solos.*
Clifton, Bill. Hillbilly (Switzerland) HRS-001: *Wanderin'.*
Clifton, Bill, and Clayton, Paul. *Bear Family* (West Germany).

    15001: *A Bluegrass Session* 1952.

Cooney, Michael. Folk-Legacy FSI-35: *The Cheese Stands Alone.*
Cravens, Red, and the Bray Brothers. *Five String 101.* (45 rpm).
Creed, Kyle, and Cockerham, Fred. County 701: *Clawhammer Banjo.*
Creswell, Grace. Rebel RRLP 3064: *Grace Creswell.*
Crook Brothers. Starday SLP 182: *Opry Old Timers.*

    Starday SLP 190: *Country Music Hall of Fame,* Volume 2.

Darby, Blind Blues. Decca 7816: *Spike Driver.*
Davis, Jean. Traditional 5117: *Old Traditions.*
Dickens, Hazel, and Foster, Alice. Folkways FTS 31034: *Won't You Come and Sing for Me?*
Dixieland Jazz Group.
Donegan, Lonnie. London 1650 (78 rpm).

    London 1650 (45 rpm).

Dyer-Bennett, Richard. Asch 4613.

    Asch-Stinson 461.

    Stinson SLP 35: *Ballads.*

    Remington 199-34: *Folk Songs.*

    Dyer-Bennett 5: *Requests.*

    Archive of Folk Music AFM 203: *Richard Dyer-Bennett.*

Easy Riders. Columbia CL1272.

Columbia Special Products CSP 123.

Eddy, Duane. Jamboree J/ST-3011: *Duane Eddy Plays Songs of Heritage.*

   Jamboree J/ST:-3021: *Million Dollars Worth of Twang.*

Edwards, Jimmy. Kanawha 319.
Edwards, Joe. Delmarti 102565.
Elliott, Jack. Everest Archive of Folk Music AFM/FS 210: *Jack Elliott* "Death of John Henry."
Emerson, Bill and His Virginia Mountaineers. Coronet CX-118: *Banjo Pickin 'n Hot Fiddlin.*
Eskin, Sam. Cook 1020: *Songs of All Times.*

Fahey, John. Takoma C 1002: Blind Joe Death.

   Takoma C 1003: *Death Chants, Breakdowns, and Military Waltzes.*

Fairchild, Raymond. Rural Rhythms RR: 256: *King of the Smokey Mt. Banjo Players.*
Faye, Frances. Bethlehem BCP-6017: *Frances Faye Sings Folk Songs.*
Flatt, Lester; Scruggs, Earl; and the Foggy Mountain Boys.

   Columbia CL 1564)CS 8364 and LE 10043: *Foggy Mountain Banjo.*

   Columbia GP 30: *20 All-Time Great Recordings.*

   Columbia KG 31964: *The World of Flatt and Scruggs.*

Fochtman, Orval. Weiser 19884: *National Oldtime Fiddlers' Folk Music Contest and Festival.*
Folk Singers of Washington Square. Continental CLP-4010: *The Folk Singers of Washington Square.* "Brooklyn John Henry."
Folksmiths. Folkways FA 2407: *We've Got Some Singin' To Do.*
Ford, Tennessee Ernie. Capitol 3421: Capitol T/DT 700. *This Lusty Land.*
Frosty Mountain Boys. Rural Rhythms RRFM-159: *Frosty Mountain Boys.*
Fruit Jar Guzzlers. Paramount 3121, Broadway 8190. "Steel Drivin' Man."
Fuller, Jesse. Good Time Jazz 12051/S10051: *San Francisco Bay Blues.*

   World Song EG-10-021: *Working on the Railroad.*

   World Song WS-1.

   Decca (England) LAG 574.

   Topic (England) 12134: *Move on Down the Line.*

Garner, Marty. Stoneways STY-167: *On the Rural Route.*
Gibbs, Terry. Time 52105/S 2105: *Hootenanny My Way.*
Gibson, Bob. Riverside RLP 12-806: *I Come for to Sing.*

   Elektra EKL/EKS 7-197: *Yes I See.*

Gibson, Bob, and Camp, Bob. EKL/EKS 7-207: *Bob Gibson and Bob Camp at the Gate of Horn.*

Glazer, Joe. Collector 1918: *Joe Glazer Sings Labor Songs.*

Gray, Arvella. Heritage HLP 1004: *Railroad Songs and John Henry.*

  Birch 60091: *The Singing Drifter.*

  Gray 14.

Greenway John. Wattle (Australia) C1: *Workin on a Buildin.* (10" LP).

Grossman, Bob. Elektra EKL-215: *Bob Grossman.* "Legend of John Henry."

Guthrie, Woody. Tradition 2058: *The Legendary Woody Guthrie—In Memoriam.*

  Sine Qua Non 102: *An Anthology of Folk Music.*

Guthrie, Woody, and Cisco Houston. Stinson 627.

  Stinson SLP 44: Folk Songs, Vol. 1.

  Everest Archive of Folk Music FS-204: *Woody Guthrie Sings Folk Songs with &c.*

  Olympic 7107: *The Immortal Woody Guthrie.*

Hank and Delma and the Dakota Ramblers. FM 461-M.

Haywood, Charles. Charles Haywood: *Program of Songs from the Library of Marian and Allan Hancock.*

Hopkins, Al, and the Buckle Busters. Brunswick 177-A.

Hopkins, Doc. Radio 1411.

  Birch 1945: *Doc Hopkins.*

Horton, Shakey. Argo 4037: *Soul of Blues Harmonica.*

Houston, Cisco. Verve/Folkways FV/FVS 9002: *Passing Through.*

Hovington, Frank. Rounder 2017: *Lonesome Road Blues.*

Howell, Peg Leg. Testament T-2204: *The Legendary Peg Leg Howell.*

Hunter, Max. Folk Legacy FSA-11: *Max Hunter of Springfield, Missouri.*

Hurt, Mississippi John. OKeh 8692.

  Folkways FA 2953 (FP 253): *Anthology of American Folk Music.*

  Biograph BLP-C4: 1928: *His First Recordings.* "Spike Driver Blues."

  Piedmont PLP 13157: *Folksongs and Blues.* "Spike Driver Blues."

  Vanguard VRS 9148/VSD 79220: *Mississippi John Hurt Today.* "Spike Driver Blues."

Ives, Burl. Columbia 38733.

  Columbia (Australia) DO 3484.

  Columbia CL 1459: *Return of the Wayfaring Stranger.*

Decca DC 8125: *Men.*

Decca ED-2237: *Men.*

Decca DXB/DXSB7-167: *Best of Burl Ives.*

Brunswick (England) OE 9202.

Ace of Hearts (England) AH 53: *Men.*

Pickwick SPC 3393: *The Best of Burl Ives.*

Jackson, Carl. Capitol ST 11166: *Banjo Player.*

"James Louis Henry (Brother of John)."

Jackson, Clarence; Frye, Charles; Slack, Johnny; and Horney, Bill.

Rural Rhythm RR-132: *Blue Grass Special.*

Jackson, John. Arhoolie 1025: *Blues and Country Dance Tunes from Virginia.*
Jackson, Tommy. Dot DLP 3580/25580: *Square Dances Played by Tommy Jackson.*
Jarrell, Tommy. County 748: *Tommy Jarrell's Banjo Album.*

Mountain 310: *Joke on the Puppy.*

Jenkins, Snuffy. Folkways FA 2314: *American Banjo: Tunes and Songs in Scruggs Style.*
Jernigan, Doug. Flying Fish FF 024: *Roadside Rag.*
Johnson, Buffalo. Rich-R-Tone 1023.
Johnson, Earl and His Dixie Entertainers. OKeh 45101.
Johnson, Henry. Trix 3304: *The Union County Flash.*
Jones, Eddie Lee. Testament T-2224: *Yonder Go That Old Black Dog.*
Jones, Louis Marshall (Grandpa Jones). Monument SLP 18138: *Grandpa Live.*

Harmony H31396: *Live.*

Jones, Tommy. Ovation QD-14-20: *Tommy's Place.*

Kazee, Buell. Folkways FS 3810: *Buell Kazee Sings and Plays.*
Kentucky Colonels. World Pacific WP/WPS-1821: *Appalachian Swing!*

World Pacific WPS-21898: *Bluegrass Special.*

Kidwell, Fiddlin' Van. Vetco LP 506: *Midnight Ride.*

LaRue, Michael; Foster, Alex; and the Drinking Gourds. Counterpoint CPT 566:
    Follow the Drinking Gourd.

Esoteric ES-560.

Laurel River Valley Boys. Judson J-3031: *Music for Moonshiners.*

Riverside RLP 7504/97504: *Dance All Night with a Bottle in Your Hand.*

Leadbelly (Huddie Ledbetter). Folkways FC 7533: *Negro Folk Songs for Young People.*

Stinson SLP 17.

Playboy PB 119: Leadbelly.

Folkways FT 31030: Shout On.

Xtra (England) 1017: Shout on.

Folkways FA 2941: Leadbelly's Last Session, Volume 1.

Leadbelly (Huddie Ledbetter) and Terry, Sonny. Asch 343-3: *Songs by Leadbelly.*

Melodisc (England) EPM 7-77. (45 rpm)

Melodisc 1187.

Stinson SLP 17: *Leadbelly Memorial,* Volume 1.

Elektra EKL 301-2.

Leadbelly; Terry, Sonny; and McGhee, Brownie. Folkways FJ 2801: *Jazz,* volume 1.
Levine, Henry, and the Dixieland Jazz Group of NBC's Chamber Music Society of Lower Basin Street. Victor 27545. "John Henry Blues."
Lewis, Furry (Walter). Vocalion 1474. "John Henry (the Steel-driving Man) Parts 1/2."

Herwin 201: *Sic 'em Dogs on Me.*

Herwin 204: *Fillin in Blues.*

Folkways FS 3823: *Furry Lewis.*

Folkways FA2692-D: *Music Down Home.*

RBF RF 202: *The Rural Blues.*

Asch 101: *The Blues.*

ASP 1: *At Home with Friends.*

Blue Star 80 602: *House of the Blues,* Vol. 2: *Fourth and Beale.*

Prestige Bluesville 1036: *Back on My Feet Again.*

Prestige 7810: *Back on My Feet Again.*

Fantasy 24703: *Shake em on Down.*

Sire SES 97015: *Stars of the 1969-1970 Memphis Country Blues Festival.*

Matchbox (England) SDR 190/Roots (Germany) SL 505: *Furry Lewis in Memphis.*

Barclay (France) 920.352T: *Beale Street Blues.*

Ampex A10140: *Live at the Gaslight at the Au Go Go.*

Lewis, Jerry Lee. Sun 344. (45 rpm)

Sun 121: *Old Tyme Country Music.*

Lewis, Ramsey. The Ramsey Lewis Trio. Mercury MG-20536/SR 60213: *Down to Earth.*
Lilly Brothers. Event E-4272. (45 rpm)

County 729: *Lilly Brothers and Don Stover.*

Limelighters. RCA Victor LPM/LSP 2907: *The Limelighters.*

Electra EKL/EKS7 180: *The Limelighters.*

Legacy 113: *Their First Historic Album.*

Little, Jack. RCA Victor LPM/LSP 2840: *Porter Wagoner—In Person.*
Living Guitars. RCA Camden ADL 2-0292: *Bluegrass Special.*
Lockmiller, Richard, and Connor, Jim. Folklore (england) F/LEUT 5.
Lomax, Alan. Tradition TLP 1029: *Texas Folksongs.* "Little John Henry."
Lomax, John Jr. Folkways FG 3508: *John A. Lomax Jr. Sings American Folksongs.*
Lost and Found. Outlet STLP-1006: *The Second Time Around.* "John Henry Jr."
Lumsford, Bascom Lamar. Riverside RLF 12-645: *Minstrel of the Appalachians.*
Lyman, Arthur. Hifi 1004: *Percussion Spectacular.*

Macon, Uncle Dave. Vocalion 15320. "Death of John Henry (Steel Driving Man)."

Vocalion 5096.

Brunswick 112-A.

Brunswick BL 59001: *Listen to Our Story*

Coral (Japan) MH 174: *American Folk Classics.*

County 502: *A Collection of Mountain Ballads.*

Historical HLP 8006: *Wait Till the Clouds Roll By.*

Vetco LP 101: *The Dixie Dewdrop.*

David Unlimited DU-TFS 101: *At Home.*

Maggie Valley Boys. Rural Rhythm RR 170: *Maggie Valley Boys.*
Mainer, J. E. Blue Grass Special EP 601. (45 rpm).
J. E. Mainer's Mountaineers. Bluebird B-6629.

Victor (Japan) RA 5520: *Blue Grass Classics.* "John Henry was a Little Boy."

King 550.

King LP 666: *Good Old Mountain Music.*

Martin, Benny. CMH 1776: *200 Years of American Heritage in Song.*
Mathis, Allison, and Stroller, Jessie. Flyright Matchbox SDM 250.
Matin, Jimmy. Decca DL/DL7 4643 and MCA 79: *Sunny Side of the Mountain.*

McAdoo, Bill. Folkways FA 2448: *Bill McAdoo Sings.*
McCall, Jim. Vetco 3010: *Pickin' and Singin'.*
McCoy, Charlie. Monument KZ 32215: *Good Time Charlie's Got the Blues.*

    Monument 25 7-8576.

McCoy, Earl; Mang, Alfred; and Garner, Clem. Columbis 15622-D. "John Henry the Steel Drivin' Man."

McCurdy, Ed. Riverside RLP 1419: *Everybody Sing.*

    Riverside RLP 12-601: *The Ballad Record.*

    Prestige International 13002: *The Best of Ed McCurdy.*

McDowell, Fred. Biograph BLP 12017: *When I Lay My Burden Down.*

    Mileston 93003: *Long Way from Home.*

    Oblivion OD1-*Live in New York.*

McDowell, Fred, and Woods, Johnny. Revival RVS 1001 and Rounder 2007: *Fred McDowell and Johnny Woods.*
McGhee, Bob. Sonora 147-171.
McGhee, Brownie, and Terry, Sonny. Choice LP 100.

    Sound of America 2001.

    Folkways FW 2327: *Brownie McGhee and Sonny Terry Sing.*

    Verve/Folkways FTS 31024: *Preachin the Blues.*

    Topic (England) 12T29: *Brownie McGhee and Sonny Terry.*

McPhail, Black Bottom. Vocalion 04220. "John."
Memphis Slim (Peter Chatman). United Artists UAL 3137/UAS 6137: *Broken Soul Blues.*

    Candid CM 8024; Barnaby ZG 31291: *Bad Luck and Troubles.*

    Folkways FG 3535: *Memphis Slim and the Real Honky Tonk.*

Memphis Slim and Willie Dixon. Folkways FA 2385: *Songs by Memphis Slim and Willie Dixon.*

    Verve V-3007: *The Blues Every Which Way.*

Merrill Jay Singers. Cabot CAB 503: *Songs of the Railroad.*
Miles, Paul; Miles, Vernon; and Miles, Wade. Library of Congress LBC 3: *Dance Music: Breakdowns & Waltzes.*

Mobile Strugglers. American Skiffle Bands. Folkways FA 2610 and FA4530: *Folk Music USA*.

Monroe, Bill, and His Bluegrass Boys. Decca 45-31540. (45 rpm)

Vocalion VL 3702/73702: *Bill Monroe sings Country Songs*. "New John Henry Blues."

Monroe, Charlie. Pine Tree PTSLP 528: *Live at Lake Norman Music Hall*.

Moore, Charlie. Vetco 3011: *Charlie Moore Sings Good Bluegrass*. "When John Henry Was a Little Boy."

Moore, Charlie, and Napier, Bill. King 5050. (45 rpm)

King 1021.

Morris, David, and Morris, John. Kidtown IFR69: *Music as We Learned It*.

Mountaineers. Cumberland SRC 69501: *Bluegrass Banjo Pickin'*.

Mountain Ramblers. Atlantic SD-1347: *Blue Ridge Mountain Music*.

Necessary, Frank, and the Stone Mountain Boys. Old Homestead OHS 90010: *Cimarron Bluegrass*.

New Christy Minstrels. Columbia CL 2187/CS 8987: *Land of Giants*. "John Henry and the Steam Drill."

New Lost City Ramblers. Folkways FA 2395: *The New Lost City Ramblers*, Vol. 5.

New Orleans Blue Nine. Grey Gull 1263.

Paramount 12003.

Nandsco 1263.

Radiex 1263. "John Henry Blues."

New River Boys. Mad Bag MB 288-289: *Country Blue Grass Jamboree*.

Niles, John Jacob. Victor 2051.

Disc album 733.

Camden CAL 330.

Tradition TLP 1023: *I Wonder as I Wander*.

Novelty Blue Boys. Grey Gull 1465.

Grey Gull 7023.

Radiex 7023.

Madison 1920. "John Henry Blues."

Odetta. Fantasy 3-15: *The Tin Angel Presents Odetta and Larry*.

Fantasy 3253: *Odetta and Larry*.

Fantasy 8345: *Odetta.*

Vanguard VRS 9076/VSD 2072: *Odetta at Carnegie Hall.*

Vanguard VSD 17/18: *Greatest Folksingers of the Sixties.*

Vanguard 43/44: *The Essential Odetta.*

Okun, Milt. Baton BL 1203: *America's Best Loved Folk Songs.*
Old Timey String Band. Blue Horizon (Sweden) LP 500: *Tennessee Travelers/Old Timey String Band.*
Osborne Brothers. MGM E/ SE 4090: *Bluegrass Instrumentals.* "John Henry Blues."
Oster, Harry. Folk Lyric LFS A2: *Louisiana Folksong Jamboree.*
Oswald, Bashful Brother (Pete Kirby). Tennessee NR 4990: *Banjo and Dobro.* "Old John Henry."

Rounder 0041. *That's Country.*

Paley, Tom. Elektra EKL-217: *Folk Banjo Styles.*
Peg Leg Sam (Arthur Jackson). Flyright (England) LP 507-508: *The Last Medicine Show.*
Peg Leg Sam and Louisiana Red. Blue Labor BL105: *Going Train Blues.*
Pegram, George. Folkways FA 2435: *Galax Old Fiddlers' Convention.*

Union Grove SS-1: *String Music.*

Rounder 0001: *George Pegram.*

Perkins, Virgil, and Jack Sims. Folkways FA 2610: *American Skiffle Bands.*

Folkways FR 4530: *Folk Music USA.*

Perry, John. Heritage 4: *Old Time Hoedown Instrumentals.*
Peters, Brock. United Artists UAL 3062: *At the Village Gate.* "John Henry Dead."
Philips, Cora. Physical PR 12-001: *Music from the Hills of Caldwell County.*
Pierce, Billy; Pierce, De De; Brother Randolph; and Bridges, Lucius. Folk Lyric FL 110: *New Orleans Jazz.*

Arhoolie 2016: *New Orleans Music.*

Pike, Pete. Rebel 1473.
Pine River Boys. Mountain 305: *Hoedown Time.*
Pinetop Slim. Kent KST 9004: *Anthology of the Blues/Blues from the Deep South.*

Colonial 106.

Poston, Fiddlin' Mutt and the Farm Hands. Rural Rhythm RRFT-157: *Howdown,* Vol. 7.
Preston, Billy. A & M 3507: *I Wrote a Simple Song.*
Puckett, Riley. Columbia 15163-D.

Old Timey LP 101: *Old Time Southern Dance Music: The String Bands,* Vol. 2. "Darkey's Wail."

Raper, Ed, and His Carolina Mountain Boys. Constellation 101.
Raney, Wayne. Starday SEP 133. (45 rpm).

Rimrock EP 296. "John Henry Blues." (45 rpm).

Reed, Jerry. RCA Victor LSP-3978: *Nashville Underground.*

RCA Victor CPL2-1014: *In Concert.*

RCA Camden ACL1-0331: *Tupelo Mississippi Flash.*

Renbourn, John. Reprise 2-6482: *John Renbourn.*

Transatlantic (England) TRA 135.

Rice, Tony. King Bluegrass KB 529.
Richardson, Larry, Red Barker, and the Blue Ridge Boys. County 702: *Larry Richardson, Red Barker, and the Blue Ridge Boys.*
Riddle, Jimmy. Cumberland MGS 29519/SRC 69519: *Classics.*
Robeson, Paul. Columbia 17381-D.

Columbia M610: *Spirituals.*

Columbia ML 4105: *Spirituals.*

Victor 19824.

Robinson, Earl. General 502.

Timely 502.

General G-30.

Rock City Singers. Cumberland MGS 29519/SRC 69519: *Classics.*
Rodgers, Jimmie. Dot 25496: *Jimmie Rodgers in Folk Concert.*
Rodgers, Will Jr., and Scott, Rom. Judson J 3013: *Great American Folk Heroes.*
Rosenbaum, Art. Kicking Mule KM 108: *Five String Banjo.*
Rubin, Rube, and the Westerners. Crown CLP 5477.

Sandburg, Carl. Caedmon TC 2025: *Carl Sandburg Sings His American Songbag.* "If I Die a Railroad Man."

Columbia ML 5339: *Flat Rock Ballads.*

Sapps, Booker T.; Matthews, Roger; and Flowers, Willy. Flyright Matchbox SDM 258: *Boot That Thing.* Library of Congress Series, Vol. 4.
Sauter-Finegan Orchestra.

Schwartz, Tracy and Eloise. Folk Variety (West Germany) FV 12007: *Home Among the Hills.*

Scott, Tom. Signature Album S-5: *Sing of America.*

    Coral CRL 56056: *Sing of America.*

Seeger, Mike. Folkways FH 5273: *Tipple, Loom & Rail.* "Death of John Henry."

Seeger, Pete. Capitol W 2172: *Folk Songs by Pete Seeger.*

    Capitol DT 2718: *Pete Seeger.*

    Columbia CL 1668/CS 8468: *Story Songs.*

    Harmony HS 11337: *John Henry & Other Folk Favorites.*

    Columbia CL 2122/CS 8922: *All Star Hootenanny.*

    Columbia 32-16-0266: *3 Saints, 4 Sinners, and 6 other People.*

    Folkways FA 2319: *American Ballads.*

    Folkways FN 2315: *Sing Out! Hootenanny.*

Seeger, Pete; Terry, Sonny; and McGhee, Brownie. Folkways FA 2201: *Country Dance Music.*

Sellers, Brother John. Vanguard VRS 9036: *Brother John Sellers Sings Blues and Folk Songs.*

Shady Mountain Ramblers. Heritage 2: *Old Time Music from the Blue Ridge Mountains.*

Sheldon, Ernie, and the Villagers. Columbia CL: 1515/CS 8315: *The Big Men: Bold and Bad.*

Shelton Brothers and Curly Fox. Decca 5173. "New John Henry Blues."

Shook, Jerry. Somerset 18400.

Shouse, Virgil; Lilly, Mike; and Miller, Wendy. Old Homestead OHS 80009: *Bluegrass.*

Skinner, Jimmie. Decca 29179.

    Decca DL 4132: *Country Singer.* "John Henry and the Water Boy."

    Vetco 3027: *Jimmie Singer Sings Bluegrass,* Vol. 2.

Bill Smith Quartet. Contemporary M3591/S7591: *Folk Jazz.*

Smith, Glen. County 757: *Clawhammer Banjo,* Vol. 3.

Smith, Harry. Folkways FA 18. *Anthology of American Folk Song.*

Smith, Pinetop. Colonial 106.

    Kent KST 9004: *Anthology of the Blues/Blues from the Deep South.*

Snow, Kilby. Folkways FA 2365: *Mountain Music Played on the Autoharp.*

Spencer Trio. Decca 1873.

    Brunswick (England) 02632.

Brunswick (France) A-505170.

Stafford, Jo. Columbia CL 1339/CS 8139: *Ballad of the Blues.*
Stamper, I. D. June Appal 010: *Red Wing.*
Stanley, Ralph. Jalyn JLP 118: *Old Time Music of Ralph Stanley.*

Rebel SLP 1530: *A Man and His Music.*

Stoneman, Ernest V. ("Pop").

Edison 51869.

Edison 5194 (cylinder).

Stoneman Family. Folkways FA 2315: *Old-Time Tunes of the South.*
Stracke, Win. Golden GLP 31: *Golden Treasury of Songs America Sings.*
Stringbean (Dave Akeman). Starday SLP 215: *A Salute to Uncle Dave Macon.*

Nashville NLP 2100: *Hee Haw Corn Shucker.*

Stuart, Joe. Atteiram API-L-1514: *Sittin on Top of the World.*
Swann, Wallace, and His Cherokee String Band. LC AFS 10. (78 rpm).

Library of Congress Archive of Folk Song L2: *Anglo-American Shanties, Lyric Songs, Dance Tunes, and Spirituals.*

Sykes Brothers. Laurel Leaf 2401314: *Twisting the Strings.*

Tanner, Gid, and His Skillet Lickers. Columbia 15 142 D.
Tanner, Gid, and Puckett, Riley. Columbia 15019-D.

Silvertone 3262.

Harmony 5144-H.

Rounder 1005: *Hear These New Southern Fiddle and Guitar Records.*

Tarlton, Jimmy. Testament T-3302: *Steel Guitar Rag.*
Taylor, Earl and His Stoney Mountain Boys. United Artists UAL 3049: *Folk Songs from the Blue Grass.*
Temple, Pick. RCA "X" LXA-3022: *Folk Songs of the People.*
Terry, Sonny. Riverside RLP 12-644: *Sonny Terry and his Mouth-Harp.*

Washington WLP 702: *Talkin Bout the Blues.*

Elektra EKL 13: *Folk Blues Sung by Sonny Terry and Alex Stewart.*

Vanguard VRS 8523/4: *From Spirituals to Swing.* "The New John Henry."

Terry, Sonny, and Bull City Red. Vanguard VRS 8523/4: *Spirituals to Swing.*
Terry, Sonny, and McGhee, Brownie. Fantasy 3317: *Shouts and Blues.*

Tomato TOM 2-7003: *A Tribute to Leadbelly.*

Terry, Sonny, and Seeger, Pete. Verve FV/FVS 9010: *Gettogether.*
Thomas, Henry. Vocalion 1094.

Origin Jazz Library OJL-3: *Henry Thomas Sings the Texas Blues.*

Herwin 209: *"Ragtime Texas" Henry Thomas.*

Thompson, Hank. Capitol 2553.

Capitol T-418: *Songs of the Brazos Valley.*

Capitol T/ST 1632: *Hank Thompson at the Golden Nugget.*

Hank Thompson's Brazos Valley Boys. Warner Brothers W/WS 1679: *Hank Thompson's Brazos Valley Boys.*
Three from Nod. International M-103.
Toomey, Welby. Gennett 6005-A. "The Death of John Henry."

Gennett 5002.

Silvertone 8146.

Silvertone 5002.

Challenge 228.

Herwin 75532.

Supertone 9245.

Champion 15198.

Travis, Merle. Capitol 48000: *Folk Songs of the Hills.*

Capitol T 891: *Back Home.*

Capitol T/ST 2662: *The Best of Merle Travis.*

Capitol (England) T 21010: *21 Years a Country Singer.*

Shasta LP 517: *The Way They Were Back Then.*

Shasta LP 523: *The Guitar Player.*

Traum, Happy. Kicking Mule SNKF 111: *Relax Your Mind.*
Trent, Charles. Smash MGS 27002/SRS 67002: *Sound of a Blue Grass Banjo.*
Turner, Lucille. Colonial C 17001.
Turner, Willie. Folkways FE 4474 (FP 474): *Negro Music of Alabama,* Vol. 6.
Two Poor Boys (Joe Evans and Arthur McClain). Perfect 181.

Romeo 5080.

Oriole 8080.

Conqueror 7876.

Origin Jazz Library OJL-14: *Alabama Country, 1927/31.* "John Henry Blues."

Uncle Josh and Hoss Linneman. Starday SLP 340: *That Dobro Sound's Goin' round.*

Starday SEP 237. "John Henry Breakdown."

Van Ronk, Dave. Folkways FA 2383: *Dave Van Ronk Sings.* "Spike Driver's Moan."

Folkways FS 3818: *Dave Van Ronk Sings Ballads, Blues, and a Spiritual.*
Verve/Folkways FV 9017: *Gambler's Blues.*

Wallace, Howard. Jewel LPS 186: *Old-Time 5-String Banjo.*
Wandering Five. Somerset SF-18600: *We're Pickin' and Singin' Folk Songs.*
Ward, Fields, Dr. W. P. Davis, and the Virginia Bogtrotters. Biograph RC-6003:
    The Original Bogtrotters 1937-1942.
Washboard Band. Folkways FA 2201: *The Washboard Band.*
Watson, Doc. Vanguard VSD 9/10: *Doc Watson on Stage.* "Spike Driver Blues."

Folkways FA 2426: *Jean Ritchie and Doc Watson at Folk City.* "Spike Driver
Blues."
United Artists LA 601: *Doc and the Boys.* "Spikedriver Blues."

Wayne, Bradley. Vee Jay VJLP 1079: *12 String Guitar Nanny.*
Welch, Guitar; Maxey, Hogman; and Mosley, Andy. Louisiana Folklore Society
    LFS A-5: *Prison Work Songs Recorded in the Louisiana State Prison at
    Angola, Louisiana.*
Wells, Sally. Pik 10. (45 rpm).
Wheeler, Billy Edd, and the Bluegrass Singers. Monitor MF 367: *Billy Edd and Blue-
    grass Too.*
White, Josh. Keynote 541.

Keynote K-125.

Decca A-447.

Decca 23563.

Decca DL 5082: *Ballads and Blues.*

Decca DL 8665: *Josh White.*

Decca 25627 (45 rpm).

Decca DL/DL7 4469: *All Time Hootenanny.*

Emarcy 1-6019.

Elektra EKL 123: *25th Anniversary Album.*

Elektra 701: *The Story of John Henry and Ballads, Blues, and Other Stories.*

Elektra EKS 75008: *The Best of Josh White.*

Mercury MG 25014: *Strange Fruit.*

Crestview CRV/CRS7: *Hootenanny.*

White, Red, and the Dixie Bluegrass Band. Rural Rhythm RR-RO-172: *Red White and the Dixie Bluegrass Band.*
Wiley, Paul. Voyager VHLP 302: *Comin Round the Mountain.*
Williams, Bill. Blue Goose 2003: *Low and Lonesome.*
Williams, Connie. Testament T-2225: *Blind Connie Williams.*
Williamson, Sonny Boy. Bluebird BB-8403. "Joe Louis and John Henry Blues."
Williamson Brothers and Curry. OKeh 45127.

Folkways FA 2951: *Anthology of American Folk Music.* "Gonna Die with My Hammer in My Hand."

Wilson, Stan. Cavalier CAV 6002.

Cavalier CAV 5001.

Wilson Brothers, Larry, and Joanna. MBC/ MRLP 1093: *Stand Tall in Bluegrass.*
Winn, George. Major MRLP-2105: *Last Train Through Lunnberg County.*
Winston, Winnie. Elektra EKL-276: *Old Time Banjo Project.*
Winter, Paul. Columbia CL-2155/CS-8955: *Jazz Meets the Folk Song.*
Wise, Chubby. Stoneway STY 146: *Sincerely Yours . . .*

Stoneway STY 157: *Grassy Fiddle.*
Stoneway 1136. (45 rpm).

Wright, Willie. Concert-Disc CS-45: *I Sing Folk Songs.*

Young, Eldee. Argo 699: *Just for Kicks.*
Young, Martin, and Grigsby, Corbett. Folkways FA 2317: *Mountain Music of Kentucky.*

SONGS ON TAPE IN THE LIBRARY OF CONGRESS ARCHIVE OF FOLKSONG

Allen, Chester (and his group). Asheville, N.C., 1941. 4790 B7.
Allen, Chester, and Sharp, Joe. (Guitar, violin, and mandolin). Skyline, Ala., 1939. 2943 A2-B1.

Amerson, Richard. Livingston, Ala., 1937. 1305 B2.

Livingston, Ala., 1940. 4045 A2 and B1 (with comment).

Anderson, Thomas. New York City, 1939. 3636 A1 and A2.
"John Henry Was a Very Small Boy." New York, 1939. 3636 B2.

Asher, M. Hyden, Ky., 1937. 1519 A2.

Atkins, Bill. Pineville, Ky., 1938. 1989 B1.

Beck, Jonesie (with washtub); Robinson, Nick (with washboard); and Beck, James (with guitar box). Charleston, S.C., 1937. 1047 A2.

Bell, Arthur. Cummins State Farm, Gould, Ark., 1939. 2668 B1.

Brown, Gabriel (on guitar). Eatonville, Fla., 1935. 355 A and B.

Brown, Joe, with guitar by Lonnie Thomas. State Farm, Raiford, Fla., 1939. 2710 B1.

Clemens, Julius. State Farm, Raiford, Fla., 1936. 689A.

Collett, Farmer (on guitar). Middle Fork, Ky., 1937. 1429 A2 and B1.

Cousts (?) String Band. (with voiced over announcement) Twenty-second Annual Mountain Dance and Folk Festival, Asheville, N.C., 1949.

Crenshew, Reese, with guitar. State prison farm, Milledgeville, Ga., 1934. 259 A2.

Crescent School students. Pittsburg, Pa., 1944. 8027 B1; 8029 B.

Davis, John. Frederica, Ga., 1935. With exclamations. 313 A.

Guitar played with bottle-neck. Frederica, Ga., 1935. 314 A.

Guitar played with bottle-neck, Frederica, Ga., 1935. 315 B.

Dunford, Uncle Alec. Galax, Va., 1937. 1363 A3 (with comment).

Dwyer Brothers. Asheville, N.C. Folk Festival, 1941. 4792 B1.

Edwards, Joe. State penitentiary, Parchman, Miss., 1936. 743 A2.

Galliher, Fred. Saltville, Va., 1942. 6729 A2; LWO 2052; R28-A side.

Godfrey, Hettie. Livingston, Ala., 1940. 4049 B5 (fragment).

Griffin, Charles, with guitar. Kilby prison, Montgomery, Ala., 1934, 238 A.

Hall, Vera. Livingston, Ala., 1937.

Hampton Institute male choir. Washington, D.C. National Folk Festival, 1938. 9836-B4.

Hampton Institute unidentified singers. Hampton Institute, 1937-41. 8316 B; 8313 B1; 8313 A1; 8312 A1; 8286 A1.

Harmon, Austin (with banjo). Maryville, Tenn., a939. 2916 B2; 2917 A1.

Harper, Gus, and group. State penitentiary, Parchman, Miss., 1937. 883 B.

Hazelburst, Harold B. Jacksonville, Fla., 1939 (with comment). 3143 A2.

Hemphill, Sid, Sid Hemphill's Band. Dundee, Miss., 1942. 6673 A6; LWO 2052; R 13-B side.

Henry, Jim. State penitentiary, Parchman, Miss., 1936. 743 A1.

Jackson, John Henry, and Smith, Norman. State penitentiary, Parchman, Miss., 1939. 3088 A2 and B1.

Jackson, Aunt Molly. New York City, 1935. (Singer from Clay County, Ky.). 828 B3.

New York City, 1939, with comment. 2551 A1.

Jones, Charley. Eatonville, Fla., 1935. 365 B2.

Josey, Albert (on banjo). Galax, Va., 1937. 2234 B3.

Kilgore, Vera. Highlander Folk School, Monteagle, Tenn., 1939. 2939 A1.

Ledbetter, Huddie (Leadbelly). New York City, 1938. (With dialog by Leadbelly and Alan Lomax. Singer from Shreveport, La.). 2503 B.

New York City, 1938. (With dialog by Leadbelly and Lomax). 2504 a.

Washington, D.C., Library of Congress, 1940. 4472 A5.

Lumsford, Bascom Lamar (with banjo). New York City, 1935. (Singer from Asheville, N.C.). 1814 A1 and A2.

Leicester, N.C., 1936. 3167 B1.

Washington, D.C., Library of Congress, 1949. 9510 A2 and A3.

Mainer, Wade and the Sons of the Mountaineers. (Tiny Dodson, The Shelton Brothers (Jack and Curly), and Howard Dixon. Announcer, Mardi Liles.) Asheville, N.C.,1941. 4490 A3.

Mainer, Wade, Wade Mainer's Mountaineers of North Carolina. Washington, D.C., 1941. 4435 A2; LWO 4844; R302 Side A.

Martin, Marcus (with banjo). Swannanoa, N.C., 1942. 7913 B.

Mathis, Allison, banjo, and Stroller, Jessie, harmonica. 1941. 5158 B-1; LWO 3493 R 11-A side.

McGhee, Brownie; Terry, Sonny; and Ledbetter, Huddie. Washington, D.C., Library of Congress, 1942. 6503 A1.

McLaughlin, Bill. Jacksonville, Fla., 1949. 9915 B1.

Memphis work house, group of Negro prisoners. Memphis, Tennessee, 1933. 174 B3.

Miles, Paul; Miles, Wade; and Miles, Vernon. (On banjo, mandolin, and guitar.) Canton, Ga., 1940. 4075 B2.

Milling, Chapman J. Columbia, S.C., 1939. 3789 B.

Mullins, J.M., with banjo. Salyersville, Ky., 1937. 1595 A1.

Oakley, Mississippi, State prison farm. Group of negro convicts. Oakley, Miss., 1933. 1867 B1.

Owens, J. State penitentiary, Richmond, Va., 1936. 730 A.

Panhandle Pete, Asheville, N.C., 1941. 4794 A5.

Parchman, Mississippi, State penitentiary, group of negro convicts. Parchman, Miss., 1933. 1864 B3; 1865 A2.

Pendleton, Silas. Huntley, Va., 1947. (Recorded at Newport, R.I.) 9059 B2.

Pittman, Sampson, with guitar. Detroit, 1939. "John Henry Was a Man." 2479 A.

Prater, Winnie, on banjo. Salyersville, Ky., 1937. 1593 A3 and B1.

Raper, "Red." Asheville, N.C., 1946. 7049 A1. (Singer from Cherokee, N.C.)

Twenty-second Annual Mountain Dance and Folk Festival, Asheville, N.C., 1949. 9997 A5.

Roark, George, with banjo. Pineville, Ky., 1938. 1997 A.

Sapps, Booker T.; Matthews, R.G.; and Flowers, Willy. Belle Glade, Fla., 1935. 371 B.

Skyline Farms Group, with guitar, fiddle, and banjo. Washington, D.C., 1938. (Singers from Scottsboro, Ala.) 1629 A.

Sloan, Jodie (aged 18), with guitar. New York, N.Y., 1947. 9096-1A.

Sloan, William, Washington, Va., 1947. 9072 B1.

Smith, Hobart, on 5-string banjo. Saltville, Va., 1942. 6724 A1 (defective); 6724 A2; LWO 2052; R27-B side.

Steele, Pete, on guitar. Hamilton, Ohio, 1938. 1711 A2.

Staffen, Bernard, and Pollock, Charles, on harmonicas. Washington, D.C., 3304 A1.
Stoneman, Glen. Galax, Va., 1941. 4937 A3.
Thomas, Bob. Tucson, Ariz., 1949. 9309 B2.
Wagoner Brothers, Elon College, N.C., 1941. 6492 A3; LWO-2052; R 29-B side.
Ward, Andy and Hasroe. Buckingham, Ky., 1946. 8485 A (R-123-L).
Ward, Fields, with guitar. Galax, Va., 1940. 4085 A1.
Ward, Fields, and Dr. W. P. Davis, with Bogtrotters Band, Galax, Va., 1937 (with
     comment). 1362 B.

APPENDIX:
INTERVIEW WITH
CHARLES LEWIS CHOICE

The interview which follows was conducted with Mr. Charles Lewis Choice, a Washington, D.C., construction worker on June 22, 1981. Mr. Choice is a resident of that neighborhood discussed in Chapter 6, who felt confident about his knowledge of the legend. The written transcript does not do justice to the expressive narrative recorded on tape, and I would like to note that many of Mr. Choice's friends who listened to the tape found it extremely humorous. I found especially interesting Mr. Choice's discussion of why he feels John Henry is a hero.

BW: Do you know who John Henry was—the original John Henry?
CC: Yeah . . . steel-drivin' man . . . railroad man.
BW: What does it mean to be a steel-drivin' man?
CC: Layin' ties . . . layin' track . . . drivin' spikes.
BW: Do you know where he worked?
CC: I don't know. West Virginia I guess.
BW: How long ago was it?
CC: How would I know? I don't know.
BW: Do you know what he looked like?
CC: No.
BW: Was he white or black?
CC: He was black. But I still don't know what he looked like.
BW: Do you know how old he was?
CC: Not really . . . no . . . but I know how old I am now, and I heard about it when I was young.
BW: You heard about it when you were young. Have you ever heard the song?
CC: Yeah, I know it . . . I mean I used to know the song years ago. . . .
BW: Really?

CC: Sure. That's about the best thing . . . that mostly I know about him; you know the song, but. . . .

BW: From hearing the song . . . not from just hearing someone tell the story?

CC: No.

BW: Did he have a wife?

CC: Yeah, but I don't know her name.

BW: Do you know anything about her?

CC: She went to the railroad track when he fell dead, I know that cause that was in the song. But basically, I don't know. . . .

BW: Did he have any children?

CC: That I can't say. I never read about it.

BW: Yes. . . .I don't think there's anything to read. I think the only way people know about it is in songs.

CC: We, this is what I say, see. This is what I'm saying, this is the only thing I would know see, cause I never lived in no West Virginia but as a kid comin' up lots of people were singin' the song, but I was just a small kid.

BW: Was that professional musicians?

CC: No, just people singin' . . . somebody had to write it though.

BW: I don't know who wrote it.

CC: I don't . . . I say somebody had to write it. If I heard it forty years ago, somebody had to write it. Or maybe longer than that, cause I wasn't in elementary school when I heard that song. I'm 57 years old now, you know good and well it's been a long time.

BW: It's an old song . . . was that in Ohio?

CC: Yeah, Ohio . . . Ohio and West Virginia . . . they're adjoining states, you know, so I wouldn't have to go to West Virginia.

BW: Did you ever sing the song?

CC: Maybe I have, I don't know. I couldn't bet on that, really . . . but I'm sure I have . . . cause if you're around somebody else singin it, maybe I'd sing it too, I don't know.

BW: Did you look up to John Henry? Do you remember kind of admiring him or anything?

CC: I like the song because he tried to beat the steam drivin' thing, you know . . . that made me think the man was a man. You know, he wasn't no boy, he was a man, a good man, he couldn't beat that machine, you know, but he tried it . . . it was in the song where he busted his heartstrings tryin'. . . .

BW: Busted his heartstrings?

CC: Well, that's what the song says.

BW: Do you know why he wanted to race it?

CC: Well, you know, it's like anything else. Somethin' come up modern and you been used to doin' it the old way, well it's just like anythin' else that's modern. You know, he wasn't used to modern things, he stood it as he was, you know . . . but, uh . . . for instance, when I was a kid we didn't have no TV, we just had radio and that was valuable, record player. . . . I remember the time I used to watch the lamplighters . . . we had fun watching them. . . .

BW: But you think he did the right thing? . . . to race the steam drill . . .

CC: Well, in his mind, he was right . . . in my own opinion, how you gonna beat a machine? But you can't change . . . what a person been all their life, you can't change that . . . he's a leader, you know . . . as far as I'm concerned, here's a man been used to doing his one thing all his life . . . all they did, come up with a modern machine, runnin' with steam, a motor.

BW: I guess that's true. But he beat it, right?

CC: Well, he worked with it. But the motor's still runnin' and he ain't.

BW: That's true.

CC: So he didn't beat it then, did he? He beat hisself. That's what he done, he beat hisself. But you still can't knock it, because he believed in hisself.

BW: Yeah, so . . . that was why you admired him?

CC: Well, I admired him for that . . . yeah, I did . . . course I didn't go to no library or anythin' like that and read up on him.

BW: But that's good, I think the only way people know about him is because other people tell them about him. . . .

CC: True, true, true. But see I never take the time out to, oh I don't know, the only time I went was when they come up with somethin' in school I had to do . . . if I didn't really have to, I didn't do it.

BW: When you met John Henry, did you think he was named for the . . .

CC: No, I basically didn't think of the name, period. It didn't ring no bell, you know. . . . It's just that I knowed a lot of people with that name . . . over the years, you know.

BW: Is it just a southern name?

CC: No, it's not really what you call a southern name. I lived in the southwest practically all my life, and that's not really southern, you know, the southwest . . . and I heard it around there. I'm not saying that's his background around there . . . but maybe somebody in the family has the name, you know. . . .

BW: So he wouldn't be named for the original man, not necessarily?

CC: I wouldn't think so . . . I mean that's my personal opinion, I don't think so. . . .

BW: I think you're right. . . .

CC: Maybe a person's named—

BW: Well, it's like my John Henry's named for his daddy . . .

CC: Yeah, yeah, that's what I'm sayin, yeah

BW: Did you ever hear him called a natural man?

CC: No, I never heard that. And I don't expect you have either. . . .

BW: No, I heard it, sometimes in the song, they'll say . . . he was a natural man, and I don't know what it means. . . .

CC: Well, what, I say, he's a natural man, he's a big, strong, healthy man, see, you know, people don't grow as big as they used to be anymore. See, a man 25-30 years old weighin' 250 . . . maybe more . . . When I was right young, you'd see a man tall and big, big muscles, big bones, big enough to break your jawbone or somethin', maybe more . . . people don't be that big anymore . . . not anymore . . . maybe every now and again, then they ain't got no big arms, they just big, that's all . . . that's true . . . you know what I'm sayin . . . unless they go out weight-liftin', well, there weren't no such thing when we were kids. That's just been the last twenty years. He was just big, that's all. Eat good, live good, get plenty of sleep. He didn't have no place to go noway. That's true, now that's a fact.

BW: Do you know anything about his life besides when he was laying tracks? Like where he was from?

CC: No.

BW: Was he a slave?

CC: No, I don't think so. No, unuh. He was strictly a railroad man. I can't say nothin' about his parents, I don't know . . . he wasn't a slave, I'm sure of that. And he wasn't no pushover either. He was a man. . . .

BW: Did you ever hear that line in the song that goes, sometimes the song has him saying, "A man ain't nothin' but a man?"

CC: Yeah! "A man ain't nothin' but a man," "You bring me back . . . somethin' like that . . ." "You bring me back a ten-pound hammer, I'll drive your steel on down," or somethin' . . . I mean if I sit down and think about it long enough I probably could remember the whole doggone song . . . it'd kinda take me a little while to get it together.

BW: Well, what does that line mean, "A man ain't nothin' but a man"?

CC: Well, the way I feel about what the line mean is this: He know what he could do. But he didn't know what the next man could do. But if he was a man, he could do it. So he must have been a big strong man, the way I see it, I never seen his pictures or nothin', but apparently, to me, I would say he was a big strong man. If he was a man, if he was a small strong man, it was allright. A man ain't nothin but a man . . . (laughs long and loud).

BW: Could you say that part over, that you just said? I'm sorry, I need that on tape. Was the steam drill gonna take his job?

CC: No, it was gonna slow his job up, that's all.

BW: I mean, you said something about bulldozers.

CC: Well, it's just like the modern equipment is slowin up, takin the, you know, when a man uses his hands, he's doin' it as a laborer, right?

BW: Uh-huh. . . .

CC: You get a machine, you don't need all this labor. You're gonna have to keep some kind of crew at all times, but you don't need as many, you can take one man and do more work than twenty men with a machine; whereas you got twenty mens out there workin'. You go buy that machine you can do the same thing, automatically do the same thing and maybe a little better, a little evener, a little faster. You don't need no men.

BW: So did you get the impression John Henry was fighting to save his job?

CC: No. I wouldn't think that. I think the man just been doing that all his life, just doin' it. For instance, I know a guy . . . says he can run as fast as Jesse Owens. Then, a friend of mine bought a horse to see if he could outrun the horse. He did, really, he outrun the horse. The horse still livin', he dead. Really. He outrun him though.

BW: So it's really not worth it?

CC: No! See, you can't . . . see the horse, therefore, he got killed. He outrun the horse, but the horse might still be kickin' around if he didn't die from old age. A man's only got two legs, the horse got four.

BW: How did they lay tracks before the steam drill? How did the men do it?

CC: Well, they still layin' track practically the same way now, only thing about that, you got to put down the ties and then you got to nail the stakes down, oh I never done, but I see enough of it, I've seen enough of it to know about what's goin' on. But they still doin' it the same way more or less, but instead of all that big sluggin' with all them big hammers and things . . . well, they still do hammer occasionally, but they got somethin' modern to level it right out, so the track don't sink . . . it's basically the same thing, but just a little faster—and less men. Oh, they still gotta keep a crew. You always gotta have a crew. But it's a whole lot different, that fast stuff they got there now, shovelin' coal and stuff, a man couldn't get around that.

BW: Do you have any idea how the steam drill got there? Did the foreman bring it on?

CC: Oh, I couldn't say anythin' about that. You see, a railroad is a company. Had to be somebody, the head, or officiatin' at the company had to stick the money out to have it made in the first place, or . . . well, you know, you can always find somebody come out of school that's really a good idea, so a man see what he can save some money by lessen the crew and gettin' the same thing, well, he gonna buy it, you know . . . a railroad is a company, so . . .

BW: So you think it would have been cheaper for the railroad to use. . . .

CC: Oh, I couldn't say a machine was all that cheap. But in fact years ago everything was cheap just so long you had the money for food and bills and stuff. So if you made yourself a dollar a day, you were doin' doggone good. I know I heard my brother say he worked for a dollar a day. Everythin's different now. You can't give a kid a dollar a day to do nothin' for you now. Might not go to the store for you!

INDEX

John Henry in, 52, 59, 60, 67, 84, 86, 116-21. *See also* Black folksong; Black heroes; Blues music; Gospel music; Slavery; Spirituals; Tricksters
Black Culture and Black Consciousness, 74-75
Black folksong, 48, 49, 50, 55, 63, 71-72. *See also* Blues music; Gospel music; Spirituals
Black heroes, 74-75, 93, 100-116-17, 119-21, 123-14. *See also* Black culture
Blair, Walter, 96
Blankenship, W. T., 56, 64, 75 n.6, 122
Blassingame, Wyatt, 91
Blues music, 72, 118, 119, 121; influencing fiction, 79, 102 n.5
Boette, Maria, 53
Botkin, Benjamin, 52, 55, 60, 81, 94
Bowman, James Cloyd, 86, 87, 93
Boyhood of John Henry, 79, 89, 91
Bradford, Roark, 52, 54, 57, 79-85, 93, 102 n.5, 115; influence of, 68, 71, 86, 88, 90, 96, 97, 100
Bradley, William, 47-48
Brannon, Peter, 50, 52
Brown, Frank C., 50, 62
Brown, Sterling, 100
Buckley, Bruce, 51
Bunyan, Paul, 84, 91, 94; compared to John Henry, 68, 77, 85-86, 90, 95, 96
Burleigh. *See* Steam drill
Burrer, Eileen, 85-86, 88
Burton, Thomas G., 51
Bush, Michael E. "Jim," 54
Butcher, Margaret, 72

C & O Railroad. *See* Chesapeake and Ohio Railroad
Cabbell, Ed, 101-2
Captain, John Henry's: in fiction, 89, 92, 94, 96, 98; in folklore, 20, 29, 78; in hammer songs, 110. *See also* Labor contractors; Johnson, W. R.
Carmer, Carl, 52, 55, 75, 94-95
Carpenter, Charles, 62
Carson, Fiddlin' John, 73, 122
Central of Georgia Railroad, 50, 52, 57, 94

Cephas, Uncle Ira, 51
Chappell, Louis, 14 n.9, 61; folksongs collected by, 50, 61, 66; influence of, 52, 53, 67, 69, 88, 93; oral histories and folklore gathered by, 17-45, 61, 65, 119, 122; in scholarly debate, 38, 41, 60, 61, 63, 64
Chesapeake and Ohio Railroad: construction of, 6, 10, 110; in folklore, 20, 21, 22, 24, 31-32; hazards on, 12, 13, 39; public relations of, 13, 39, 113; in song, 112. *See also* Railroading
Chicago, 50, 113
Childhood of John Henry, 79, 89, 91
Child of John Henry: in fiction, 93, 95, 96, 97; in song, 48, 58, 72, 124
Children's literature, 90-91, 97-99
Cincinnati, 6
Civil War, 86
Coal mining, 5, 11, 72, 97, 110, 111
Coffin, Tristram, 94
Cohen, Hennig, 94
Cohen, Norm, 56, 64, 65, 66, 73, 75 n.6, 111, 114, 122, 123-24
Combs, Josiah, 47, 61, 62, 65, 122
Contest with the steam drill, 8, 11-12, 20, 31; in drama, 85-86, 89, 101; in fiction, 79, 87-92, 97-98; in folklore, 18, 20, 24, 25, 26, 30-33, 37, 78-79; in oral history, 34-36, 38-39, 40, 44, 45; in song, 48, 50, 57, 72, 124
Contractors. *See* Labor contractors
Cooke, Marion, 67
Cooper, Charles O., 100
Cooper, Lee, 125 n.9
Copland, Aaron, 57
Courlander, Harold, 51, 55, 72, 81
Cox, John Harrington, 17, 21, 61, 62, 63, 65
Crockett, Davy, 117
Cruzee (Cursey) Mountain, 25-27, 94
Curtis-Burlin, Natalie, 48

Daddy Joe, 115
Daniel, Pete, 14 n.6
Davis, Arthur, 50
Davis, Henry, 48
Death of John Henry: in folklore, 30,

McCaslin, Nellie, 99
Machines and John Henry, 60, 68, 70, 74, 111, 115
Macon, Uncle Dave, 73
McCorkle, W. A. (Governor), 21-22, 61, 63, 65
McCormick, Kyle, 53
Magarac, Joe
Malcolmson, 95-96
Maloney, Daniel, 101
Manning, Thomas G., 51
Marriage of John Henry. *See* Woman with John Henry
Marx, Leo, 112
Mason, Robert, 51
Miller, Jeffrey, 69, 100
Miller, Kurt, 75
Miller, Olive, 95
Mississippi, 48, 49, 97, 100
Mississippi River, 80, 91
Moore, Dash, 54
Morris, Alton, 51
Mother of John Henry. *See* Parents of John Henry
Mountain influence. *See* Ballad of John Henry: mountain white influence on
Mulcahy, Mary Lou, 70, 122
Murray, Robert, 67

Naming practices, 3-4, 120
Nash, Roderick, 74, 111
Natural Man theme, 49, 52, 53, 82, 96, 121
Nelson, James, 6
New Orleans, 83, 87, 96
New South, 123
New York, 98
Nine-Pound Hamemr motif, 25, 73, 109-10. *See also* Hammer songs.
1950s: art from, 100-101, 103 n.5; curricular material from, 97-99; drama from, 85, 99; fiction from, 88-90; music from, 51, 53, 56, 101
1940s: art from, 87, 101; curricular material from 97, 98; literature from, 86-88, 95-96, 98, 100; music from, 51, 52-53, 55-56
1960s: art from, 90, 91; curricular

material from, 99; fiction from, 90, 97; music from, 51, 56
1970s: art from, 100, 123; fiction from, 91-93; music from, 51, 56
1930s: art from, 55, 70-71, 101; drama from, 81-85; fiction from, 79-91, 94-95; folklore from, 78-79; music from, 50-51, 52, 55
1920s: folklore from, 17-45; folksongs collected in, 48-50, 55
Nitroglycerin, 6, 7, 8
Nordhoff, Charles, 14 n.9
Norfolk and Western Railroad, 27
North Carolina, 4, 5, 20; in fiction, 97; in folklore, 18, 42, 77-79, 97; songs from, 23, 47, 48, 50

Oakley, Giles, 72
Odum, Howard, 48-49, 52, 62, 77-78, 97, 99
Ohio, 51
Ohio and Kentucky Railroad, 19
Oliver, Paul, 14 n.6, 72, 119
Only a Miner, 72-73
Parents of John Henry: in fiction, 86, 91, 92, 94, 95, 96; in song, 48, 124
Partner. *See* Shakers
Perrow, E. C., 47, 65, 122
Philadelphia, 51
Pippins, L. C. "Bunk," 54
Plantations, 3, 4; in fiction, 86, 87, 91-92. *See also* Slavery
Poetry, 100
Polly Ann: in drama, 98; in fiction, 86-88, 92-93, 96, 98; in song, 49, 50, 54. *See also* Woman with John Henry
Populism, 113
Porcello, Patricia, 75
Pound, Louise, 60
Prison: folklore of, 18, 20-21, 24; songs of 50, 51, 118
Prophecy of John Henry: in fiction, 91, 96; in folklore, 77; in song, 48, 62, 68, 112, 124
Protest songs, 54, 55

Race with the Steam drill. *See* Contest with the Steam drill
Radio programs, 85, 98-99, 102

About the Author

BRETT WILLIAMS is Associate Professor of Anthropology and American Studies in the American Studies Program at American University. She is the coeditor with Robert Gordon of *Exploring Total Institutions* and the author of several articles.